BETWEEN DEBT AND THE DEVIL

BETWEEN DEBT AND THE DEVIL

MONEY, CREDIT, AND FIXING GLOBAL FINANCE

ADAIR TURNER

PRINCETON UNIVERSITY PRESS

PRINCETON AND OXFORD

Copyright © 2016 by Princeton University Press
Published by Princeton University Press, 41 William Street, Princeton, New Jersey 08540
In the United Kingdom: Princeton University Press, 6 Oxford Street,
Woodstock, Oxfordshire OX20 1TW

press.princeton.edu

Jacket/frontispiece illustration: *Faust and Mephisto*, engraving by Tony Johannot, 1845–1847.
From Johann Wolfgang von Goethe, *Faust: Der Tragödie erster Teil*, ed. Hans Henning, 1982.

Library of Congress Cataloging-in-Publication Data

Turner, Adair, author.
  Between debt and the devil : money, credit, and fixing global finance / Adair Turner.
    pages cm
  Includes bibliographical references and index.
  ISBN 978-0-691-16964-4 (hardback) — ISBN 0-691-16964-0 (hardcover)   1. International
finance.   2. Finance.   3. Financial institutions.   4. Credit.   5. Financial crises.   6. Mone-
tary policy.   7. Economic policy.   I. Title.
  HG3881.T88 2015
  332'.042—dc23

                                                                           2015015015

British Library Cataloging-in-Publication Data is available

This book has been composed in Minion Pro and Helvetica Neue

Printed on acid-free paper. ∞

Printed in the United States of America

10 9 8 7 6 5 4 3 2 1

To Orna

CONTENTS

ACKNOWLEDGMENTS

T HERE ARE MANY PEOPLE without whom this book could not have been written, and my acknowledgements here are incomplete.

My first thanks must go to the Institute for New Economic Thinking (INET), which has supported me throughout the past 2 years, and to Robert Johnson, the executive director of INET, who has continually inspired me with the depth of his intellectual interests, encouraged me to think radically, and provided a never-ending stream of ideas for further research and reading.

In addition I must particularly thank two others. The first is George Soros, one of INET's founders, with whom I have discussed my emerging ideas since we first met in 2009, and whose own writing has posed a profound challenge to the simplicities of pre-crisis economic orthodoxy. The second is Martin Wolf. For several years Martin and I have been on a very similar intellectual journey, and his *Financial Times* columns and latest book, *The Shifts and the Shocks*, have played an important role in the development of my thinking.

My special thanks also go to friends who read and commented on early drafts of the book, including in particular Bill Janeway, Anatole Kaletsky, and Robert Skidelsky. And I am indebted also to Mervyn King, who, in the depths of the financial crisis of autumn 2008, first helped me understand the inherent instability of modern banking systems.

There are also many people with whom I have discussed my emerging ideas, or who have inspired me through their own writings. They include Anat Admati, Olivier Blanchard, Claudio Borio, Marcus Brunnermeier, Jaime Caruana, Ulf Dahlsten, Brad DeLong, Barry Eichengreen, Roman Frydman, Charles Goodhart, Andrew Haldane, Will Hutton, Otmar Issing, Oscar Jorda, Richard Koo, Paul Krugman, Michael Kumhof, Jean-Pierre Landau, Richard Layard, Paul McCulley, Atif Mian, Liu Mingkang, Rakesh Mohan, John Muellbauer, Avinash Persaud, Michael Pettis, Thomas Piketty, Adam Posen, Zoltan Pozsar, Enrico Perotti, Raghuram Rajan, Hélène Rey, Kenneth Rogoff, Moritz

Schularick, Andrew Sheng, Joe Stiglitz, Larry Summers, Nassim Taleb, Gillian Tett, Jose Vinals, Paul Volcker, Richard Werner, and Bill White. Some of them will almost certainly disagree strongly with some of my arguments, but all have played a role in making me think.

I also thank many colleagues at the UK Financial Services Authority, and in particular Hector Sants and Andrew Bailey, who had to put up with my musings on fundamental causes and theory even as we were struggling with day-to-day crises, or who provided vital research input to analysis of these issues. And thanks also to the many members of the international Financial Stability Board with whom I worked closely for four years to redesign global financial regulation. There are far too many to mention them all, but in addition to Chairman Mark Carney, and Executive Director Svein Andresen (without whom we could never have made as much progress as we did), I pay particular tribute to fellow hawks in our debates, such as Philipp Hildebrand from Switzerland, Dan Tarullo and Sheila Bair from the United States, and my fellow Brit, Paul Tucker. We achieved a lot, even if I argue in this book that there is more to do.

I am also greatly indebted to my two research assistants, Lisa Windsteiger and Yuan Yang, who have helped me identify and analyze key arguments in the academic literature, have challenged my emerging ideas, and have been tenacious fact finders. My assistant Lina Morales has also played a vital role in the book's production, working in particular on the bibliography.

No book can ever see the light of day without the hard work and encouragement of the publisher, and I am very grateful to Seth Ditchik at Princeton University Press for his excellent advice, which helped give the book a strong central focus, as well as to Cyd Westmoreland and Karen Fortgang for their vital role in editing and production. And my thanks also to my excellent agent, Georgina Capel.

Finally and most importantly my deepest thanks go to my wife Orna, who has lived with this book not for the year that I thought it would take to write, but for the two it actually required. Without her encouragement I would never have finished it. And without her unflagging support during five demanding years at the Financial Services Authority, I would never have been able to start it. This book is dedicated to her.

THE CRISIS I DIDN'T SEE COMING

O N SATURDAY, SEPTEMBER 20, 2008, I became chairman of the UK Financial Services Authority. Lehman Brothers had failed the previous Monday; AIG had been rescued by the Federal Reserve on the Tuesday. Seventeen days later I was with Alistair Darling, UK finance minister, and Mervyn King, governor of the Bank of England, discussing with the major UK banks the need for public capital injections. The UK government ended up owning 85% of the Royal Bank of Scotland and 45% of Lloyds Bank Group. We faced the biggest financial crisis in 80 years. Seven days before I started, I had had no idea we were on the verge of disaster.

Nor did almost everyone in the central banks, regulators, or finance ministries, nor in financial markets or major economics departments. In April 2006, the International Monetary Fund (IMF) had described in detail how financial innovation had made the global financial system more stable. In summer 2007 the first signs of distress were seen as manageable liquidity problems. In summer 2008 most experts agreed that the point of maximum danger in this financial crisis had already passed. And even after the meltdown of autumn 2008, neither official commentators nor financial markets anticipated how deep and long lasting would be the post-crisis recession. Almost nobody foresaw that interest rates in major advanced economies would stay close to zero for at least 6 years. Almost no one predicted that the eurozone would suffer a severe crisis.

I held no official policy role before the crisis. But if I had, I would have made the same errors. As a director of a major bank, I was careful to understand evolving macroeconomic and financial risks. My career had involved extensive experience in private finance, but in the 1990s I had also advised finance ministries and central banks in Eastern Europe and Russia about overall financial system design. I thought I understood financial system risks. But in some crucial ways I did not.

My lack of foresight did not reflect blind faith in free financial markets. I always believed that financial markets were susceptible to surges of irrational exuberance: I was unconvinced by the Efficient Market Hypothesis. In a book I wrote in 2001 I included a chapter titled "Global Finance: Engine of Growth or Dangerous Casino?" As chair of the United Kingdom's Pensions Commission in 2006 I argued that we needed strong state intervention to ensure that long-term savers got value for money. But I had no inkling that advanced economy financial systems could collapse as they did in autumn 2008, nor that crisis would be followed by a near decade of lost growth.

From 2009 on I played a major role in global financial reform. In endless meetings with colleagues from around the world, we forged the new Basel III bank capital standard; we designed special regulations for globally systemically important banks. We inched forward toward regulations to curtail shadow banking risks.

In those debates I was a hawk—arguing for higher capital and liquidity requirements and tighter market controls. I think we achieved a lot. But as the depth of our post-crisis problems became apparent, I was increasingly convinced that our reforms failed to address the fundamental issues, and that we were wrong to assume that economies would recover if only we could restore confidence in the banking system.

The reforms we agreed to sought to make the financial system itself more stable and banks less likely to fail. That is very important. But financial system fragility alone cannot explain why the post-crisis Great Recession was so deep and recovery has been so weak.

To understand that, I found I had to return to questions usually ignored amid practical policy design. We need to ask why debt contracts exist, what benefits they bring, and what risks they inevitably create. We need to question whether banks should exist at all. And we need to recognize that developments seemingly only tangentially related to financial stability—the fact that richer people devote an increasing share of their income to buying real estate, and that inequality has increased across the advanced economies—are as important to the story as the technical details of financial regulation.

Radical policy implications follow. I now believe that banks should operate with leverage levels (the ratio of total assets to equity) more like five than the twenty-five or higher that we allowed before the crisis. And I argue that governments and central banks should sometimes stimulate economies by printing money to finance increased fiscal deficits. To many people the first proposal is absurdly radical and the second dangerously irresponsible; to many, too, they appear contradictory. But I hope to convince you that they are entirely consistent and appropriate, given the causes of the 2007–2008 crisis and the severe post-crisis recession. In 2008 I had no idea that I would make such proposals.

Nor in 2008 did I understand the huge risks facing the eurozone. Earlier indeed, I had argued in principle in favor of European monetary union. I recognized some of the risks involved, but not the most crucial ones. Radical changes are essential if the eurozone is to succeed: if they cannot be agreed to, it would be better for it to break up.

The 2007–2008 crisis also has major implications for the discipline of economics. Most mainstream economics failed to provide the insights that could have alerted us to danger; worse indeed, influential theories and models assumed that extreme instability was impossible. Of course the failure was not universal: there were always many schools of thought. And many economists, whom I cite in this book, have done excellent work explaining why financial markets are imperfect and how financial systems can amplify instability. But I still found it striking that to understand the causes and consequences of 2008, I had to return to the insights of early and mid-twentieth-century economists, such as Knut Wicksell, Friedrich Hayek, John Maynard Keynes, and Irving Fisher. And I had to discover the writings of Hyman Minsky, a late twentieth-century economist largely marginalized by the mainstream of the discipline.

In August 2009 some comments I made caused a stir: I said that some pre-crisis financial activity had been "socially useless." Originally reported in a worthy but small-circulation intellectual magazine, my phrase gained notoriety but also considerable support. Most people assumed I was referring to the exotica of "shadow banking," to the complex structured credit securities traded between major financial firms in ever increasing volumes in the pre-crisis years. That was indeed what I then had in mind. I felt then and still do that if amid the turmoil of 2008 we had managed to mislay the instructions for how to create a CDO-squared, humanity would be no worse off.

But increasingly I came to believe that the most fundamental problems of financial and economic instability are created not by activities that we would quite happily see disappear entirely, but by activities—such as lending money to someone to buy a house—which in moderate amounts are clearly valuable, but on an excessive scale can cause economic disaster. This book makes that argument.

BETWEEN DEBT AND THE DEVIL

|||||||||||||||||||||||||||||||||||||||||||||||||||||||||||||||||||||||||||||||||||||||||||||||||||||||||||||||||||||||||||||||||||||||||||||||||||||||||||||||||||||||||||||||||||||

TOO IMPORTANT TO BE LEFT TO THE BANKERS

FOR MANY DECADES BEFORE THE 2007–2008 CRISIS, finance got bigger relative to the real economy. Its share of the U.S. and UK economies tripled between 1950 and the 2000s. Stock-market turnover increased dramatically as a percentage of GDP. On average across advanced economies private-sector debt increased from 50% of national income in 1950 to 170% in 2006.[1] Trading in foreign exchange grew far faster than exports and imports; trading in commodities far faster than commodity production. Capital flows back and forth among countries grew far more rapidly than long-term real investment. From 1980 on, the growth was turbocharged by the financial innovations of securitization and derivatives; by 2008 there were $400 trillion of derivative contracts outstanding.

This growth rang few alarm bells. Most economists, financial regulators, and central banks believed that increasing financial activity and innovation were strongly beneficial. More complete and liquid markets, it was confidently asserted, ensured more efficient allocation of capital, fostering higher productivity. Financial innovations made it easier to provide credit to households and companies, enabling more rapid economic growth. Empirical studies suggested that "financial deepening"—an increase in private-sector debt as a percentage of GDP—made economies more efficient. More sophisticated risk-control systems, meanwhile, ensured that complexity was not at the expense of stability, and new systems for originating and distributing credit, rather than holding it on bank balance sheets, were believed to be dispersing risks into the hands of those best placed to manage it.

Not only, moreover, had the financial system become safer and more efficient: economies had also become more stable because of better central bank policies based on sound economic theory. Provided independent central banks ignored short-term political pressures and achieved low and stable inflation, a "Great Moderation" of steady growth seemed assured. Robert Lucas, then president of the American Economic Association, concluded in 2003 that "the central problem of depression prevention has been solved, for all practical purposes, and has in fact been solved for many decades."[2]

The Great Moderation ended in the crisis of 2007–2008, and in a severe post-crisis "Great Recession." The economic harm caused by this crisis has been enormous. Millions of people lost homes because of unaffordable debts; millions also suffered unemployment. The percentage of the U.S. population that is employed fell to a 35-year low, and despite limited recovery after 2013 is still far below the pre-crisis level.[3] The Spanish unemployment rate grew from 8% in 2007 to 26% in 2013 and has so far fallen only to 24%.[4] In the United Kingdom surprisingly strong jobs growth was accompanied until 2014 by falling real wages, and per capita income remains below its 2007 peak. Public debts have increased dramatically, and fiscal austerity programs have been introduced in response. Economic recovery is now under way, but in the United States it has been weak, in the United Kingdom dangerously unbalanced, and in the eurozone anemic. The fact that we are now slowly recovering from a deep and long-lasting recession must not blind us to the reality that the 2007–2008 crash was an economic catastrophe.

This catastrophe was entirely self-inflicted and avoidable. It was not the result of war or political turmoil, nor the consequence of competition from emerging economies. Unlike the problems of stagflation—simultaneous high inflation and high unemployment—which afflicted several developed countries in the 1970s, it did not derive from underlying tensions over income distribution, from profligate governments allowing public deficits to run out of control, or from powerful trade unions able to demand inflationary pay claims.

Instead this was a crisis whose origins lay in the dealing rooms of London and New York, in a global financial system whose enormous personal rewards had been justified by the supposedly great economic benefits that financial innovation and increased financial activity were delivering.

Many people are therefore legitimately angry about individual banks and bankers, and are concerned that few have been punished. Many bankers lent money recklessly to U.S. subprime mortgage borrowers or to Irish, Spanish, or British real estate developers. And some acted dishonestly, manipulating the LIBOR[5] rate or knowingly selling securities whose value they doubted to investors whose acumen they disparaged.

But important though the incompetence and dishonesty of some bankers was, it was not a fundamental driver of the crisis, any more than the misbehavior of individual financiers in 1920s America was of more than peripheral importance to the origins of the 1930s Great Depression.

As for regulatory reform, much focus has been placed on making sure that no bank is "too big to fail" and that taxpayers never again have to bail out the banks as they did in autumn 2008. That is certainly very important. But focus on the too-big-to-fail problem also misses the vital issue. Government bailout costs were the small change of the harm produced by the financial crisis. In the United States the total direct cost of government support for the banking system is likely to be negative: the Federal Reserve has sold all its capital injections into banks at a profit, and made a positive return on its provision of liquidity to the financial system. Across the advanced economies overall bailout and support costs will be at most 3% of GDP.[6]

The full economic cost of the crash and post-crisis recession is far bigger. On average in advanced economies public debt increased by 34% of GDP between 2007 and 2014.[7] But even more importantly, national incomes and living standards in many countries are 10% or more below where they could have been and are likely to remain there, not for a year, but for year after year in perpetuity. It is on this loss we should focus, and such a loss could be suffered again even if we managed to create a regulatory regime that ensured we never again had to put public money into failing banks.

Neither bankers threatened by prison nor a no-bailout regime will guarantee a more stable financial system, and a fixation on these issues threatens to divert us from the underlying causes of financial instability.

The fundamental problem is that modern financial systems left to themselves inevitably create debt in excessive quantities, and in particular debt that does not fund new capital investment but rather the purchase of already existing assets, above all real estate. It is that debt creation which drives booms and financial busts: and it is the debt overhang left over by the boom that explains why recovery from the 2007–2008 financial crisis has been so anemic.

But from the point of view of private profit-maximizing banks, even when run by good competent honest bankers, debt creation that is excessive in aggregate can seem rational, profitable, and socially useful. It is like a form of economic pollution. Heating a house or fueling a car is socially valuable, but the carbon emissions produced have a harmful effect on the climate. Lending a family money to buy a house can be socially useful, but too much mortgage debt in total can make the economy unstable. So debt pollution, like environmental pollution, must be constrained by public policy.

One objective of this book is therefore to define the policies needed to prevent excessive debt creation leading to future financial crises: these policies need to go far beyond current regulatory reforms. The second is to propose how to escape from the debt overhang which past policy errors have bequeathed and which continues to depress economic growth across the developed world: doing that will require policies previously considered taboo. Finally I aim to identify why mainstream modern economics failed to see the crisis coming, and why it so confidently asserted that increasing financial activity had made the world a safer place. To do that, we need to return to the insights about credit, money, and banks on which an earlier generation of economists focused, but which modern economics has largely ignored.

Inefficient Markets and Dangerous Debt

All financial markets are to different degrees imperfect and subject to surges of exuberance and then despair, which take prices far from rational equilibrium levels and can result in inefficient misallocation of capital resources. That reality, explored in Chapter 2, means that more financial activity is not always beneficial, and should make us very wary of strongly free market approaches to financial regulation. Free financial markets can generate more trading activity than is socially beneficial: so financial transaction taxes are in principle justified. And financial firms enjoy more opportunities than in other sectors of the economy to make money without truly adding value—to extract economic "rent." Policy interventions to protect investors against exploitation are justified and often essential. Free financial markets alone, moreover, are not sufficient to ensure adequate support for the investment and innovation that drive forward economic progress: governments have often played important roles.

But the inevitable inefficiency and irrational volatility of financial markets does not in itself justify a fundamental shift in policy approach. Even imperfect and inefficient markets can still play a valuable economic role. The irrational exuberance of the Internet boom and bust of the late 1990s and early 2000 certainly produced large economic waste, but it also helped foster the development of the Internet. A perfect planner could have done better but no such perfect planner exists. And in her absence, financial markets will usually allocate capital better than governments will.

We must therefore focus not on some unattainable perfection, but on the most important causes of the 2007–2008 crisis and post-crisis recession. Those lay in the specific nature of debt contracts, and in the ability of banks and shadow banks to create credit and money.

Many religions and moral philosophies have been wary of debt contracts. Aristotle described money lending as the "most hated sort" of wealth getting, since "it makes the gain out of money itself and not from the natural object of it." Islam condemns debt contracts as inherently unfair: they make the borrower pay a fixed return even if the economic project which the borrowing financed has failed. But many economists and economic historians argue that debt contracts play a crucial role in capitalist growth, and their arguments are convincing. The very fact that debt contracts deliver a predefined return almost certainly made it possible to mobilize savings and capital investment—whether for nineteenth-century railways or twentieth-century manufacturing plants—which would not have been forthcoming if all investment contracts had to take a more risky equity form.

But the fixed nature of debt contracts also has inevitable adverse consequences. As Chapters 3 and 4 explain, it means that debt is likely to be created in excessive quantities. And it means that the more debt there is in an economy, beyond some level, the less stable that economy will inevitably be.

The dangers of excessive and harmful debt creation are inherent to the nature of debt contracts. But they are hugely magnified by the existence of banks, and by the predominance of particular categories of lending. Read almost any economics or finance textbook, and it will describe how banks take money from savers and lend it to business borrowers, allocating money among alternative capital investment projects. But as a description of what banks do in modern economies, this is dangerously fictitious for two reasons. First, because banks do not intermediate already existing money, but *create* credit, money, and purchasing power which did not previously exist.[8] And second, because the vast majority of bank lending in advanced economies does not support new business investment but instead funds either increased consumption or the purchase of already existing assets, in particular real estate and the urban land on which it sits.

As a result, unless tightly constrained by public policy, banks make economies unstable. Newly created credit and money increases purchasing power. But if locationally desirable urban real estate is in scarce supply, the result is not new investment but asset price increases, which induce yet more credit demand and yet more credit supply. At the core of financial instability in modern economies, this book argues, lies the interaction between the infinite capacity of banks to create new credit, money, and purchasing power, and the scarce supply of irreproducible urban land. Self-reinforcing credit and asset price cycles of boom and bust are the inevitable result.

Such cycles are inherent to any highly leveraged banking system. But they can also be generated by the complex chains of nonbank debt origination, trading, and distribution—"the shadow banking system"—which developed ahead of the 2007–2008 crisis. Indeed, as Chapter 6 argues, the development of more complex and liquid markets in credit securities increased the dangers of volatility; and the very techniques that were supposed to control risk actually increased it. If debt can be a form of economic pollution, a more complicated and sophisticated debt creation engine can make the pollution worse. The net effect of pre-crisis financial innovation was to give us the credit cycle on steroids, and the crash of 2008.

The depth of the recession that followed, however, is explained less by the internal features of the financial system than by the simple fact that after years of rapid credit growth, many companies and households were overleveraged. Once confidence in rising asset prices cracked, they cut investment and consumption in an attempt to reduce their debts. That attempted deleveraging in turn has stymied economic recovery.

The crash itself was thus caused both by excessive real economy leverage and by multiple deficiencies in the financial system itself; but the main reason recovery has been slow and weak is not that the financial system is still impaired, but the scale of the debt burden accumulated over the preceding decades.

The Conundrum: Do We Need Ever More Credit to Grow Our Economies?

For 50 years, private-sector leverage—credit divided by GDP—grew rapidly in all advanced economies; between 1950 and 2006 it more than tripled. But that poses a crucial question: was this credit growth necessary?

Leverage increased because credit grew faster than nominal GDP. In the two decades before 2008 the typical picture in most advanced economies was that credit grew at about 10–15% per year versus 5% annual growth in nominal national income. And it seemed at the time that such credit growth was required to ensure adequate economic growth. If central banks had increased interest rates to slow the credit growth, our standard theory suggests that that would have led to lower real growth. The same pattern and the same policy assumptions can now be seen in many emerging economies, including in particular China: each year credit grows faster than GDP so that leverage rises, and that credit growth appears necessary to drive the economies forward.

But if that is really true, we face a severe dilemma. We seem to need credit to grow faster than GDP to keep economies growing at a reasonable rate, but that leads inevitably to crisis, debt overhang, and post-crisis recession. We seem condemned to instability in an economy incapable of balanced growth with stable leverage.

Is that true, and are future crises, as bad as 2007–2008, therefore inevitable? My answer is no, and I argue in this book that it should be possible and is essential to develop a less credit-intensive growth model. But I also argue that it will only be possible if we recognize and respond to three underlying drivers of increasing credit intensity.

The first is the increasing importance of real estate in modern economies. Real estate accounts for more than half of all wealth, for the vast majority of increases in wealth, and for the vast majority of lending in all advanced economies. For reasons which Chapter 5 explains, this is the inevitable consequence of trends in productivity, in the cost of capital goods, and in consumer preferences—that is, what people want to spend their income on. Real estate is bound to become more important in advanced economies: but that has consequences for financial and economic stability that need to be carefully managed.

The second driver is increasing inequality. Richer people tend to spend a lower proportion of their income than do middle income and poorer people. Increasing inequality will therefore depress demand and economic growth, unless the increased savings of the rich are offset by increased borrowing among middle or low income earners. In an increasingly unequal society, rising credit and leverage become necessary to maintain economic growth but lead inevitably to eventual crisis.

The third driver is global current-account imbalances unrelated to long-term investment flows and useful capital investment. These imbalances must inevitably be matched by the accumulation of unsustainable debt.

These three factors each result in a growth of debt that, contrary to the textbook assumption, does not support productive capital investment and does not therefore generate new income streams with which debt can be repaid. As a result, they drive increases in leverage that are not required to spur economic growth but will produce severe economic harm.

Financial and economic stability will only be attainable if we address these underlying factors.

What to Do—Building a Less Credit-Intensive Economy

This analysis of the causes of the crisis and post-crisis recession—set out in Parts I–III—poses two questions, which Parts IV and V address. First: how to build a less credit-intensive and more stable economy, reducing the risks of future crises? Second: how to deal with the debt overhang inherited from a half-century of credit-intensive growth?

On the first, policies to ensure better run banks and more competent and honest bankers will never be a sufficient policy response. For if excessive debt is like pollution, its growth imposes on the economy a negative externality which it will *never* be sensible for profit-maximizing banks to take fully into account. Indeed as Chapter 10 argues, even lending which from a private perspective looks like and is "good lending"—loans that can be and are paid back in full—can still produce harmful instability for the whole economy. Even good competent bankers can, through the collective impact of their actions, make economies unstable. And as Chapter 6 describes, even the banks that most expertly applied the new techniques of Value at Risk modeling and mark-to-market accounting, and that survived 2007–2008 relatively unscathed, contributed just as much to the crisis as did the incompetents who went bust. Certainly we should use public policy sanctions—such as changes to directors' responsibilities or to compensation rules—to penalize incompetent or reckless behavior. Certainly we should address the too-big-to-fail problem. But such policies will never be sufficient to achieve a more stable economy.

Nor, either, will central bank policy still operating within the assumption that we can have one objective—low inflation, and one instrument—the interest rate. In the decades before 2008 central bank practice and modern macroeconomic theory gravitated to the belief that achieving low and stable inflation was sufficient to ensure financial and macroeconomic stability, and that any dangers arising from credit creation would show up in present or prospective inflation. But a central argument of this book is that we can have excessive credit growth that *never* results in excessive inflation but still produces crisis, debt overhang, and post-crisis deflation. We enjoyed low and stable inflation in the pre-crisis "Great Moderation": and in its aftermath inflation has remained below central bank targets. And yet excessive credit growth still produced a financial and economic disaster.

An alternative approach, favored by several economists associated with the Bank for International Settlements, would be to lean against excessive credit growth by increasing interest rates even when inflation is low and stable. This may sometimes be appropriate. But it can never be sufficient. For if we rely on interest rates alone to slow down credit booms, we are likely, as Chapter 11 discusses, to do so at the expense of curtailing desirable investment and growth.

Policy must therefore address both the underlying causes of excessive credit creation and the inherent instability created by the nature of debt contracts and banks. Policies related to urban development and to the taxation of real estate can be as crucial to financial stability as the technical details of financial regulation or interest rate decisions. So too is action to address growing inequality and large global imbalances. But we must also recognize that financial instability is inherent in any financial system that is allowed to create credit, money, and purchasing power, and we must decide how radically to address that fact.

Several economists who lived through the boom of 1920s America and the subsequent Great Depression, such as Irving Fisher and Henry Simons, concluded that the answer had to be very radical. They believed that "fractional reserve banks," which keep only a small fraction of their liabilities in central bank reserves or in notes and coins, and which as a result can create credit and money, were so inherently dangerous that they should be abolished. Milton Friedman made the same case in an article written in 1948. Instead they proposed that banks should hold reserves equal to 100% of their deposits and should play no role in the extension of credit, being instead simply custodians of money savings and providers of payment services. Loan contracts would still exist in the economy, but they would be outside the banking system and would involve no new creation of money and purchasing power.

For reasons I set out in Chapter 12, I believe that proposal is too extreme. But the powerful arguments that Fisher, Simons, and others put forward for 100% reserve banking certainly justify a program of reform far more radical than has been implemented so far. We need to impose far higher bank capital requirements than those set out in the Basel III standard, but we must also use reserve requirements directly to limit banks' money creation capacity. We should change tax regimes to reduce the current bias in favor of debt finance and against equity. We should equip central banks as macroprudential regulators with powers to impose far larger countercyclical capital requirements than have so far been established. And we should place tough constraints on the ability of the shadow banking system to create credit and money equivalents, and must not be diverted from that path by spurious arguments about the dangers of inadequate liquidity in credit markets.

We should also use public policy to produce a different allocation of credit than would result from purely private decisions, deliberately leaning against the private bias toward real estate and instead should favor other potentially more socially valuable forms of credit allocation. Minimum risk weights that determine the capital needed to support different categories of lending should be set by regulators and not, as under current Basel agreements, on the basis of individual banks' assessments of risks. Constraints on mortgage borrowers through maximum loan-to-value (LTV) and loan-to-income ratios (LTI) have an important role to play. And we should be willing to place some limits on the free flow of international capital; some fragmentation of the global financial system can be a good thing.

Governments of emerging economies, meanwhile, observing the mess into which overconfidence in the merits of free market finance took the advanced economies, should be wary of the supposed benefits of rapid and comprehensive financial liberalization.

These proposals will be attacked as anti-growth and anti-market. But the argument that they are anti-growth is based on the delusion that we need rapid credit growth to achieve economic growth, and on a failure to recognize that rising leverage will lead inevitably to crisis and post-crisis recession. And the argument that they are anti-market ignores the reality that all financial markets are imperfect and banking markets are even more so.

Irving Fisher and Henry Simons were in general very strong proponents of free markets and were deeply suspicious of government intervention. But they believed that the processes of credit and money creation were so distinct and so inherently social in nature, that free market principles should not apply to them. They believed, rightly, that credit creation is too important to be left to the bankers: future policies need to reflect that fact.

Escaping the Debt Overhang Mess

But those policies were not in place before the crisis. Instead, credit was treated as a product like any other, its supply, demand, and allocation left almost entirely to free market forces.[9] As a result we suffered a huge crisis and now face an enormous debt overhang, severely constraining economic growth. While designing a better system for the future, we must therefore also navigate as best possible out of the debt overhang left by past policy mistakes. Doing so, I argue in this book, requires unconventional policies previously considered taboo.

Once economies have too much debt, it seems impossible to get rid of it. All we have done since the 2007–2008 crisis is to shift it around, from the private to the public sector, and from advanced economies to emerging economies, such as China. Total global debt to GDP, public and private combined, has continued to grow.

Faced with large inherited debt burdens, all policy levers appear to be blocked. Fiscal deficits can stimulate the economy, offsetting the deflationary effect of private deleveraging, but the result is increasing public debt to GDP, raising concerns about debt sustainability. As for ultra-easy monetary policies—interest rates close to zero and quantitative easing—they are certainly better than nothing: without them the advanced economies would have suffered still deeper recessions. But they can only work by reigniting the very growth in private credit that got us into our current problems: they create incentives for risky financial engineering, and their impact on asset prices exacerbates inequality. Reducing the value of debt through restructuring and writedowns, meanwhile, should certainly play a role, but can in some circumstances exacerbate deflationary pressures.

As a result we seem condemned to continued weak growth and fiscal austerity in the eurozone, to a mediocre recovery in the United States, and to an unbalanced recovery in the United Kingdom. Japan meanwhile, faces an ever-growing level of public debt that will never be repaid in the normal sense of the word. And as 2015 progresses, it looks increasingly likely that China's credit boom is ending in a potentially dangerous downturn.

It seems that we are out of ammunition—the policy magazine is empty. But if the problem we face is inadequate nominal demand, the magazine is never empty, and there is always one more option left. That option is "fiat" money creation, using central bank-printed money either to finance increased public deficits or to write off existing public debt. In Chapter 14 I argue that we should be willing to use that option. Failure to use it until now has produced an unnecessarily deep and long-lasting recession, and has increased the dangers of future financial instability, which inevitably result from continued very low interest rates.

My proposals will horrify many economists and policymakers, and in particular central bankers. "Printing money" to finance public deficits is a taboo policy. It has indeed almost the status of a mortal sin—the work of the devil. In September 2012, Jens Weidman, president of the Bundesbank, cited the story of Part II of Goethe's Faust, in which Mephistopheles, agent of the devil, tempts the emperor to print and distribute paper money, increasing spending power and writing off state debts. Initially the money fuels an economic upswing, but, inevitably in Weidman's eyes, the policy "degenerates into inflation, destroying the monetary system."[10]

But it is striking that the mid-twentieth century economists who proposed the 100% reserve banking model, though as strongly committed to low inflation as they were to free markets, believed that fiat money creation was a *safer* way to stimulate nominal demand than relying on private credit creation.[11] Their belief sprang from deep reflection on the nature of credit and money, and on possible sources of nominal demand growth.

Between Debt and the Devil—A Choice of Dangers

There are essentially two ways to achieve nominal demand growth—through government money creation or through private credit growth. Each has advantages and disadvantages. Each can be beneficial up to a point but becomes dangerous in excess.

History provides many examples of governments that successfully stimulated sustainable economic growth with printed money. During the American Civil War, the U.S. Union government printed greenbacks to pay for the war without generating dangerously high inflation; Japanese finance minister Takehashi used central bank funded fiscal deficits to pull Japan's economy out of depression in the early 1930s.[12] But the counterexamples of the Confederate states in the U.S. Civil War, Weimar Germany, and modern Zimbabwe illustrate the danger that once the option of printing money is first allowed, governments may print so much that they trigger hyperinflation.

Private credit can also be beneficial up to some point: for instance, strong arguments can be made that countries like India would benefit if they had higher levels of private credit to GDP. But free markets left to themselves will keep on creating private credit and money beyond the optimal level and will allocate it in ways that generate unstable asset price cycles, crises, debt overhang, and post-crisis recession.

We face a balance of benefits and dangers, not a choice between perfection on one side and inevitable perdition on the other.

In the pre-crisis years economic orthodoxy was characterized by an anathema against government money creation and a totally relaxed attitude to whatever level of private credit free markets generated. But the latter led to a disaster from which many ordinary citizens throughout the world are still suffering. To prevent future crises we need far tighter controls on private credit creation than we had before the crisis. And to get out of the debt overhang, we need to break the taboo against the money finance of fiscal deficits, while ensuring that the option is not used to excess.

The Book's Structure

I set out my argument in five parts.

Part I describes the dramatic growth of the financial system and the confident pre-crisis assessment of its great benefits. It argues that all financial markets are in fact imperfect and potentially unstable. As a result, more finance is not necessarily good. But it also recognizes that even imperfect financial markets play a useful role and cautions against any delusion that we can or should pursue absolute perfection.

Part II focuses on the core driver of financial instability—excessive credit creation. It explains how banks and shadow banks create credit and money, and the positive as well as adverse consequences stemming from that ability. It identifies the underlying reasons that growth has been so credit intensive, and the severity of the debt overhang we now face as a result of excessive debt creation over the past half-century. It argues that we cannot leave either the quantity of credit created or its allocation among different uses entirely to free market forces. It concludes by describing the alternative potential sources of nominal demand growth, and the danger that without radical policies we could face a "secular stagnation" of chronically deficient demand.

Part III considers the role of credit creation in economic development and the impact of international capital flows. It describes how the most successful developing countries used credit direction to foster rapid economic growth but also identifies the potential dangers in that approach. It rejects the pre-crisis orthodoxy that global financial integration is limitlessly beneficial and argues that some fragmentation of the international financial system is a good thing. It also considers the special case of the eurozone, whose flawed political design left it ill-equipped to deal with the consequences of unsustainable private credit creation and capital flows, and which cannot deliver economic success without radical reform.

Parts IV and V set out policy implications. Part IV describes the policies required to build a less credit-intensive economy in the future, reducing the risks of future crises. Part V addresses how to escape the debt overhang left behind by past policy mistakes and how to address the dangers of secular stagnation.

The Epilogue asks why modern economic theory left us so ill equipped to see the crisis coming, and how, in a sort of strange amnesia, it came to ignore the crucial insights of earlier generations of economists. It argues for a major change not just in policies, but also in ideas and in the approach to the social science of economics. We must, it suggests, avoid the "fatal conceit" that economics can deliver precise answers or that either the market or the state can deliver perfect results.

PART I

Swollen Finance

||||||||||||||||||||||||||||||||||||||||||||||||||

F OR 40 YEARS BEFORE THE 2007–2008 CRISIS, finance grew far faster
than the real economy, private credit grew faster than GDP, trading
volume soared, and the financial system became far more complex. And
as Chapter 1 describes, most experts were confident that increasing size
and complexity had improved capital allocation, stimulated economic
growth, and posed no threat to economic stability as long as inflation
was low and stable.

But as the 2007–2008 crisis showed, that confidence was profoundly
mistaken and was based on shaky intellectual foundations. For as Chapter 2 sets out, all financial markets can be imperfect, inefficient, and unstable, and finance has a distinctive ability to grow beyond its socially
useful size, making private profit from activities that add no true social
value.

Public policy should not therefore be driven by the assumption that
ever more financial innovation, market completion, and liquidity is by
definition good: less finance can be better, and policies such as financial
transaction taxes might make economies more efficient.

But policy should also reflect the reality that state-driven capital allocation can be even more deficient, and that even imperfect financial
markets can play valuable roles. Policy reform must therefore focus on
the specific areas where swollen finance has the greatest potential to
cause harm. That is above all where it creates excessive debt.

||||||||||||||||||||||||||||||||||||||||||||||||||||||||||||||||||||||||||||||||||||||||||||||||||||||||||||||||||||||||||||||||||||||||||||||||||||||||||||||||||

ONE

THE UTOPIA OF FINANCE FOR ALL

In the last thirty years, dramatic changes in financial systems
around the world amounting, de facto, to a revolution have
brought many ... advances. We have come closer to the utopia
of finance for all.

—*Raghuram Rajan and Luigi Zingales,* Saving Capitalism from the
Capitalists[1]

FINANCE LOOMS FAR LARGER in both advanced and emerging economies than it did 30 or 40 years ago. Few readers will need convincing
of that fact. Newspapers and television programs report regularly on the
huge size of global capital markets and trading activity. Financial centers
such as New York, London, or Hong Kong have ballooned in importance. Huge bonuses paid to bank trading staff and management are
highly contentious in many countries, but the money earned by hedge
fund managers dwarfs that of mere bankers. Finance has become the
destination of choice for top graduates from elite universities and business schools throughout the world. Some commentators talk about the
"financialization" of our economies. It is an ugly word, but it seems to
capture the reality: more finance, better paid, playing a more pervasive
role in economic life.

Impressions often deceive. But in this case, sober analysis confirms
what anecdote suggests. Significantly in most advanced economies but
dramatically in the United States and the United Kingdom, finance has
accounted for a growing share of national income. And across the world,
in many different financial markets, trading activity has massively increased, its growth far outpacing that of real economic activity.

Finance has grown more rapidly than the real economy since modern capitalism first developed in the nineteenth century. Analysis by Andrew Haldane shows finance in the United Kingdom growing on average by 4.4% per year from 1856 to 2008, while the economy grew at 2.1%.[2]

But Haldane's analysis also reveals big variations in growth over time. From 1856 to 1914, the value-added of UK financial services grew 3.5 times more rapidly than national income. The economy became more complex as industry grew at the expense of agriculture; companies issued bonds and stocks on public markets; individuals began to accumulate savings; and London became a financial center servicing global capital flows. As a result the financial industry became far more important.

From 1914 to 1970 finance grew less rapidly than total GDP, even though the economy, despite two world wars, grew faster than in the previous period: by 1970 finance accounted for a smaller share of a far bigger economy than in 1914. But from 1970 on, and in particular after 1980, the picture changed again. From 1970 to 2008 UK finance grew twice as fast as UK national income, with the outperformance becoming greater as each decade progressed.

The U.S. experience, illustrated in Figure 1.1, was similar. Between 1850 and the crash of 1929, finance's share of national income grew from 2% to 6%, with a particularly strong increase throughout the 1920s. That share collapsed in the 1930s and even in 1970 stood at a significantly lower 4%. From 1970 to 2008 it more than doubled. In 2007 finance played a bigger role in advanced economies, as measured by share of GDP, than ever before.[3]

The growth of finance from the 1970s on, and the acceleration of that growth over the subsequent decades, would be an important issue for economic research even if we had not suffered the financial crisis of 2007–2008. Finance, after all, is not a consumer product or service, valued in itself, like a car or a restaurant meal or clothing. No one gets up in the morning and says "I feel like enjoying some financial services today." Finance is a necessary function to enable the production of the goods and services we actually enjoy. And it makes up a large enough proportion of the economy that the cost efficiency with which the financial industry performs these functions has a significant impact on people's living standard. Even if there had been no crisis, it would be worth asking whether we are getting value for money.

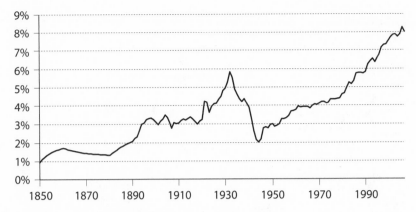

Figure 1.1.   Share of the financial industry in U.S. GDP

Source: Philippon (2008) (as referenced by Haldane, Brennan, and Madouros 2010). Used with permission.

But it is the financial crisis of 2007–2008 that makes it not merely interesting but vital to ask searching questions about the economic impact of this huge increase in financial intensity. For the crisis and its aftermath have been an economic catastrophe, a setback to the success of the market economy system only previously matched by the two world wars and the Great Depression of the 1930s.

We cannot therefore avoid the questions: Which aspects of this growing financial intensity were beneficial and which harmful? Which led to the crisis, and how radically must we now reform to prevent a repeat?

Increasing Real Economy Borrowing ... and Saving

The first step is to identify which specific financial activities contributed most to finance's remarkable growth. Research by Robin Greenwood and David Scharfstein shows that two factors dominated.[4]

First, finance made much more money out of providing credit to the economy, and in particular credit to households. Second, asset management activities and profits grew dramatically; that growth reflected increased fees flowing to a wide range of financial institutions such as securities firms, mutual funds, hedge funds, and venture capitalists. But

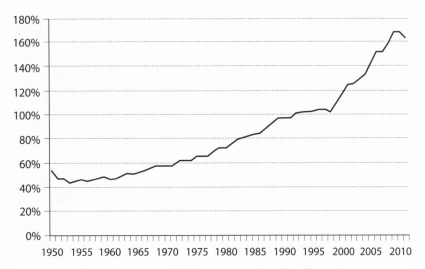

Figure 1.2.   Private domestic credit as a percentage of GDP: Advanced economies, 1950–2011

Source: IMF Working Paper 13/266 *Financial and Sovereign Debt Crises: Some Lessons Learned and Those Forgotten.* Authors: C. Reinhart and K. Rogoff, December 2013.

it also entailed the extensive trading, market-making, and funding ac-tivities that form inputs to the asset management process.

Other aspects of finance also grew, but less dramatically. Insurance for instance grew slowly as a percentage of GDP but without the sharp acceleration in growth that marked debt and asset management–related activities.

Greenwood and Scharfstein's findings reflect a startling and import-ant fact—that the role of debt in the U.S. economy, and in most other advanced economies, grew dramatically. Finance made lots more money from providing credit, because households and companies borrowed much more. In 1945 total private sector debt—household and business combined—was about 50% of U.S. GDP; by 2007 it had reached 160%. In the United Kingdom in 1964, total household debt stood at 15% of GDP; by 2007 it was 95%. In Spain total private debt was 80% in 1980 and 230% by 2007.[5] Figure 1.2 shows the picture for all advanced econ-omies combined. The private sector became dramatically more leveraged: households—and in some countries, businesses—owed much more debt relative to their income.

Increasing borrowing also helps explain rising asset management revenues. For every debt in an economy, every financial liability, there has to be some matching asset. Sometimes that match may be easy to see: a corporate bond owed by a business can be an asset owned by a pension fund. Sometimes the match is indirect and more difficult to discern: a mortgage debt indirectly funded, through multiple intermediate steps, by investors in money market mutual funds.

But overall the growth of debt liabilities as a percentage of GDP had to be matched by increases in fixed income assets, by money or bonds of some sort. In the United Kingdom household bank deposits grew from 40% to 75% of GDP between 1964 and 2007;[6] in the United States money market funds grew from zero in 1980 to $3.1 trillion in 2007.[7] Institutional holdings of bank debt and of non-bank credit securities also dramatically increased, indirectly or directly funding increased borrowing.

Fixed-income financial assets thus inevitably grew as a percentage of GDP, rising in the United States from 137% in 1970 to 265% in 2012.[8] So too did financial assets in an equity form. Total U.S. equity market value rose from 58% of GDP in 1989 to 142% in 2007.[9] There were many more assets to manage, so the business of managing assets grew.

Part of the reason finance grew is therefore simply that the real economy—households and businesses—owed more financial liabilities and owned more financial assets. To assess the impact of increasing financial intensity, we must therefore assess whether this increased use of financial services by the real economy was beneficial.

In most other sectors of the economy we wouldn't even ask such a question. If people choose to spend more of their increasing income on a particular service—more restaurant meals or travel—we usually trust that they have used their income in the way best suited to increase their welfare. But financial services are different, because their provision and consumption can have important effects on overall economic growth and stability.

Seen from the asset side, increased financial consumption might appear clearly beneficial: people holding more financial assets sounds like a good thing. But the dramatic increase in private sector leverage had important and harmful effects. Indeed, a central argument of this book is that the high level of private debt built up before the crisis is the most fundamental reason the 2007–2008 crisis wrought such economic harm.

Increasing Complexity in the Financial System

But the dramatic acceleration of finance's growth that occurred after the 1970s was not just the result of greater use of financial services by real economy households and businesses. Equally striking is that for each unit of financial services consumption by the real economy, the financial system itself did far more, and more complex, activities.

One way to capture that increased complexity is shown in Figure 1.3, which sets out the scale of debt liabilities in the U.S. financial system. It illustrates the gradual growth of corporate leverage and the more significant growth of household leverage. But the most striking feature of Figure 1.3 is the growth of intrafinancial system assets—of debt and other contracts between different financial institutions. Financial institutions did much more business with one another than they had done before 1970.

Look at the typical bank balance sheet in the 1960s, and apart from government bond holdings and cash, it was dominated by loans to and deposits from households and businesses. In the United Kingdom in 1964 loans to the real economy plus government bonds and reserves at the

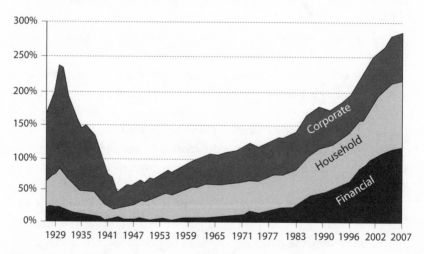

Figure 1.3.   U.S. debt as a percentage of GDP by borrower type

Source: Oliver Wyman.

Bank of England accounted for more than 90% of aggregate bank balance sheets.[10] By 2008 much more than half the balance sheets of many of the biggest banks in the world—such as JP Morgan, Citibank, Deutsche Bank, Barclays, RBS, or Société Générale—were accounted for by contractual links, whether in loan / deposit or in financial derivative form, between these and other banks, and between them and other financial institutions, such as money market funds, institutional investors, or hedge funds.

That reflected in part a dramatic increase in trading activity. Financial institutions buy and sell financial instruments back and forth between each other to a far greater extent than they did 40 years ago, and financial trading has grown dramatically relative to underlying real economic flows. The value of oil futures trading has gone from less than 10% of physical oil production and consumption in 1984 to more than 10 times that of production and consumption now.[11] Global foreign exchange trading is now around 73 times global trade in goods and services.[12] Trading in derivatives played a minimal role in the financial system of 1980, but it now dwarfs the size of the real economy; from zero in 1980, the total notional value of outstanding interest rate derivative contracts had soared by 2007 to more than $400 trillion, about nine times the value of global GDP.[13]

This growth of trading activity was spread across numerous different asset classes and contract types. But one of the most important changes was increased trading of credit securities, a key element in the phenomena we label "securitization" and "shadow banking."

Tradable credit securities, bonds that represent a debt claim against some counterparty, have existed for as long as bank loans: government and corporate bonds were extensively issued and somewhat less extensively traded in 1950, when finance accounted for just 2% of U.S. GDP. But from the 1970s, the scale of credit security creation soared, above all in the United States, but with consequences across all advanced economies and major financial centers. The credit intermediation system that connected end borrowers with end savers was transformed.

The new system was built on the innovations of credit securitization, credit structuring, and credit derivatives. Securitization enabled loans to homeowners, car buyers, students, or businesses to be pooled into composite credit securities and sold to end investors rather than held to maturity on bank balance sheets; it extended bond-based finance from governments and major corporations to a wider set of borrowers. Credit structuring divided up the risk and return inherent in a portfolio of loans and allowed the creation of different tranches of credit securities— from low-risk low-return "super senior" claims to high-risk mezzanine or equity. It gave us the alphabet soup of collateralized loan obligations (CLOs), collateralized debt obligations (CDOs), and even CDO-squareds. CDOs did not even exist in 1995; in 2006 $560 billion of new CDOs were issued.[14] Credit default swaps (CDS) were invented to allow banks to hedge credit risk, but they also enabled banks and other investors or dealers to seek profit from position taking: their value grew from zero in 1990 to almost $60 trillion by 2007.[15]

Together these innovations enabled credit exposures originated by banks (or nonbanks) in one country to be distributed to end investors across the world. Mortgage lending to British homeowners could be turned into securities and funded indirectly by U.S. money market funds. Subprime mortgage loans to U.S. low-income households could be financed by German Landesbanks seeking higher return without, it was hoped, more risk.

But the common description of this system as one of "origination and distribution" fails to do justice to its complexity. In fact credit securities and the credit derivatives that referred to them could be traded back and forth numerous times between multiple institutions. And the same credit security could pass from borrower to ultimate investor through multiple intermediate steps. An investor in an apparently low-risk and instantly available money market fund could indirectly finance 30-year mortgages, with the finance passing through contracts in the asset-backed commercial paper (ABCP) market, via structured investment vehicles (SIVs) or Conduits, or through the repo market and hedge funds.

The sheer complexity of the securitized credit and shadow banking system on the eve of the crisis is mind boggling. The Federal Reserve Bank of New York attempted to capture all of its possible paths and interconnections on a single map. It printed the results on a poster 3 feet × 4 feet in size and recommended that anyone attempting to understand the system should do the same: anything smaller and it becomes difficult to read the labels.

The overall impact was as Figure 1.3 illustrates. For each unit of real economy borrowing or saving, the financial system itself did more, and more complex, activities.

Therefore, in addition to assessing the impact of increasing real economic leverage, we need to assess the consequences—positive or negative—of this increasing complexity in the financial system itself. Although there may have been some positive effects, Chapter 6 argues that the net impact was severely negative. Increased complexity made the financial system inherently less stable, and it facilitated excessive credit extension and leverage in the real economy. As a result it both made the crisis more likely and the consequences more severe.

More Finance, Higher Pay

The financial system thus became both bigger and more complex. It also paid much better. Even in 2012, 4 years after the crisis, more than 2,500 bankers in London were earning more than £1 million per year.[16]

As with anecdotes of increasing financial activity, so with financiers' pay, quantitative analysis confirms what impressions suggest. Pay rates in finance increased far faster than in the rest of the economy. Thomas Philippon and Ariel Reshef have analyzed the "excess wage" of the U.S. financial sector—the amount by which pay in the financial sector exceeds that of people with comparable skill levels in other sectors of the economy.[17] The size of that excess has mirrored the swings in the relative size of the financial sector. In the 1920s, as finance played an increasing role in the economy, it soared from zero to about 40%. After the 1929 crash and the regulation of finance that followed, it fell as dramatically, varying around zero to 5% from the 1930s to the 1980s (at times indeed it was negative). By the eve of the 2007–2008 crash, it had grown back to 50%.

Rising inequality has been a striking feature of most advanced economies over the past 30 years, and the financialization of the economy has played a major role in that increase. Not surprisingly, finance has drawn to itself a disproportionate share of highly skilled people. Finance has become, in a way that it was not in the 1950s and 1960s, the predominant destination of choice for top graduates from elite universities and business schools, and the dealing rooms of the world are filled with numerous top math and physics graduates, devoting their skills to trading strategies and financial innovation, rather than to scientific research or industrial innovation. This is socially useful if those trading strategies and innovation help make the market economy more efficient, or the financial system more stable. If not, these skills are being wasted.

Finance's Impact: The Benign Pre-crisis Assessment

So finance got bigger, more complex, and better paid. And until the crisis of 2007–2008 most policymakers and academic economists believed the impact of this growth was either positively beneficial or at least not at all concerning.

Three distinct strands of that favorable assessment can be distinguished. Finance theorists and many regulators saw financial innovation and increased liquidity as axiomatically beneficial. Practical policymakers saw increased credit supply as essential to economic growth. And macroeconomists and central bankers developed economic models from which the financial system was entirely absent, its activities of no macroeconomic importance. The precise arguments differed, but the strands combined to justify a benign or relaxed attitude toward increasing financial intensity.

Market Completion, Efficiency, and Stability

A strongly positive assessment dominated among finance academics and at least implicitly among regulators. It reflected the assumption that free competition was bound to result in useful rather than harmful activity, and that increased financial activity, by making more markets complete and efficient, must be improving capital allocation across the economy.

Given this faith in free markets, it was not actually necessary to understand precisely how a specific financial innovation worked its economic magic. But the general theory of why financial intensity made the economy more efficient was clear. Increased liquidity in markets, generated by increased trading activities, ensured better "price discovery," and the more accurately financial contracts were priced, the more efficient would be capital allocation in the real economy. Securitization and credit derivatives, meanwhile, allowed the wisdom of the market to set transparently observable and rational prices for credit, to which lenders of money could refer when setting their loan terms. In 2004, a paper by Glenn Hubbard and Bill Dudley confidently concluded that "the increasing depth of U.S. stock, bond, and derivatives markets has improved the allocation of capital and risk throughout the U.S. economy." As a result this had "led to more jobs and higher wages."[18]

Greater efficiency, moreover, was accompanied by increasing stability. Credit structuring enabled investors to choose the precise combination of risk, return, and liquidity that best matched their preferences. Risk was thus distributed into the hands of those best placed to manage it. And securitization and shadow banking were accompanied by the development of new and apparently sophisticated risk management techniques—mark-to-market accounting, the use of secured debt contracts and Value at Risk models—which, it was argued, made the system more resilient.

In April 2006, only 15 months before the onset of the financial crisis, the IMF's Global Financial Stability Report noted with approval the "growing recognition that the dispersal of credit risk by banks to a broader and more diverse group of investors ... has helped make the banking and overall financial system more resilient." That improved resilience, it suggested "may be seen in fewer bank failures and more consistent credit provision. Consequently the commercial banks may be less vulnerable today to credit or economic shocks."[19]

That benign view was common among financial regulators across the world. When I became chairman of the UK Financial Services Authority in autumn 2008, I was soon aware that the presumption in favor of market completion and market liquidity—as many financial contracts as possible as widely traded as possible—was an accepted article of faith. As a result, most policymakers, far from seeking to constrain finance's remarkable growth, favored deregulation, which could unleash yet more financial innovation. Old-fashioned barriers between investment and commercial banks were dismantled, derivatives markets developments were encouraged, and financial liberalization was urged on emerging markets as a key component of successful economic development strategies.

More Credit to Drive Economic Growth

As Chapter 2 describes, the assumption that market completion and liquidity would inevitably generate favorable results rested on an overt and sophisticated, though mistaken, theory. The conclusions followed if the Efficient Market Hypothesis applied. The second strand of the benign assessment was more pragmatic and less theoretically based: it simply assumed that growing banking and shadow banking systems could provide more credit to businesses and households, and it assumed that that in turn was good, because more credit supposedly drove economic growth and enabled more people to become home owners.

Simple though this argument was, it was extremely influential. In the design of the Basel II capital standard for banks, one overt aim for some regulators was to enable banks to "economize on the use of scarce capital" and thus be able to extend more credit to the real economy. Even after the crisis, in an interview with *The Economist* magazine in 2012, a senior American regulator argued that "securitisation is a good thing. If everything was on banks' balance sheets, there would not be enough credit."[20] Hubbard and Dudley noted approvingly that more liquid bond and derivative markets meant that "at times home-owners can obtain 100% financing to purchase a home."[21] And when in early 2009, as chairman of the Financial Services Authority, I was thinking about what to say about credit derivatives in the report on the crisis which the UK Treasury had asked me to produce, staff experts in the Financial Services Authority warned me that if we restricted CDS market liquidity, that would make it harder for banks to provide more credit.

And indeed the first part of the argument—that a bigger bank and shadow banking system makes possible more real economy credit, is not only obvious but also true by definition. The issue discussed in Parts II and III, however, is whether additional credit creation was beneficial or harmful.

Modern Macroeconomics and the Financial System Veil

Most financial experts and policymakers thus treated more finance as positively beneficial. But in one area of policymaking—in central banks—

financial system developments were primarily viewed as neither positive nor negative, but simply neutral. Financial services might have important microeconomic effects, fostering efficiency or satisfying consumer demands, but at the macro level, they were irrelevant.

Earlier economists who experienced the financial and economic upheavals of the 1920s and 1930s—such as Friedrich Hayek, Irving Fisher, or John Maynard Keynes—believed that the operation of the financial system, and in particular of the banking system, carried vital implications for overall macroeconomic stability. But increasingly from the 1970s on, their insights were rejected or ignored.

Instead modern macroeconomics and central bank practice gravitated to the assumption that the monetary workings of the economy could be captured by models from which the banking system was almost entirely absent, and that provided central banks manipulated interest rates successfully to achieve low and stable inflation, stable macroeconomic performance would follow. Finance was described as a mere "veil," through which real economy contracts passed but whose size and structure carried no important implications. As Mervyn King, then governor of the Bank of England, put it in a lecture in autumn 2012, the dominant theoretical model of modern monetary economics "lacks an account of financial intermediation, so money, credit and banking play no meaningful role."[22]

Rising leverage, whether in the real economy or in the financial system, thus became by definition of no macroeconomic importance. Central banks could concentrate on containing inflation and leave financial system issues to the financial regulators. And increasingly it seemed that the policies needed to contain inflation and thus achieve macroeconomic stability had been discovered. The "Great Moderation" of low and stable inflation and of macroeconomic stability seemed to have been achieved.

From a different direction, modern macroeconomics thus provided further support for the benign assessment of increasing financial intensity and market liberalization. If the banking and wider financial system were of no macroeconomic importance, what mattered was finance's micro implications. And most financial theorists and regulators were confident that increasing financial intensity and complexity were making the economy more efficient.

Overall there was much to applaud and little to fear.

Financial Deepening — The Empirical Evidence

Three strands of theory thus seemed to justify a benign assessment of finance's dramatic growth. Historical and empirical research appeared to support the theoretical assertions.

Although proof is difficult, economic history strongly suggests that the development of modern financial systems played an important supportive role in the early stages of economic development. Bond and equity markets, and banking systems, enable business projects to be financed by multiple dispersed investors, rather than relying on the capital of individual entrepreneurs. It is difficult to imagine the canal and railway investments that fueled early British industrial growth without such markets and institutions. German industrialization in the late nineteenth century depended heavily on the banking system; U.S. stock markets played a major role in the growth of new industries in the early twentieth century. The fact that in the nineteenth century finance grew far more rapidly than the economy may well have been essential to the economic development process.[23]

Economists have attempted to supplement the narrative descriptions of economic history with quantitative analysis. A comprehensive review of the relevant literature by Ross Levine in 2005 found a broad consensus that "financial deepening" was beneficial.[24] In particular he reported positive correlations between such measures as private sector credit as a percentage of GDP and economic growth, and stock market turnover and growth. Both more credit and more market liquidity were, it seemed, socially useful.

Theoretical assertion and apparent empirical support therefore coalesced into a strong pre-crisis consensus: more finance was good for the economy, making the latter both more efficient and more stable. In 2004 a book on the impact of financial markets on the real economy felt able to conclude that "in the last thirty years, dramatic changes in financial systems around the world amounting, de facto, to a revolution have brought many ... advances.... We have come closer to the utopia of finance for all."[25]

But the consensus turned out to be completely wrong. In 2007 to 2008 the advanced economies suffered the biggest financial crisis since the 1930s, followed by a severe post-crisis recession. And both the origins of the crisis and the causes of the anemic recovery were rooted in specific elements of the increased financial intensity and complexity that the pre-crisis orthodoxy had either lauded or ignored.

The pre-crisis orthodoxy utterly failed to warn of the impending crisis: worse indeed, it overtly asserted that the very developments that produced the crisis had made it less likely. That failure reflected two profound intellectual errors.

The first was a failure to recognize that financial markets are different from other markets—such as those for restaurants or automobiles—and that the propositions in favor of market liberalization, strong in many other sectors of the economy, are far weaker in many areas of finance.

The second, still more important, was a failure to recognize the crucial macroeconomic implications of credit and money creation, of banks and shadow banks, and of debt contracts in general and specific types of debt in particular.

As a result, even though finance plays a crucial role in a market economy and increasing financial intensity is positive for economic development up to a point, the relationship is not linear and limitless. Beyond some point, and in particular where debt is concerned, more finance can be harmful, and free market finance can fail to serve well society's needs.

|||||||||||||||||||||||||||||||||||||||||||||||||||||||||||||||||||||||||||||||||||||||||||||||||||||||||||||||||||||||||||||||||||||||||||||

TWO

INEFFICIENT FINANCIAL MARKETS

The high recent valuations in the stock-market have come about for no good reasons. The market level does not, as so many imagine, represent the consensus judgement of experts who have carefully weighed the long-term evidence. The market is high because of the combined effect of indifferent thinking by millions of people, very few of whom feel the need to perform careful research on the long-term investment value of the aggregate stock market, and who are motivated substantially by their own emotions, random attentions, and perceptions of conventional wisdom.

—*Robert Shiller,* Irrational Exuberance[1]

OVER THE PAST 200 YEARS economic growth has delivered a remarkable breakthrough in human welfare, and market economies have proved far superior to planned ones. And without a vibrant and fairly complex financial system, market economies could not operate.

Finance supports the mobilization and allocation of capital. Capital markets and banks enable entrepreneurs or businesses with ideas and investment projects to attract capital from savers: without these markets and banks, capital accumulation would either be limited by the wealth of the individual entrepreneurs or would have to rely on the state.

Some of that capital mobilization can be achieved through equity contract markets, but, as Chapter 3 explores, debt instruments also play a crucial role. Some capital resources would not be made available except in exchange for the fixed return promises that debt contracts promise.

Both equity and debt capital in turn need to be allocated between alternative competing investment projects. In the equity arena that requires either liquid equity markets in which multiple investors interact to set prices, basing their decisions on investment analysis, or the allocation of equity through private equity funds. In the debt arena it requires bond market analysis and price discovery, or banks making decisions on who should receive loans.

Equity and debt markets and banks can also play a crucial role in liquidity or maturity transformation.[2] Liquid equity or debt markets enable investors to fund long-term investment projects while holding assets that they can sell for cash at short notice. Banks enable depositors holding short-term deposits to fund longer-term loans. Without liquidity- or maturity-transforming devices, capital mobilization would be more difficult to achieve.

It is therefore impossible to imagine the development of an advanced market economy without the development of a complex financial system. Britain's leadership role in the industrialization of the nineteenth century probably reflected, among many other factors, its more advanced financial system. Haldane's finding that from 1856 to 1914 finance grew much faster than the economy is not surprising. Nor is Ross Levine's finding that across some range of increasing debt to GDP ratio or stock-market turnover to GDP ratio, there is a positive correlation between increasing financial intensity and economic growth potential.[3] The case for more finance, up to some level, is strong.

But, the crucial question relates not to the early stages of finance's growth, but to growth over the past half-century in those countries which by 1950 or 1960 already had advanced industrial economies and reasonably complex financial systems. The United States in the 1950s was a highly successful capitalist economy with a financial system that accounted for less than 3% of its GDP. The subsequent expansion of finance to 8% of GDP by 2007 cannot have been essential to ensure that the American economy continued to grow. It is possible that that expansion was the inevitable consequence of economic growth, and it may have facilitated the spread of home ownership. It may, as the proponents of financial deepening suggest, have helped in some particular ways to improve economic efficiency. But it cannot be assumed in all respects to have been beneficial just because the earlier stages of economic growth required a growing financial sector.

In fact financial markets, when left to free-market forces, can generate activity that is privately profitable but not socially useful. There can be too much finance, too much trading, and too much market completion.

Theoretical Foundations of the Pre-crisis Orthodoxy

As Chapter 1 describes, arguments for the beneficial impact of further financial deepening are often based not on observed empirical effects, but simply on confidence that freer and more liquid markets are bound to deliver improved economic efficiency. Whether explicitly or not, indeed, such arguments build on one of the most important theoretical propositions in economics—that if all markets existed and operated in a perfectly informed and rational fashion, maximum economic efficiency would inevitably be attained.

That proposition—implicitly grasped by free market economists since Adam Smith's *Wealth of Nations*[4]—was proved mathematically by Kenneth Arrow and Gerard Debreu in a famous 1954 article.[5] They illustrated that if all markets existed and worked efficiently, the production and consumption resulting would be such that it would be impossible to make any one person better off without making others worse off. The result would be what economists label "Pareto efficient":[6] there could be debates about the appropriate distribution of the economic cake, but the cake would be as efficiently produced as possible.

In fact, all markets are to a degree incomplete and imperfect. Much of Kenneth Arrow's subsequent work was devoted to identifying the many circumstances in which the conditions required for the attainment of a "competitive equilibrium" do not and cannot exist. But at least in some sectors of the economy, markets work sufficiently well that the general proposition in favor of market liberalization and thus market completion (enabling households and businesses to strike as many different contracts as they wish) is justified. The market for restaurants works sufficiently well that there are few debates about whether restaurants are socially useful or restauranteurs overpaid.

One possible response to market imperfections is to seek to reduce the imperfections by ensuring more transparent information, by encouraging more participants to enter the market, and by "completing" markets with new types of contract. The pre-crisis orthodoxy was built on the idea that even if financial markets were in some ways imperfect, market liberalization and completion would at least bring us closer to perfection. CDS contracts would, it was believed, complete the market for credit risk, enabling better price discovery and better hedging of risks. More trading would result in greater liquidity and thus more efficiently determined prices.

Competitive equilibrium theory thus appeared to provide a rigorous theoretical underpinning for the assumption that financial innovation and increased financial intensity must be beneficial. Of course this would only be true if free financial markets operate in an efficient fashion, reflecting the rational assessments of individual economic "agents," whether households, businesses, or financial institutions. But the orthodoxy was able to draw on theories suggesting that those conditions indeed applied. Two theoretical propositions in particular played a central role in the pre-crisis orthodoxy in both finance and macroeconomics— the Efficient Market Hypothesis (EMH) and the Rational Expectations Hypothesis (REH).

The EMH defines an efficient financial market as one in which securities prices fully and rationally reflect all available information, and in which therefore price movements reflect newly available information rather than analysis of information already available or the impact of irrational sentiment.[7] It suggests that the average investor—whether individual, pension fund, hedge fund, mutual fund, or bank dealing unit— cannot consistently beat the market. In particular it suggests that "chartist" analysis, which seeks to predict future stock price movements on the basis of past observed patterns, is a waste of time and resources: in securities markets investing, there is no free lunch.

Three arguments in turn explained why the EMH must apply. First, people are in general rational. Second, even if some people are irrational, their irrationality is random, with as many people likely to irrationally buy as irrationally sell: as a result, their behavior cancels out and leaves no impact on stock or bond prices. And third, even if there are enough irrational investors to produce divergences from efficient rational values, the action of rational arbitrageurs, who spot the divergences and trade to gain from the reversion to efficient rationality, will ensure that the reversion is swift. Moreover, extensive empirical evidence seemed to prove the theory correct. Michael Jensen, one of the creators of the EMH, claimed in 1978 that "there is no other proposition in economics which has more solid empirical evidence supporting it than the Efficient Markets Hypothesis."[8]

Meanwhile, the REH applied the assumption of human rationality to develop propositions also relevant to macroeconomics. It proposed that individual agents in the economy—be they individuals or businesses— operate on the basis of rational assessments of how the future economy will develop. The REH thus provided a theoretical underpinning for the EMH. But it also suggested that significant macroeconomic instability could only result from truly exogenous shocks (such as new resource discoveries or technologies), whose impact was unlikely to be very large, or from the harmful and unanticipated policy interventions of governments. Provided governments and central banks pursued sensible rule-driven policies, the macroeconomic problems of the past must disappear. Free financial markets, populated by rational agents, could not generate economic instability from within.

But real-world evidence and more realistic theory contradict both hypotheses. They show that human beings are not fully rational, and that even if they were, market imperfections could produce unstable financial markets that diverge far from rational equilibrium levels. They explain why market imperfections are inherent and unfixable, and why as a result market completion, financial innovation, and financial deepening— far from bringing us closer to the nirvana of efficient equilibria—can sometimes make economies less efficient and less stable.

Inefficient and Irrational Markets: The Real World Reality

Financial markets have been susceptible to surges of irrational exuberance followed by panics and despair, to volatility inexplicable in terms of economic fundamentals, for as long as trading in financial markets, or indeed in real assets, has existed. Charles Kindleberger's book *Manias,*

Panics and Crashes[9] describes multiple examples stretching from the Dutch tulip bulb bubble of 1635–1637, through the South Sea and Mississippi bubbles of 1719–1720, to the U.S. equity boom of the late 1920s and its bust in 1929, and the NASDAQ boom of the late 1990s.

In some, such as the Tulip bubble, investors paid rapidly rising prices for assets whose real "value" was inherently arbitrary: in early autumn 1636 a pound of "Switsers" (a particular bulb variety) cost 60 guilders; by February 1, 1637, the price had reached 1,400; two weeks later it reached its peak price of 1,500. In the subsequent crash, some prices fell as much as 99%.[10] In other manias, such as the South Sea bubble, investors for a time believed fantastic stories about projects that were largely fraudulent. And in the booms and busts that were most harmful, speculation financed by credit played a crucial role—the key theme to which Parts II and III return. But in all cases, price setting was driven by beliefs and actions inexplicable in terms of the EMH and REH.

That is most obviously the case in the extreme examples explored by Kindleberger and before him by Charles MacKay in his 1841 book *Extraordinary Popular Delusions and the Madness of Crowds.*[11] It is also obvious in the case of sudden and extreme market crashes: there was no "new information" that made it rational for the Dow Jones Industrial Average index to fall 23% between the opening and closing bells on Monday, October 19, 1987.

But as the economist Robert Shiller has illustrated, this observation is more generally true: the volatility of equity markets during the twentieth century is too great to be explained by believable variations in the prospective cash flows on which efficient market theory proposes that equity prices are based.[12] The overall level of stock market prices continually oscillates for reasons unrelated to new information about future business prospects, and at times it can diverge dramatically from any reasonable assessment of fundamental value. Figure 2.1 shows the NASDAQ index of high-tech stocks during the dot-com boom and bust, rising from 1,000 in July 1995 to a peak of 5,048 in March 2000 before falling back to 1,108 in October 2002. Its aggregate value at its peak in 2000 could not possibly be justified by the prospective cash flows available from all companies in the index combined: when that reality dawned, the subsequent fall inevitably followed. This was irrational exuberance at work.

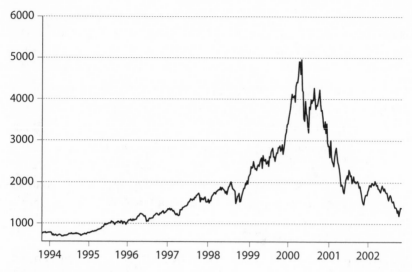

Figure 2.1.   Nasdaq index, 1994–2002

Source: Used with permission.

Five factors explain why these bubbles and subsequent crashes are bound to occur. The first is that human decisionmaking is not entirely rational. As Andrew Haldane has put it "when making difficult inter-temporal decisions we are quite literally in two minds."[13] Our brains combine a prefrontal cortex capable of patient rational analysis and a lim-bic system that disposes us to instinctive emotional responses. We are products of evolution, which has given us a unique ability for rational thought but which also makes us naturally susceptible to herd effects—because keeping up with the herd, the crowd, the tribe, is an impulse that at some stage in our evolutionary history was important for survival.[14]

Second, the impact of this irrationality is not, as efficient market theory suggests, independent and random, but highly correlated, with unsophisticated investors tending to move as a herd, their beliefs about the future strongly influenced by the beliefs that other investors hold. And even professional investors can be subject to the same biases, be-cause end investors may assess their managers' performance by looking at how well they did relative to the market in general.

Third and crucially, the theory that rational arbitrageurs will bring prices rapidly back to efficient equilibrium levels, though perhaps valid in relation to the price of individual stocks or bonds relative to others, is wholly invalid in relation to the level of prices in general across the market, as it is impossible to hedge the whole market in a riskless fashion. As Andrei Shleifer puts it in his Clarendon lectures on *Inefficient Markets:* "an arbitrageur who thinks that stocks as a whole are overpriced cannot sell short stocks and buy a substitute portfolio, since such a portfolio does not exist.... Thus arbitrage does not help to pin down price levels of stocks and bonds as a whole."[15]

Fourth, and as a consequence of the first three factors, it can be entirely rational for sophisticated, thoughtful investors, who are themselves not susceptible to irrational herd effects, to act in ways that for a time drive prices even further from rational equilibrium levels. John Maynard Keynes famously likened professional investment to a particular form of "spot the beauty" competition popular in 1930s newspapers, in which "the competitors have to pick out the six prettiest faces from a hundred photographs, the prize being awarded to the competitor whose choice most nearly corresponds to the average preferences of the competitors as whole."[16] Success therefore depended on "anticipating what average opinion expects the average to be." But such a focus can be entirely rational. And rational investors who observe irrationally exuberant surges in price can often profit from the upswing, provided they are clever enough to get out before the eventual bust. Privately rational behavior can drive a collectively unstable and irrational result. Financial markets are thus driven by what George Soros labels "reflexive" processes, which can drive prices far from long-term equilibrium levels.[17]

Fifth and finally, both the EMH and REH are flawed, because they fail to recognize that the future is characterized by inherent irreducible uncertainty and not mathematically modelable risk.[18] That distinction is fundamental to understanding the potential instability of financial markets but was too often ignored by mainstream economics and by regulators and risk managers in the pre-crisis years. It implies, as Chapter 6 explores, that the Value at Risk models that firms and regulators believed would contain the risks of increased trading activity were fatally flawed. And it means, as the work of Roman Frydman and Michael Goldberg has illustrated, that occasional significant divergences of market prices from equilibrium values are inevitable.[19]

Together these factors explain why financial markets are bound to be susceptible to inefficiency and collective irrationality. In particular they suggest that the overall level of equity prices, and of bond prices and yields, can diverge radically from rational equilibrium levels. But some of the empirical propositions of the EMH may still be valid. There may indeed be very few opportunities to make money from simple trading rules, such as chartists propose, and new flows of relevant information may indeed be rapidly reflected in individual stock prices. Markets as a result may do a fairly efficient job at establishing the appropriate relative price of one equity or one bond versus another.

But that could be true even if the overall level of market prices often moved in an irrational fashion. As the economist James Tobin put it, "information arbitrage efficiency" and "fundamental valuation efficiency" are two quite different concepts.[20] The fact that there is "no free lunch," or that relative prices are sensibly determined, in no way implies that in some absolute sense "the price is right."

Implications of Market Inefficiency: Zero Sum Activity and Unnecessary Cost

If financial markets can be inefficient, axiomatic arguments in favor of financial innovation and increased financial intensity, on the grounds that they complete markets and make them more liquid and efficient, are not convincing. Instead we have to recognize that increased financial activity and market completion can have both positive and negative effects.

Two possible negative consequence need to be distinguished. The first is that more financial activity might simply burden the economy with the dead weight of additional and unnecessary cost. The second arises if more financial activity generates increased market volatility or in other ways made the economy less stable.

To many outside observers, it appears obvious that there is pointless activity and unnecessary cost in the financial system. As Chapter 1 describes, the past 30 years have seen a dramatic increase in activity in the financial system, as banks, investment banks, and numerous other financial institutions have traded ever more intensively with one another.

Indeed, in most financial markets the value of deals between different financial firms is a huge multiple of the underlying flows of investments and trade to which they relate. Tom Wolfe's book *The Bonfire of the Vanities* has a scene where Sherman McCoy's wife Judy mocks the supposed social value of her husband's bond trading by explaining to her daughter that it is like passing a cake that one did not bake back and forth multiple times, picking up on each pass a few golden crumbs of trading profit and commission. To many ordinary citizens, the idea that much financial trading is socially useless hardly needs proof.[21]

But some financial trading does deliver important if indirect benefits. And though the main purpose of this book is to argue that we can have too much finance, it is important to understand the positive role that financial trading can play. Liquid markets can facilitate capital investment and help ensure well-informed capital allocation. And liquid markets in turn may require market-makers, who are willing to buy when end investors want to sell, and sell when they want to buy—but that requires position taking, and position taking is a form of betting. A financial system that performed only socially useful functions would still be one in which many firms and individuals earned large incomes from trading activities whose value will seem to many people mysterious.

But the fact that market-making, trading, and market liquidity can be valuable up to a point does not make them limitlessly valuable; left to themselves, free financial markets will generate far more intrafinancial system trading than is socially optimal.

Joseph Stiglitz's Nobel Prize lecture describes why.[22] Economic theory explains why trade in goods and services among businesses, individuals, or countries will increase human welfare: if one person prefers apples and another oranges, or if one is better at producing apples and the other oranges, both will be better off if they can trade and consume a mix of different fruits than they produce. But while trade in goods and services is driven either by inherent differences in preferences or by productive capabilities, financial trade is driven by differences in expectations, reflecting either different analysis or different sources of information. As a result, financial market participants may devote large resources to predicting movements in price minutely ahead of the rest of the market, in ways that can be profitable for the individual firm but cannot possibly increase the size of the overall economic cake. Indeed, for society as a whole the impact is negative because of the costs of skilled labor, computers, and physical premises involved.

The response of EMH devotees is that this activity must still be valuable, because it improves "price discovery," ensuring the more rapid and efficient processing of new information and thus better informing the allocation of capital in the economy. Given the timescales over which real investment decisions are made, however, this argument is utterly unconvincing. If a company's share price will reflect tomorrow some newly available information, real economy capital allocation decisions will not be better made because the information is anticipated today. Any marginal "price discovery" benefits of yet more trading must decline once liquidity has already reached a reasonable level.

As for how much liquidity is enough, there is no science with which we can estimate that point. But with the advent of high-frequency trading, we know we are far beyond it. When trading decisions are made by computers millisecond by millisecond, they cannot possibly reflect analysis of information relevant to real-world capital allocation, but simply hardwire market responses to immediately preceding movements in the market price. Nor can it possibly matter to useful price discovery whether prices move a millisecond earlier than they otherwise would. But as Michael Lewis describes in *Flash Boys*, firms using high-frequency trading are now spending enormous sums on computers and communication systems to ensure that their orders enter the market a millisecond ahead of the competition.[23] The result is an arms race of expenditure on technology and skilled people for an activity with no social value.

Free financial markets can thus create private incentives for levels of intrafinancial activity that go far beyond those required to deliver true social value. And the phenomenon extends far beyond the esoteric world of high-frequency trading: numerous studies have shown that much active asset management adds no additional value but does add significant cost, compared with passive index-linked strategies.

Indeed, major questions arise about whether investors get good value for money from asset management. Private equity and hedge fund fees absorb a startling proportion of total gross returns. And large increases in assets under management as a percentage of GDP have not been matched by economy of scale effects—cost per unit of output falling as volumes rise—which are observed in most other sectors of the economy.

But while the deadweight cost of unnecessary financial activity is important—and could justify strong public policy objectives—it is not my focus in this book. The financial crisis of 2007–2008 did not occur because asset management fees charged to end investors were swollen by unnecessary costs. Poor value for money may well be costing end customers a percentage point or so of GDP, but the far bigger problem is that advanced economy GDP levels are now some 10–15% below where they would have been on pre-crisis trends.

The crucial question is whether increasing financial intensity makes financial markets and the macroeconomy more unstable.

Financial Intensity, Market Completion, and Instability

Financial markets can clearly be subject to collectively irrational price movements that contravene the EMH. But that still leaves open a different question—whether more trading and financial innovation make markets at least somewhat more efficient and stable, or further exacerbate instability and inefficiency.

That question has been extensively debated by economists and is unlikely ever to be fully resolved. But neither theory nor empirical evidence support axiomatic confidence that market completion and increased trading activity always deliver benefit: in some circumstances they can clearly cause harm.

In theory the impact of increased trading on volatility must depend on trading strategies and time horizons. More activity by irrational "noise traders," who are driven by herd behaviors, could make markets more volatile and inefficient. So too could trading by investors who are entirely rational but whose strategy is to invest with the momentum of the market but get out in time before the market turns. In contrast, the more trading by rational arbitrageurs who spot divergences from fundamental value and trade to gain when prices return to rational levels, the more efficient and stable markets will be. Financial transaction taxes, which penalize short-term trading, in theory could reduce harmful volatility, because they would discourage herd-driven traders but leave unaffected the rational investors focusing on long-term fundamental value.[24]

The empirical evidence however is debated and ambivalent. Some studies suggest that volatility is increased by higher trading volumes, but others argue the contrary. Some studies of financial transaction taxes suggest that they reduce volatility, but others have found no significant effect.[25] The best conclusion is that the impact of increased financial trading on price volatility is uncertain and differs across different markets and circumstances. But the proposition that increased trading and market liquidity always reduces volatility and improves the efficiency of price discovery is unjustified.

The impact of increased market liquidity on the efficient mobilization of capital is similarly ambivalent. Reasonably liquid equity markets enable savers to fund long-term investments without making long-term savings commitments. But market liquidity also reduces the need for thoughtful analysis of long-term investment prospects and increases investor focus on anticipating short-term market trends. In debt markets increased liquidity can certainly be a double-edged sword. Liquid government bond markets, for instance, reduce the need for investors to assess whether governments can really afford the commitments they are taking on, focusing instead on how sentiment and yields will change over the very short term. If the Greek government bond market had been less liquid in the years before the crisis, investors might have focused more attention on debt sustainability, rather than being willing in 2006 to lend money to Greece at an interest rate only 30 basis points (0.3%) higher than to Germany.

As for financial innovations that "complete markets" by making possible previously absent forms of contract, these too can have positive as well as negative effects. In theory more complete markets make possible better management of risk and better allocation of capital—and that may be true in some cases. For instance, a reasonable case has been made that the expansion of the market in oil and gas futures has facilitated the emergence of independent energy companies, which have increased the efficiency of U.S. energy markets.

But as Joseph Stiglitz has pointed out, if markets are to a degree inherently imperfect, taking one specific step toward market completion can produce less efficient results.[26] And any new instrument that can be used to hedge a position and reduce risk can also be used simply to bet. As mentioned above, some betting is required to create a reasonably liquid market. But large-scale betting can also create socially useless volatility and financial instability. The development of CDS enabled hedging of credit risk and made the price of credit more transparent. But as Chapter 6 describes, the price that emerged was subject to the same overshooting instability that Figure 2.1 illustrates in the equity market; and the large-scale use of CDS to place bets played a major role in the explosion of complexity and interconnectedness that made the shadow banking system an engine of instability.

The market became more complete—and the social impact was negative.

What Follows ... and What Does Not

Financial markets are not always efficient, and the overall level of market prices will sometimes diverge greatly from rational equilibrium values. Some trading activity adds significant cost without delivering value, some forms of market completion through financial innovation can have harmful economic effects, and it is possible that more trading in some markets might make prices more volatile and price discovery less efficient.

But these facts do not in themselves justify major constraints on financial market activity. They simply argue that our attitude to finance, as to the market economy in general, should be based on reality, not on quasi-religious belief.

The case for a market capitalist economy is not that it is perfect but simply that it is better than the alternative of a predominantly planned economy. And the valid case for active financial markets is not that they are always efficient and rational but that having them is better than not.

Financial markets will occasionally be subject to large irrational overshoots, but they still perform important economic functions. And we cannot get the benefits without some of the disadvantages. Trading activity may in some markets be greater than socially optimal, but some trading is beneficial, and we have neither the science to tell us what the perfect level is nor the policy tools to achieve it.

Moreover, even irrational equity markets may play a vital role in the inevitably chaotic processes of market-driven innovation and investment.

As the venture capitalist and economist Bill Janeway has described in his book *Doing Capitalism in the Innovation Economy*, the benefit of major innovations can almost never be estimated by considering in an entirely rational fashion the probability distribution of future cash flows. And major waves of innovation often arise either as by-products of government strategic objectives—relating for instance to defense, transport, or health, or from research and development pursued by large corporate R&D departments almost for its own sake.[27] But as Janeway also illustrates, irrational equity markets surges, interacting with the venture capital industry, can deliver beneficial side-effects. NASDAQ prices in mid-2000 were irrational, and a significant misallocation of real resources resulted. Lots of young people set up Internet companies that had no real prospects of success, and many investors lost large amounts of money. But the NASDAQ boom and bust left behind it the companies, infrastructure, and ideas that have driven a new wave of innovation. A perfectly informed economic planner could have done a better job, delivering all the upside and none of the chaotic value destruction. But since no such perfect planner exists, we are better off with an occasionally irrational equity market than with none at all.

So the fact that financial markets are different from other markets and can be inefficient, irrational, and impose deadweight cost does not in itself prove that significantly less financial activity would necessarily be better.

But it does mean that we should reject axiomatic arguments in favor of ever more market liberalization and market completion. We should pragmatically consider public policy interventions to address issues of value for money. And we should identify those financial activities that have the greatest potential to produce not merely unnecessary cost but also macroeconomic instability. That potential is greatest where debt contracts and banks are involved, and confidence in the limitless benefits of increased financial activity and market completion did most harm when applied to the market for credit. Parts II and III explain why.

Dangerous Debt

||||||||||||||||||||||||||||||||||||||||||||||||||

THE MOST IMPORTANT REASON the 2008 crisis was followed by such a deep recession and weak recovery was excessive private credit creation in the preceding decades. Part II focuses on why that growth occurred, why it caused harm, and how it was possible even though inflation remained low and stable.

Chapter 3 describes why debt contracts can be valuable but also dangerous and how banks create credit, money, and purchasing power. Chapter 4 analyses the different economic functions of various categories of credit and explores the implications of the rising importance of urban real estate in modern economies. Together these two chapters explain why banking systems left to themselves are bound to create too much of the wrong sort of debt, instability, and crisis.

Excessive leverage growth before the crisis produced a severe post-crisis debt overhang, faced with which all policy levers appear blocked. As Chapter 5 describes, that means that fixing the banks will not be sufficient to fix the economy. More radical policies will be required.

Chapter 6 discusses how securitization and shadow banking fit into the story. Increased interbank trading activity and financial innovation, far from making the system more efficient and stable, amplified the inherent instability of the credit cycle and made the debt overhang effect worse. And the very risk management tools that were meant to reduce risks actually magnified them. Meanwhile, at the aggregate level intense intrafinancial system activity in the asset management industry is a zero-sum game, making society no better off, but generating costs that reduce end customer returns. The summary scorecard on three decades of financial innovation is thus almost entirely negative.

Chapter 7 addresses an apparent dilemma. Excessive credit growth before 2008 produced crisis and debt overhang, but it seemed at the time that we *needed* rapid credit growth to achieve adequate economic growth. Chapter 7 argues, however, that we could grow modern economies without excessive credit growth, but only if we address three drivers of "unnecessary" credit growth—rising real estate values, increasing inequality, and global imbalances—and only if we recognize that direct government stimulus of demand, through money financed deficits, is sometimes less dangerous than private credit creation. It may indeed be the only effective response to secular stagnation, that is, to a long-term rather than merely cyclical problem of chronically deficient demand.

‖‖

THREE

DEBT, BANKS, AND THE MONEY THEY CREATE

The cycle of manias and panics results from procyclical changes in
the supply of credit ... Money always seems free in manias.
  —*Charles Kindleberger,* Manias, Panics and Crashes: A History of
  Financial Crises, *1978*[1]

C HARLES KINDLEBERGER'S CLASSIC HISTORY of financial crises doc-
uments the never-changing potential for financial markets to generate booms, busts, and financial instability. His examples cover equities, tulips, real estate, and various commodities and are drawn from
Scandinavia, Japan, Korea, the United States, the United Kingdom, and
many other countries. The precise patterns of behavior and economic
implications vary. But his conclusion, supported by numerous other
researchers, is clear: the booms and busts that result in the greatest economic harm (rather than merely losses for some speculators) are driven
by "procyclical" credit supply, with a rapidly growing and easily available supply of credit in the boom, followed by a dearth of credit in the
subsequent downswing. The potential for irrational exuberance exists in
all asset markets, but when it is financed by debt, severe economic harm
results.

In the decade running up to the 2007–2008 crisis, private credit grew
rapidly in almost all advanced economies: in the United States at 9%
per year, in the United Kingdom at 10% per year, in Spain at 16% per
year.[2] In most it grew far faster than nominal GDP; as a result, private
leverage—the ratio of private credit to GDP—significantly increased. But
that ten-year pattern was a continuation of the far longer-term sixty-
year trend of increasing real economy leverage described in Chapter 1.

Total UK private-sector leverage grew from 50% in 1964 to 180% by 2007; in the United States it grew from 53% in 1950 to 170% in 2007. More recently the pattern has been repeated in emerging economies. South Korea's private leverage grew from 62% in 1970 to 155% before the Asian financial crisis of 1997: it is now even higher at 197%. The ratio of Chinese debt to GDP has grown from 124% in early 2008 to more than 200% today.[3]

Real economy leverage grew, because private credit grew faster than nominal GDP. That suggests a fundamental question: was such rapid credit growth needed to deliver a reasonable rate of economic growth, or could we have achieved economic growth without ever rising indebtedness? Chapter 7 addresses that issue. This chapter and the next three explain why rising debt levels led to crisis and post-crisis recession.

The Positive Role of Debt Contracts ... and Banks

A recent history of debt by the anthropologist David Graeber is titled *Debt—The First 5000 Years*.[4] Human societies have used debt contracts for as long as they have used money—indeed, Graeber argues for longer. And for much of that time, some philosophers and religions condemned interest-bearing debt as intrinsically unjust. In a debt contract the lender is due a return even if the borrower's business project fails: tenant farmers, for instance, have to pay interest to a landlord who lends them money even if the harvest is poor. Interest-bearing debt contracts can therefore magnify initial inequalities and not just in agricultural societies; Chapter 7 discusses the two-way link between debt and inequality in advanced societies today. Islam prohibits usury; medieval Christianity was deeply suspicious of it. Aristotle in *The Politics* described usury as a "most hated sort" of way to accumulate wealth.[5]

But modern economic theory sees debt contracts as vital to spur economic growth. Moreover, it is precisely their fixed nature—the fact that the returns to lenders are largely independent of the success of the business project—that makes them valuable.

Financial systems facilitate the mobilization of capital. In theory that could be achieved entirely by an equity market: all capital could flow from investors to entrepreneurs and businesses in the form of equity contracts, savers would hold all their claims on businesses as equities, and businesses would be 100% equity financed.

But from the earliest days of the Industrial Revolution, capital accumulation in fact involved a major role for debt capital markets and banks as well as equity markets. And economic theory provides good reasons for believing that without debt contracts, capital mobilization would be more difficult.

In an equity contract, the return to the investor varies with the success of the business projects being financed. But those results are unknown in advance to either entrepreneur or investor. And once projects are completed, entrepreneurs or business managers know far more about the true results achieved than do investors. So they can act to the investors' disadvantage, for instance, by paying themselves higher salaries, which reduce investors' returns.

Equity contracts thus leave investors facing risks that they cannot control. Finding out the full truth about project returns is expensive and difficult: in the language of finance theory, investors face the challenge of "costly state verification." In contrast, debt contracts offer a return that is specified in advance and is fixed as long as the business project does not actually fail.[6] As a result, they support capital mobilization from savers who would be unwilling to fund investment projects if all contracts had to take an equity form. Without railway company debt issues as well as equity issues, private-sector investment in the railways of nineteenth-century Britain would almost certainly have proceeded more slowly.

This benefit could be delivered by debt contracts that take a simple "direct" form, with an investor holding bonds issued by companies. And liquid bond markets can make it possible for the investor to fund long-term investments while holding an asset they can sell for cash in the short term. As Chapter 2 describes, such liquidity transformation, in either debt or equity markets, can also play an important role in enabling capital mobilization.

But banks that intermediate between savers and borrowers further enhance this transformation function, since they enable depositors to hold claims that not only are rapidly or immediately available but also maintain an apparently certain capital value. The development of "fractional reserve banks" (that is, banks that hold only a small proportion of their deposits in liquid money form while lending the rest out on longer maturities than their liabilities) therefore also probably played an important role in enabling economic development. Writing in *Lombard Street*, his famous 1878 description of the British banking system, Walter Bagehot argued that Britain's more developed banking system, compared with that of much of continental Europe, enabled wider pools of savings to become "borrowable" by entrepreneurs, rather than merely hoarded.[7] The economic historian Alexander Gerschenkron argued that investment banks in late nineteenth-century Germany played a role as important as industrial technologies in driving economic growth.[8]

It is therefore not surprising that empirical studies have found evidence of a beneficial effect of financial deepening—measured as either the ratio of private debt to GDP or that of bank assets to GDP—as countries progress through the early stages of economic growth. And in some emerging countries today, such as India, a strong case can be made that the extension of banking into small towns and rural areas would facilitate capital formation by small and medium enterprises, which would not occur if capital accumulation required either equity or direct debt contracts between investor and entrepreneur.

Debt Contract Dangers

But while debt contracts and banks play economically valuable roles, the very character that makes them valuable also makes them potentially harmful. Debt contracts appear to provide certain returns—but that very fact increases the danger of irrational booms and amplifies the impact of subsequent busts. Five related features of debt contracts make them potentially dangerous.

First, debt contracts can fool us into ignoring risks. Their return does not depend in a precise fashion on the success of the business projects they finance. But that does not mean that debt contracts are riskless: instead, the risks take a particular form.

When an investor buys an equity, she knows that the most likely expected return is only one among many possible results, and that both considerably higher or considerably lower return is possible. Moreover, the daily variation in equity prices makes the investor continually aware of this inherent risk. In contrast, a debt contract has a high likelihood of one specific return—the debt paying off in full and with prespecified interest—and there is no possibility of an upside above that fixed return. But there is a small probability of a very significant downside.

This pattern of return tends to induce myopia, or as the economist Andrei Shleifer and colleagues have labeled it, "local thinking": investors in good times assume that full payout is not only likely but certain, and they exclude from their consideration the possibility of loss.[9] In the upswing of the crisis, there is thus a danger that risky loans and bonds are treated as close to riskless. As a result many bonds may be bought by investors and many bank loans made, which, as Shleifer and colleagues put it "owed their very existence to neglected risk." This was undoubtedly the case in the United States in the years running up to 2008. Market imperfections of the sort described in Chapter 2 can lead to price instability in all financial markets. But in the debt market, they can generate debt contracts that in a rational market would never even have existed.

Second and as a result of feature 1, debt markets can be susceptible to "sudden stops" in new credit supply as investors or bankers who previously ignored risks suddenly become aware of the full range of possible results and are therefore unwilling to lend new money. The nature of debt contracts therefore creates the danger that debt finance, whether by bonds or banks, will be first provided on excessively easy terms and then denied at almost any price. Credit supply in Ireland grew on average at almost 20% per year from 2004 to 2008; from 2009 to 2013 it contracted by about 1.3%.[10] Both the bonanza and the sudden stop caused harm.

Sudden stops in debt finance are far more harmful than in equity finance, because of the specific maturity of debt contracts and the need for debt rollover. Once made, equity investments are permanent: there is no commitment to return the capital at some specific time, and even income payments (dividends) are to a degree discretionary. As a result one could imagine an economy in which new equity investment markets closed entirely for a number of years. Over time there would be economic costs, but business operations and new investment would still continue. An economy with large debt contracts outstanding relies, however, on the supply of new credit, without which many debt-dependent companies would cease investment and in some cases close. A more debt-intensive economy—in particular, one with extensive short-term debt commitments—is more vulnerable to sudden falls in investor confidence or to sudden reductions in bank lending capacity than an equity-intensive one would be.

Third, when debt contracts become unsustainable they do not adjust smoothly. As former Federal Reserve Chairman Ben Bernanke has commented, "in a complete markets world" (that is, in the world described by the Arrow Debreu model, discussed in Chapter 2) "bankruptcy would never be observed."[11] Debt contracts would instead specify in advance how losses should be shared between borrowers and lenders, enabling viable businesses to continue trading even if investors suffered disappointing returns. But in the real world, bankruptcy procedures often result in disruption, in large administrative costs, and in "fire sale" losses as assets are sold at just the wrong point in the economic cycle.

Fourth, asset price falls induced by a sudden stop in confidence and credit growth can further depress both confidence and credit supply. Fire sales resulting from default and bankruptcy can result in lower prices for the assets of failing companies. But reduced credit supply can make those asset price falls more widespread, as companies and households are less able and willing to buy assets with credit. And reduced asset prices can impair the solvency of banks, leading to yet further constraints on credit supply.

Fifth and finally, falling asset prices can produce a deflationary debt overhang effect. Faced with falling asset prices, borrowers may become suddenly concerned that they are overleveraged and cut consumption (in the case of households) and investment (in the case of businesses) in an attempt to reduce their debts and ensure their solvency. But the combined impact of this behavior by multiple households and companies depresses aggregate demand, economic growth, asset prices, and confidence. Chapter 5 argues that the severity of the debt overhang we now face is the most important reason that recovery from the 2007–2008 crisis has been so anemic.

The quasi-fixed nature of debt contracts, combined with inherently imperfect markets and potentially myopic human beings, can thus be powerful drivers of financial and macroeconomic instability. Together they drive overexuberant booms; and together they produce post-crisis recessions. In 1933 the economist Irving Fisher argued in a famous article that the United States faced a Great Depression because excessive

Fisher's debt deflation dynamics: key features

1. Debt liquidation leads to distress selling

2. Contraction of deposit currency (i.e., bank money)

3. Fall in the level of prices

4. Still greater fall in the net-worths of businesses, precipitating bankruptcies

5. A like fall in profits

6. Reduction in output, in trade, and in employment

7. Pessimism and lack of confidence

8. Hoarding and slowing down still more the velocity of circulation

9. Complicated disturbances in rates of interest—fall in nominal rates, rise in real rates

Figure 3.1.

credit creation had been followed by a self-reinforcing "debt deflation." Figure 3.1 summarizes his description of the processes at work.[12] The run-up to the 2007–2008 crisis and the subsequent Great Recession have seen us repeat that experience.

So debt could be dangerous, even if all debt took a direct, bond financed, form (particularly if the bonds were relatively short term). But the dangers are greatly increased by the fact that banks create credit, money, and purchasing power.

Banks and the Money They Create

Read an undergraduate textbook of economics, or advanced academic papers on financial intermediation, and if they describe banks at all, it is usually as follows: "banks take deposits from households and lend money to businesses, allocating capital between alternative capital investment possibilities."[13] But as a description of what modern banks do, this account is largely fictional, and it fails to capture their essential role and implications.

Banks create credit, money, and thus purchasing power. They make loans to borrowers, crediting an asset on the banks' balance sheet; at the same time they put money in the borrowers' account, creating a bank liability. The loan is repayable at a later date, but the money is immediately available. It is this "maturity transformation" that creates effective purchasing power. The borrower may, and almost certainly will, then pay out the money to another business or household, but that creates money in that person's account. The vast majority of what we count as "money" in modern economies is created in this fashion: in the United Kingdom 98% of money takes this form, and only 2% represents the notes and coins liabilities of the state.[14]

By creating credit and money, banks can increase purchasing power, and bank money creation therefore plays a crucial role in stimulating nominal demand growth. And bank credit and money creation can, as Chapter 8 describes, skew purchasing power toward investment, driving at least for a time faster economic growth. But it can also skew purchasing power toward asset speculations of the sort described by Kindleberger. How much credit banks create and to what purposes that credit is devoted are therefore issues of vital importance.

In fact, the ability to create credit and purchasing power, for good or ill purposes, is not unique to banks. If a company selling products or services to a customer is willing to accept a promissory note rather than cash, a form of credit is created. And if the creditworthiness of the customer is undoubted, the supplier may be able to use the promissory note to pay its own suppliers: in which case the credit note becomes in effect money. Spontaneously arising trade credit can thus increase spending power in an economy, and speculative booms are possible even without banks. Banks were largely irrelevant to the Dutch tulip bulb mania of 1638: instead innovations in vendor finance made possible a self-reinforcing rise in both prices and the value of trade credit outstanding. Shadow banking activities—as Chapter 6 describes—can create credit and money equivalents outside the formal banking sector.

But the existence of fractional reserve banks greatly increases the potential for credit and purchasing power creation. The Swedish economist Knut Wicksell provided a beautifully clear description of why this is the case in his 1898 book *Interest and Prices*.[15] In a system of bank-based credit—or as he labels it, "organized credit"—bank money becomes the dominant medium of exchange. For reasons of convenience and security, households and businesses hold almost all their money in bank deposits, and almost all payments involve transfers from one account to another, effected through the interbank clearing system. As a result, once bank money has been created by the extension of new credit, it is almost certain to remain in the banking system: very little is taken out and used in the form of notes and coins.

Wicksell concluded that banking systems can therefore greatly increase potential purchasing power in the economy. And their ability to do so is further enhanced by interbank lending markets: for while any one bank alone might seem constrained by the need to hold some assets in liquid reserves (in case depositors wish to transfer their money to other banks), if the money can be borrowed back in the interbank lending market, the constraint disappears. The more liquid are interbank lending markets, the less constrained is the banking system's ability to create new credit and money.[16]

Wicksell therefore worried that, left to itself, a free market banking system might create too much credit and as a result induce harmful inflation. He proposed two responses to this concern. The first was that bank credit creation would be constrained if banks were *required* to hold a fixed proportion of their money liabilities as liquid reserves at the central bank, and if the central bank controlled that proportion. In fact, however, modern central banks have tended to move away from such quantitative controls.

The second was that the quantity of credit created would be appropriate and inflationary dangers avoided if central banks kept market interest rates in line with what Wicksell labeled "the natural rate of interest," that is, the rate of return available on real physical investment projects. As long as this relationship was maintained, Wicksell argued, entrepreneurs would only have an incentive to borrow money for investments likely to produce an increase in real productive potential in line with the additional purchasing power created. Purchasing power and output would therefore grow in a balanced noninflationary fashion

Pre-crisis central bank orthodoxy built, at least indirectly, on this strand of Wicksell's thought. Indeed, one of the most important statements of the pre-crisis orthodoxy, Michael Woodford's *Interest and Prices*, is titled in homage to Wicksell.[17] And central banks gravitated to the belief that, provided interest rates were maintained at levels that ensured low and stable inflation, the amount of credit that the banking system created would be of no concern. Low and stable inflation was sufficient to ensure financial and macroeconomic stability.

But the crisis of 2007–2008 proved that assumption quite wrong. Excessive credit produced a crisis, even though inflation remained subdued. The explanation lies in two facts. First, all credit extension creates debt contracts, which can have the adverse consequences described in this chapter. Second, most credit in advanced economies is not used to finance new capital investment. Chapter 4 describes that reality.

||||||||||||||||||||||||||||||||||||||||||||||||||||||||||||||||||||||||||||||||||||||||||||||||||||||||||||||||||||||||||||||||||||||||||||||||||||||||||||||||||||||||||

FOUR

TOO MUCH OF THE WRONG SORT OF DEBT

With very few exceptions, the banks' primary business consisted
of non-mortgage lending to companies in 1928 and 1970. In 2007
banks in most countries had turned primarily into real estate
lenders.... The intermediation of household savings for productive investment in the business sector—the standard textbook
role of the financial sector—constitutes only a minor share of the
business of banking today.

—Òscar Jordà, Moritz Schularick, and Alan Taylor, "The Great
    Mortgaging"[1]

TEXTBOOK DESCRIPTIONS OF BANKS usually assume that they lend
money to businesses to finance new capital investment. Explanations of why financial deepening is valuable focus almost entirely on the
beneficial impact of better credit flow to businesses and entrepreneurs.[2]
But in most modern banking systems most credit does not finance new
capital investment. Instead, it funds the purchase of assets that already
exist and, above all, existing real estate.

In some ways that is inevitable, since real estate accounts for the
majority of all wealth in advanced economies. Seen from an individual
borrower's perspective, moreover, mortgage lending is clearly socially
useful. And seen from a private bank's perspective, lending against real
estate can appear the easiest and safest thing to do.

But the increasing importance of real estate and of lending against
it has huge implications for financial and macroeconomic instability.
Different categories of credit perform different economic functions and
have different consequences. Only when credit is used to finance useful

new capital investment does it generate the additional income flows required to make the debt certainly sustainable. Contrary to the pre-crisis orthodoxy that the quantity of credit created and its allocation between different uses should be left to free market forces, banks left to themselves will produce too much of the wrong sort of debt.

Categories of Credit

Credit can be extended for the textbook purpose of funding new capital investment. But it can also fund increased consumption, and it can be used to finance the purchase of an asset that already exists, whether that be a painting, a house, an office building, or a company.

Figure 4.1 shows the breakdown of bank lending in the United Kingdom in 2012. Residential mortgages accounted for 65% and unsecured consumer loans for 7%. Of loans to companies, the majority funded commercial real estate development or investment.[3] These figures cannot be mapped precisely to the division among finance for investment, consumption, and existing assets. Residential mortgages can finance increased consumption as well as house purchase, and the houses purchased can be existing or newly built; commercial real estate lending finances a mix of investment in existing properties and new developments. But it is clear that credit to finance investment in non–real estate assets accounts for no more than 14% of the UK total, and the same broad pattern is found across the advanced economies and increasingly in emerging ones. To understand the roots of the 2007–2008 crisis and of the Great Recession that followed, we have to understand the different economic impacts of the various categories of credit.

Credit-Financed Consumption

In most advanced economies only a small share of credit is explicitly and wholly related to consumption finance. In the United Kingdom, unsecured lending to households (by means of personal loans, overdrafts, and credit cards), is around 10% of GDP;[4] in the United States the equivalent figure is about 5%.[5] But these figures understate the role of

100% = £1600bn

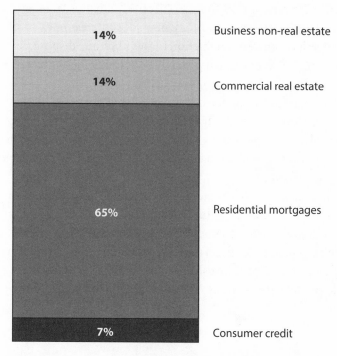

Figure 4.1.   Categories of bank lending in the United Kingdom, 2012
Source: Bank of England.

credit-financed consumption, since mortgage borrowing can also be used to support consumption growth. Rapid growth of U.S. mortgage credit before the 2007–2008 crisis played a major role in spurring U.S. personal consumption.

Personal loans and credit cards enable people to smooth consumption in the face of fluctuating income: mortgage-financed consumption can allow them to smooth consumption across different periods of life, within the constraints of their total lifetime income. Such consumption smoothing has nothing to do with the mobilization or allocation of credit, but it can still be valuable—or "welfare enhancing," in formal economic terms.[6]

But consumption credit can also have harmful effects, both for individuals and for the macroeconomy. Particularly in the face of rising inequality, individuals may borrow too much in an impossible attempt to maintain consumption that is objectively unaffordable, given their future income prospects. And they may face interest rates so high that the net result is a material reduction in their lifetime disposable income. As Chapter 7 discusses, rising indebtedness can be both part consequence and part cause of rising inequality.

Debts incurred to finance consumption can also contribute to post-crisis debt overhang effects. If secured against real estate, they can look increasingly affordable as long as house prices rise. But when prices fall, defaults and attempted deleveraging by overindebted households can depress the economy.

The overall point is simple. If credit finances consumption rather than useful investment, it is more likely that the debts created will subsequently prove unsustainable. We have always recognized that fact in relation to public debt: fiscal deficits that finance consumption rather than growth-enhancing investment are more likely to produce unsustainable public debt burdens. The same is true for private-sector credit creation.

Credit-Financed Investment . . . and Overinvestment

If credit is extended to finance useful investment, which increases future productive potential, it will be affordable: the investment will itself generate the income from which the debt is repaid. But the word "useful" is a crucial qualification, since even finance that results in new capital investment can produce waste and instability.

Credit creation can facilitate capital investment, and Chapter 8 discusses how directed bank credit creation was used by some developing countries to drive higher levels of investment and faster rates of growth than could otherwise have been achieved. But as both Friedrich Hayek and Hyman Minsky explored, it can produce cycles of overinvestment that leave behind wasted real resources and a debt overhang problem.[7]

Two factors combine to produce those cycles—inherent uncertainty about future returns and the length of time required to build new capital assets. Given these factors, there is no perfect market mechanism that ensures that the level of investment chosen by free markets will be reasonable in the face of subsequent demand for the goods and services produced. Expectations of increased demand for a particular product or service, and thus for the capital assets required to produce it, can generate increases in the price of the current stock of those assets that stimulate a far bigger quantity of new investment than subsequently appears wise.

Cycles of credit-financed overinvestment have therefore been features of capitalism throughout its history, from the railway booms of the nineteenth century to the U.S., Spanish, and Irish real estate building booms of the 2000s. By 2006 Ireland was building 90,000 homes per year in a country of just over 4 million people.[8] Many of the builders and developers who built those homes have subsequently gone bankrupt. At least 20,000 homes on "ghost estates" are now being demolished, their construction an utter waste. But in the upswing of the cycle, building them and lending money to the builders appeared profitable. Indeed, from a purely private point of view it often was. The lucky builders who completed and sold their developments before summer 2008 made money, and the loans due for repayment before then were typically repaid in full. Up until 2008 free market price signals validated increased investment.

But the collective result was a disaster. Specific investments made money, but only because new credit supply for a time drove up the price of completed projects. In the terms defined by Hyman Minsky, the system had progressed from one in which credit was "Hedge" in form (financing assets with debt that could be repaid out of the income generated by that investment) to a "Speculative" system, in which new credit supply was essential to finance repayment of existing debts.[9]

A free market credit system can thus produce cycles of overinvestment, which in turn cause two types of harm. The first is misallocation of real resources: in Spain the construction sector swelled from 8% to more than 12% of GDP between the late 1990s and 2007, in Ireland the increase was from 4% to 9%, and in both the share of construction in total employment grew rapidly.[10] High unemployment was the inevitable post-crisis consequence, as it was too in several U.S. states that experienced construction booms, such as Florida and Arizona. The second is the debt overhang effect.

The problem of debt overhang can also arise even if the credit boom results in no new investment but is instead focused entirely on already existing assets. Indeed, credit booms focused on already existing real estate assets can result in a supercharged version of the credit cycles described by Hayek and Minsky.[11]

Credit to Finance Existing Assets—The Dominance of Real Estate

Credit can finance the purchase of many different sorts of existing asset. In theory we could face a credit bubble that drove up the price of works of art valued only for their subjective aesthetic value. In the bubble of 1638, Dutch tulips were valued simply for their beauty.

Some non–real estate business finance, meanwhile, is also focused on existing assets. For instance, many private equity buyouts essentially leverage up existing companies, increasing potential return at the expense of increased risk but with no necessary consequences for the level of investment.

But by far most lending against existing assets is against real estate, and lending against already existing real estate represents the majority of all bank lending in most advanced economies and an increasing number of emerging ones.

It wasn't always like that. As research by Jordà, Schularick, and Taylor shows, what banks do in advanced economies has changed dramatically in the past 45 years (see Figure 4.2). In 1928 real estate lending averaged about 30% of all bank lending; by 1970 it had edged up to 35%; by 2007 it was approaching 60%. In addition, a significant proportion of the remaining 40% is likely to finance commercial real estate.[12] As Jordá, Schularick, and Taylor put it

> with very few exceptions, the banks' primary business consisted of non-mortgage lending to companies both in 1928 and 1970. In 2007, banks in most countries had turned primarily into real estate lenders. The intermediation of household savings for productive investment in the business sector—the standard textbook role of the financial sector—constitutes only a minor share of the business of banking today.

Some of that real estate lending finances investment in new real estate, whether residential or commercial. But the vast bulk finances the purchase of real estate assets that already exist, with households borrow-

Figure 4.2.   Share of real estate lending in total bank lending for seventeen advanced economies

Source: Jordà, Schularick, and Taylor (2014a). © 2014 by Òscar Jordà, Moritz Schularick, and Alan M. Taylor. All rights reserved. Used with permission.

ing to purchase already existing houses, and companies and institutional investors borrowing to make investments in existing commercial property. For instance, the UK mortgage credit and house price boom of 2000–2007—unlike the credit and price booms in Florida, Spain, or Ireland—was primarily an existing assets boom, with only a relatively small rise in new construction.

It is vital indeed to understand that an advanced economy in which there was *no* new investment in real estate at all would also almost certainly be one in which most new bank credit was extended to finance real estate. That reflects the inevitably rising importance of real estate as a share of wealth in increasingly rich societies.

The Rising Importance of Real Estate in Wealth

Thomas Piketty's *Capital in the Twenty-First Century* has focused attention on the remarkable increase in the ratio of wealth to income in advanced economies over the past 40 years.[13] In 1970 wealth typically amounted to about three times national income; by 2010, that number had grown to five to six times.

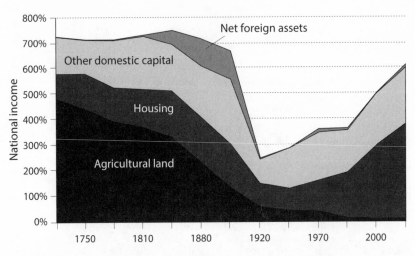

Figure 4.3.   Capital in France, 1700–2010: Percentage of national income

Source: Reprinted by permission of the publisher from Piketty (2014), translated by Arthur Goldhammer, p. 117, Cambridge, MA: The Belknap Press of Harvard University Press, Copyright © 2014 by the President and Fellows of Harvard College.

Several factors have driven this change. But by far the most important is the huge increase in the value of housing, which in most countries accounts for the majority of all wealth and for most of the increase in the wealth / income ratio. In France and United Kingdom, for instance, housing accounts for more than half of all wealth, and the increase in housing wealth relative to national income explains about 90–100% of the increase in the total wealth / income ratio since 1970. Housing wealth in the United Kingdom was about 120% of national income in 1970 and had reached 300% by 2010; in France, as Figure 4.3 shows, housing wealth grew from 120% of GDP in 1970 to 371% by 2010. In addition, though not separated in Piketty's figures, commercial real estate accounts for a significant share of non-housing wealth.

Much of this housing wealth—and in many countries the lion's share of the increase—reflects not the constructed value of the buildings but the urban land on which the buildings sit. In major cities such as London, Paris, New York, San Francisco, or Hong Kong, actual new expenditures on construction explain only a trivial part of the increase in real estate value. For advanced economies on average, 80% of house price increases between 1950 and 2012 can be attributed to rising land prices and only 20% to increases in the constructed value of the housing.[14] An increasing share of wealth in all rich societies, and more recently in many emerging economies too, thus derives not from capital stock accumulated out of capital investment but from urban land, and in particular from land in the most desired and therefore highest-valued locations.

That may seem strange. Many economists talk of our "weightless" modern economy in which physical goods are of declining importance and in which software and applications play an increasing role: but the most physical thing of all—land—is increasing in importance. But paradoxically, the rising importance of land is in part the direct consequence of the remarkable progress of information and communications technology (ICT). And the faster ICT progresses in the future, the more the value of real estate and land may increase.

A recent book by MIT economists Eric Brynjolfsson and Andrew McAfee, *The Second Machine Age*, argues persuasively that ICT is a uniquely powerful technology because of two distinctive features: first, the price of hardware capacity along many different dimensions—processing power, memory, bandwidth—keeps collapsing roughly in line with Moore's law, halving every 1.5–2 years or so; second, once software has been developed, it can be replicated at close to zero marginal cost.[15]

These features enable ICT companies to create huge wealth with very little capital investment. In mid-2014 Facebook had an equity valuation of $150 billion: the software "machine" that runs it took at most 5,000 or so software engineer years to build. Compared with the investment that went into building automobile, airline, or traditional retail companies, this is trivial. And more generally, the two distinctive features mean that wherever the "machines" that drive businesses include a large ICT software or hardware element, they keep falling in price relative to current goods and services. IMF figures show that the price of capital equipment relative to prices of current goods and services fell by 33% between 1990 and 2014.[16]

The inevitable consequence is that an increasing share of investment is accounted for by those categories of capital expenditure where prices are not falling—and the most important of those is physical construction. A world in which the *volume* of information and communication capacity embedded in capital goods relentlessly increases is a world in which real estate and infrastructure constructions are bound to account for an increasing share of the *value* of all investment.

Meanwhile, the changing pattern of consumption increases the relative importance of locationally desirable land. As people on average get richer, they choose to spend their increasing income on a different mix of goods and services. In some expenditure categories, people approach satiation, and both the volume and value of food, clothing, or household appliances consumed therefore grow more slowly than income. In some other categories, volumes consumed may continue to soar, but prices collapse in an offsetting fashion—so that while ever more tablets, mobile phones, and computer games are bought, total expenditure at best keeps pace with income.

Offsetting these "low-income-elasticity" goods and services, are others whose income elasticity of demand is far greater than 1, that is, for which expenditure grows faster than income. The most important of these is locationally specific housing, as consumers devote an increasing share of their income to competing for the ability to live in the most desired parts of town. But if the supply of desirable locations is scarce, and the land on which desired real estate is irreproducible, the only thing that can adjust is the price.

Thus the rising importance of real estate—and of the underlying land—in part reflects fundamental technological and consumer preference factors. Advanced economies are getting more real estate intensive, because they are more ICT intensive, and because they are on average getting richer. But awareness of rising real estate prices in turn gives further impetus to the effect, as real estate has become an "asset class" in which people invest not only to enjoy housing services but also in the anticipation of capital gain.

At the top end of the housing market, the "asset investment" motivation may indeed be the dominant one, with many super-luxury apartments in London, Dubai, or New York bought but rarely occupied. But the phenomenon reaches far beyond the top of the market. If people buy houses earlier in life than they otherwise would for fear of losing out as prices rise, they are effectively treating housing as an investment. For many people their own home is by far the most important investment they will ever make. And in the United Kingdom, investment in residential housing for rent—"buy to let" investment—has grown to account for 15% of the housing stock.

Advanced economies would therefore become more real estate–intensive even if leverage played no role. But increasing leverage is the inevitable consequence: and in turn it amplifies the effect.

Real Estate and Leverage—The Bias and the Cycle

Unlike 50 years ago, most bank lending—and in the United States most lending through capital markets—now finances the purchase of real estate. In part that reflects simply the increasing role of real estate in total wealth. In part it reflects the valuable social role that mortgage credit plays in lubricating the exchange of homes between different people, including different generations. But it also reflects a bias for banks to prefer to lend against the security of real estate assets.

Lending to finance non–real estate business investment requires difficult and expensive assessment of project prospects and future cash flows: and if the project fails, the assets financed often have little resale value. But real estate, whether commercial or residential, usually has value for many alternative users. Taking security against real estate therefore seems to simplify risk assessment. Banks seeking rapid market share growth nearly always focus on real estate; safely expanding other types of lending requires the gradual and difficult build-up of customer relations and knowledge. And at least in residential real estate, though not commercial, actual loan losses are often low even in the face of major economic recession. In the latest crisis, it is true that U.S. losses from residential mortgage lending have reached 7% of total loan volumes, reflecting very aggressive subprime lending in the pre-crisis period. But while the United Kingdom also experienced a big mortgage credit boom, losses in the latest crisis have been less than 1%.[17]

Seen from the private perspective of individual banks, lending against real estate often therefore seems, and sometimes actually is, lower risk and easier to manage than other categories of lending. Before the mid-twentieth century, banks in several advanced economies were restricted or at least discouraged from entering real estate lending markets: in different ways, for instance, Japan, the United Kingdom, and Canada all constrained bank mortgage lending. Once the constraints were removed, these institutions increasingly became real estate lenders.[18]

But lending against real estate—and in particular against existing real estate whose supply cannot be easily increased—generates self-reinforcing cycles of credit supply, credit demand, and asset prices. Figure 4.4 illustrates the upswing. More credit supply produces rising real estate prices, which in turn increase both the net worth and the confidence

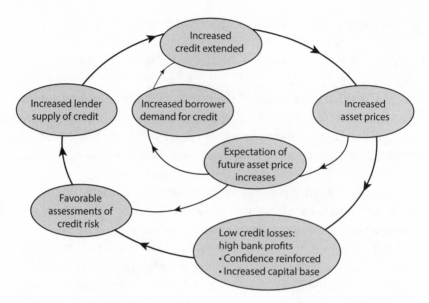

Figure 4.4.   Credit and asset price cycles

of borrowers and lenders. As prices rise, lenders experience only small loan losses, which increases their capital bases, which makes it possible for them to make more loans; but low loan losses also reinforce bank management and loan officer confidence that further loans will be safe. Meanwhile, borrowers see their net worth rise, which enables them to borrow more for any given loan to value ratio (LTV), and the experience of rising prices generates expectations that further rises will continue at least for the medium term. Throughout modern economic history real estate credit and prices move together. In the latest upswing, from 2000 to 2007, mortgage credit in the United States increased by 134% and house prices by 90%; in Spain the increases were 254% and 120%; in Ireland, 336% and 109%.[19]

These cycles sometimes generate booms in new real estate investment. Ireland and Spain saw pre-crisis construction booms, and so too did U.S. states such as Florida and Nevada. But they can also generate booms and subsequent busts in the price of already exiting real estate, and of the irreproducible land on which the real estate sits. In the United Kingdom the boom and bust was mainly in existing house prices, as it was in U.S. cities where the ability to build is more constrained, such as

Manhattan and San Francisco.[20] Even in the countries or regions where a housing construction boom occurred, dramatic rises in the price of existing houses (for example, of central Dublin properties) played a major role in making new construction appear profitable.

At the very core of financial instability in modern economies thus lies an interface between an infinite capacity and an inelastic constraint. Banks, unless constrained by policy, have an infinite capacity to create credit, money, and purchasing power; so do shadow banking systems, as Chapter 6 explores. But the supply of locationally desirable real estate (and ultimately land) is always somewhat inelastic and in some cities close to fixed. Potentially infinite nominal demand and finite supply combine to make the price of locationally specific real estate indeterminate and potentially volatile. The resulting credit and asset price cycles are not just part of the story of financial instability in modern economies, they are its very essence.[21]

The upswing of the cycle drives real estate prices higher, accentuating the rising importance of real estate wealth apparent in Piketty's figures. But it also leaves the economy vulnerable to financial crisis and post-crisis recession as the cycle illustrated in Figure 4.4 swings into reverse. In the downswing, falling asset prices reduce both the net worth and confidence of both lenders and borrowers, curtailing credit supply and demand. The economy is left facing a debt overhang effect. Chapter 5 describes the consequences.

||||||||||||||||||||||||||||||||||||||||||||||||||||||||||||||||||||||||||||||||||||||||||||||||||||||||||||||||||||||||||||||||||

FIVE

CAUGHT IN THE DEBT OVERHANG TRAP

Economic disasters are almost always preceded by a large increase in household debt. In fact, the correlation is so robust that it is as close to an empirical law as it gets in macro-economics.
  —*Atif Mian and Amir Sufi,* House of Debt[1]

Contrary to widely held beliefs, six years on from the beginning of the financial crisis in the advanced economies, the global economy is not yet on a deleveraging path. Indeed the ratio of global total debt over GDP has kept increasing at an unabated pace and breaking new highs: up 38 percentage points since 2008 to 212%.
  —*Luigi Buttiglione, Philip R. Lane, Lucrezia Reichlin, and Vincent Reinhart,* Deleveraging, What Deleveraging? The 16th Geneva Report on the World Economy[2]

T HE FINANCIAL CRISIS OF 2007–2008 was followed by a credit crunch—a sudden stop to the rapid pre-crisis credit growth. Fixing the financial system and in particular the banks therefore seemed a top priority. Higher bank capital requirements and stress tests sought to remove market concerns about bank solvency and constraints on bank funding; public capital injections and central bank liquidity lines were designed to enable banks to start lending again. These policies were appropriate and essential: but they were also inadequate.

That's because the biggest problem we faced was not an impaired financial system but a severe debt overhang in the real economy. And fixing the banks cannot itself fix that problem. Faced with severe debt overhang, indeed, all policy levers have seemed inadequate. The result has been seven years of recession and only weak recovery.

Japan—The Canary in the Mine

Ahead of the crisis, the relentless rise in private-sector leverage shown in Figure 1.2 in Chapter 1 provoked little concern. But it should have, because from the 1990s on, Japan provided a warning of the huge damage a debt overhang can cause. Richard Koo explained how in an important book published in 2008—*The Holy Grail of Macroeconomics: Lessons from Japan's Great Recession.*[3]

Japan successfully used a form of directed credit policy to achieve high investment and rapid economic growth during the 1950s to 1980s. From the early 1980s on, however, its banks were increasingly allowed to enter real estate lending and had incentives to do so. In addition many nonfinancial companies became heavily involved in real estate speculation alongside their core manufacturing or consumer service activities.

The result was a massive credit-fueled real estate boom, with domestic bank credit increasing 65% from 1985 to 1989, real estate lending increasing four times, and land prices rising 245%.[4] In total Japan's land was valued at around 5.2 times GDP, driving Japan's total wealth to income ratio from about 510% in 1980 to a peak of 800% in 1990.[5] Market prices suggested that the gardens surrounding the Imperial Palace in central Tokyo, if available for building, would be worth as much as all the land in California: the market value of land in one of Tokyo's districts, central Chiyoda, was said to exceed that of the whole of Canada.[6]

In 1990 the bubble burst, and commercial property prices fell in some locations by as much as 80%.[7] Japanese companies, which had borrowed money in expectation of further real estate price increases, suddenly focused on the need to pay back swollen debts out of operational cash flow. They therefore cut investment in an attempt to deleverage. Rather than being net borrowers from other sectors of the economy, they switched to being net savers and continued to be so even when interest rates were cut to nearly zero. In Koo's terms, Japan had entered a "balance sheet recession," in which companies were so determined to improve their balance sheets by paying down debt that low interest rates were power-less to stimulate expenditure. Two decades of slow growth and gradual price deflation followed.

But before the crisis of 2007–2008, the lessons from Japan's experience were largely ignored by Western economists, regulators, and central banks. Japan, it was commonly assumed, was so different and exceptional that what happened there carried few general implications. But the analysis of Jordá, Schularick, and Taylor shows that debt overhang effects resulting from real estate lending have become steadily more important across the advanced economies.[8] Recessions are on average much deeper and longer lasting when preceded by large build-ups of mortgage debt, and debt overhang effects resulting from mortgage lending have become more important as banking systems have become more biased toward real estate. Moreover, these authors show that "recessions tend to be considerably deeper and the recovery much slower when the preceding boom saw a strong expansion of mortgage debt," *irrespective* of whether there was a financial crisis involving the failure of a major bank or other financial institution. The early 1990s recession in the United Kingdom is a case in point. A strong credit and house price boom in the late 1980s was followed by falling house prices, depressed demand, a recession, and then very slow recovery, even though loan losses were never high enough to threaten the solvency of the banking system.

Financial crises and bank insolvencies can cause great harm, but the debt overhang created by excessive private credit creation can be more harmful still.

America and the House of Debt

Advanced economy private-sector leverage, and in particular leverage against real estate, had never been higher than in 2007. The impact of the post-crisis debt overhang has therefore been severe. Atif Mian and Amir Sufi's book *House of Debt* provides a compelling account of how excessive debts wrought great harm in the U.S. economy.[9]

They explain how the debt overhang effect works for the individual household. During the boom, households are tempted into borrowing, which appears to make sense because of rising house prices. But when house prices fall, borrowers suffer a fall in net worth, and the higher their leverage is, the greater the percentage loss they experience. With a 90% loan to value mortgage, a 5% fall in house prices wipes out 50% of the household's equity in their house.

Faced with falling net worth, many households cut consumption. This follows in part from a simple "wealth effect": when people feel less wealthy, they tend to consume less and save more. But it is amplified if debtors are worried that the fall in their net worth could go so far as to make them insolvent, facing them with the additional costs of bankruptcy, repossession, and the sale of their home at a fire sale price. Fear that default might make it impossible to borrow in the future (except at exorbitant rates) may also be an important concern.

So when house prices fall, highly leveraged households focus strongly on reducing their debt levels—the household equivalent of the Japanese companies that Richard Koo analyzed—and their reduced expenditure depresses demand in the economy. But this reduction is not offset by increased expenditure on the part of net creditors elsewhere in the economy:[10] indeed, if asset house prices mean falling prices for credit securities, or concerns about bank solvency, net creditors may themselves reduce expenditure.

Using county-specific data on mortgage borrowing relative to home value, Mian and Sufi are then able to illustrate this debt overhang effect at work. They report four important findings.

First, the biggest rises and then falls in house prices before and after the 2007–2008 crisis occurred in those cities where it was most difficult, because of population density and zoning restrictions, to expand housing supply. This illustrates the impact of the inelastic supply of land discussed in Chapter 4.

Second, there was a strong correlation between those counties where households were most highly leveraged (and therefore suffered the greatest falls in net worth) and those where consumer expenditure fell most dramatically after 2008.

Third, these were also the counties where employment in locally oriented businesses—such as shops, auto dealerships, or restaurants—fell most significantly.

Fourth, business investment by such companies fell, not because companies faced a restricted supply of credit, but because reduced household spending had cut demand for their goods and services.

These findings, in line with Koo's argument and the research of Jordà, Schularick, and Taylor, carry a simple but extremely important implication: fixing the banks will not be sufficient to fix the economy.

Fixing the Banks Will Not Fix the Economy

After the crisis, credit growth collapsed in all the affected economies. In the United States it fell from 8.8% per year in the decade before the crisis, to –2.5% in 2009; in Spain from 17% per year before the crisis to –3% per year over the years 2009–2014.[11] Restoring robust credit growth seemed essential to drive economic recovery.

But credit supply seemed blocked by weaknesses in the banking system: banks were short of capital to support new lending, and worries about bank solvency were reflected in the increased cost of bank funding. Central banks worried that the "monetary policy transmission mechanism" was impaired—that rock bottom interest rates and quantitative easing were failing to translate into easy credit supply for households and companies.

To remove these blockages, prudential regulators and central banks implemented a complex combination of policies, striking difficult trade-offs among conflicting objectives. Stress tests, asset quality reviews, and increases in required bank capital ratios sought to restore market confidence in bank solvency. But since banks could respond to higher bank capital requirements by cutting lending yet further, we also debated long and hard about the merits of rapid versus slow progress toward the new standards. Governments put new capital into banks, or provided backstops to private capital raising, in an attempt to ensure that higher capital ratios meant more capital—not less lending. And several central banks introduced new facilities that directly funded real economy lending. The Bank of England's Funding for Lending Scheme, introduced in 2012, provided cheap funding for banks, provided they increased lending to households and companies. The European Central Bank's Targeted Long-Term Repo Scheme, introduced in September 2014, copied that approach.

I was involved for 4 ½ years in the debates that led to these policies, and I believe they were important. Restricted credit supply can hold back growth. In Chapter 3's analysis of debt contracts, the risk that debt rollover and new supply might suffer a sudden stop was one of the dangers I identified. But both Japan's experience in the 1990s and Western experience after the 2007–2008 crisis show that restoring potential credit supply is insufficient to restore growth.

Many analyses of Japan in the 1990s focus on the role of a broken banking system. But as Richard Koo illustrates, by the mid-1990s that banking system was offering loans to businesses at close to zero interest rates, but corporate borrowing remained depressed. Monetary policy was effectively transmitted to cheap credit supply, but the demand was not there, because borrowers were already overleveraged.

Similarly, in the United Kingdom we had intense discussions from 2009 to 2013 about why the banks were not lending the money made available to them through quantitative easing. But we always had strong indications that lack of demand was the more important problem. Even when banks had already granted lending facilities to companies, actual utilization remained low: and the Bank of England's Credit Conditions survey repeatedly found that lack of demand for business products and services was a more important brake on business activity than the availability of credit.

As for the eurozone, after 2011 the European Central Bank placed great emphasis on the need to restore confidence in the banking system, arguing that high bank funding costs and lending rates in several countries hampered the transmission of monetary policy and held back growth. But major declines in bank funding and lending rates between 2011 and 2014 failed to translate into significant credit growth. And when the ECB launched its version of a funding for lending scheme in September 2014, offering to lend money to banks for four years at only 0.1% per year, banks chose to borrow only €80 billion out of the €400 billion made available. Credit supply at low price was ensured, but credit demand was lacking because of the debt overhang effect.

Atif Mian and Amir Sufi argue indeed that the dominance of the debt overhang effect is so clear that we should shift the policy focus entirely from a "banking view," in which restoring bank health is the key priority, to a "debt view," which should lead, for instance, to significant personal debt forgiveness. My own judgement is that both credit supply and credit demand matter. But Mian and Sufi are right that public debate after the 2007–2008 crisis was skewed far too much toward the credit supply problem and that we were slow to realize the severity of the debt overhang challenge.

In part that skew probably reflected wishful thinking. For fixing the banks, while demanding, is clearly doable. In contrast, a severe debt overhang appears to make all policy levers ineffective.

Debt Doesn't Go Away—It Simply Shifts Around

Between 1990 and 2010 Japanese corporate debt fell from 139% to 103% of GDP: Japanese companies reduced their leverage.[12] But Japanese gross government debt increased from 67% of GDP to 215% of GDP.[13] And the increase in government debt was an automatic consequence of corporate-sector deleveraging. Companies cut investment, and the economy entered recession, so government deficits increased as tax revenues fell and social expenditures rose.

Those public deficits played a valuable role in offsetting the deflationary impact of private-sector deleveraging: if the Japanese government had insisted on balanced public budgets in the face of corporate deleveraging, Japan would almost certainly have suffered not just two decades of slow growth but a massive depression. But the deficits leave a problem: what to do about the rising public debt stock? The leverage has not gone away: it has simply shifted from the private to the public sector.

That pattern has been replicated in numerous countries after the 2007–2008 crisis (Figure 5.1). U.S. private debt to GDP has fallen by 12 percentage points (from 192% of GDP in 2008 to 180% of GDP in 2013 with significant household sector deleveraging), but public debt has increased from 72% to 103%. Spanish private debt to GDP, having risen sharply in the years before 2008, has fallen from 215% of GDP to 187%, but public debt has increased from 39% of GDP in 2008 to 92% in 2013.[14] Figure 5.2 shows the overall picture for advanced economies— household debt is down as a percentage of GDP since 2009, corporate debt is flat, but public debt has dramatically increased. Total debt for the real economy (that is, excluding intrafinancial system debt) has continued to increase.[15]

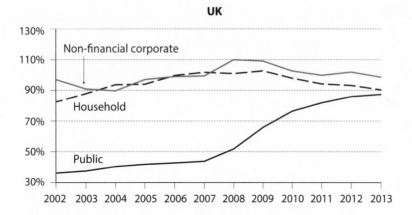

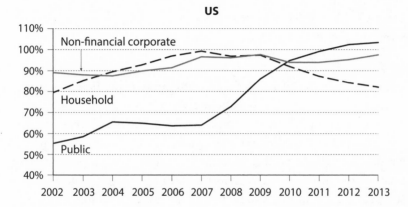

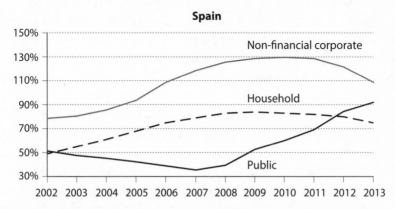

Figure 5.1.   Shifting leverage: Private and public debt to GDP, Spain, the United Kingdom, and the United States

Source: International Monetary Fund; Organisation for Economic Co-operation and Development; McKinsey Global Institute.

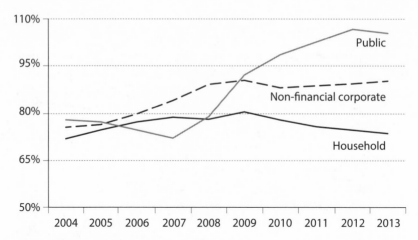

Figure 5.2.   Developed economies: Debt to GDP

Source: Buttiglione et al. (2014).

Increasing public debt has focused attention on public expenditure: it seems to imply that the roots of current problems lay in profligate government spending. In a few countries, in particular Greece, they did: excessive public spending relative to taxation was central to what went wrong. And all advanced economies face pressures on long-term public finances that need careful management. But in most countries the reason public debt has increased rapidly since the crisis is simple: excessive private credit creation produced a crisis and post-crisis recession.

Moreover, in almost all countries it was the post-crisis recession that played havoc with public finances, not the direct costs of rescuing the banking system. In the United Kingdom the total net costs of bailing out the banks—including equity injections, guarantees, and central bank liquidity support—have amounted to about 1.3% of GDP,[16] but public debt as a share of GDP has soared from 44% in 2007 to 92% in 2013.[17] In the United States the total cost of rescuing the formal banking system was negative—the authorities made a profit, but federal debt has gone from 76% to 103% of GDP. Only in Ireland and Greece does the direct cost of bank rescue explain a significant part of the increase in public debt. Elsewhere public debt increased almost entirely because excessive growth in private leverage before the crisis resulted in a debt overhang, private-sector deleveraging, and a deep recession.

So leverage has not fallen but has simply shifted from the private to the public sector. In addition it has shifted between countries. Chapter 8 describes China's post-2009 credit boom, with "total social finance" up from 124% of GDP in early 2008 to 200% in 2014 and still rising.[18] That increase was a direct consequence of the 2007–2008 crisis and thus in turn of the pre-crisis growth of advanced economy private leverage. Faced with a severe global recession in autumn 2008, and fearful that this would produce a socially dangerous slowdown of Chinese growth, the Chinese authorities used rapid credit expansion as the only tool apparently available to maintain growth. Private deleveraging and recession in advanced economies thus drove a policy of credit-fueled growth in China: leverage has not gone away, it has simply shifted from one country to another.

Indeed, even where individual countries have achieved deleveraging, their ability to do so has been crucially dependent on growing leverage in other countries. Germany is one of the few countries where private leverage today, at 108% of GDP, is below the level of both 2007 and 2000. But Germany's economic growth has still been driven by unsustainable increases in debt: it is simply that in Germany's case the credit growth occurs in its export markets. Before the 2007–2008 crisis, Germany's export growth and large current-account surplus were made possible by rapid growth in private credit and demand—and the resulting current-account deficits—in the United States, the United Kingdom, and peripheral eurozone countries, such as Spain. After the crisis Germany's now yet larger surpluses have been underpinned by public debt increases in, for instance, the United Kingdom and the United States, and by China's huge credit boom.

To understand excessive credit creation and debt overhang, we must therefore take a global perspective. The global picture is shown in Figure 5.3, which shows total advanced economy leverage increasing though not as fast as before 2007, but global debt to GDP increasing even faster than before the crisis as emerging economy debt soars.[19] In aggregate, attempts to deleverage have been utterly ineffective.

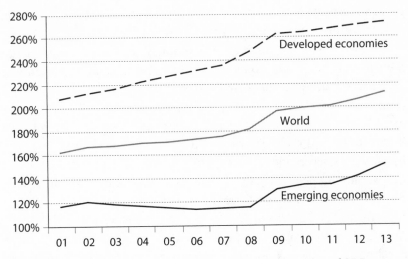

Figure 5.3.   Global debt excluding financial corporations: Percentage of GDP

Source: Buttiglione et al. (2014).

No Good Policy Options?

The lack of progress with deleveraging reflects the fact that once debt has first grown to excessive levels, all traditional policy levers appear blocked or have adverse side effects. Debt overhang seems to be a trap from which there is no clear escape.

Fiscal Policy Constrained

Fiscal deficits undoubtedly have a short-term stimulative effect, and the large deficits run by many countries in 2009–2010 helped avoid still deeper recession than actually occurred. Fiscal austerity in turn undoubtedly depresses short-term growth, and aggressive fiscal consolidation in several eurozone countries generated severe recessions after 2010. As Chapter 14 discusses, a strong case can be made that in several countries fiscal policy was tightened too rapidly after 2009, depressing the pace of recovery.

But once large public debt levels have already been accumulated, some fiscal consolidation—through public expenditure cuts or tax increases—

appears essential. Surely, it seems, we need an answer to the question: how will public debts ever be repaid?[20]

Once high leverage already exists, fiscal policy seems to be stuck between a rock and a hard place.

EASY MONEY'S COLLATERAL DAMAGE

Faced with large accumulated debts, meanwhile, monetary policy levers may prove imperfectly effective or have adverse side effects. All such policy levers work by cutting one or another interest rate. Conventional policy can reduce the short-term policy rate to zero or even slightly below: quantitative easing and forward guidance can reduce long-term rates and expectations of future short-term rates. "Funding for lending" type schemes seek to cut the interest rates actually paid by companies or households.

These reductions will, it is hoped, in turn stimulate real economy effects. Faced with lower funding costs, banks may be more willing to lend, and faced with lower loan rates, households and companies more willing to borrow. Lower yields on safe government bonds—and resulting increases in bond and other asset prices—may stimulate now-wealthier households to consume more and investors and companies to fund business investment in search of higher returns. And it is highly likely that the policies pursued have indeed reduced the danger of price deflation and enhanced real growth. The Bank of England estimated in 2012 that UK nominal GDP was about 1.5% higher as a result of its quantitative easing program.[21]

But that success comes with collateral damage. Since quantitative easing stimulates the economy through rising asset prices, it is bound to increase wealth inequalities. Bank of England estimates suggest that quantitative easing may have increased total household wealth by just over £600 billion, the equivalent of £10,000 per capita if assets were evenly distributed across the population.[22] But since the top 10 % of households own over 70% of all household financial assets, the vast majority of this benefit has accrued to the better off.[23] Quantitative easing has been good for the rich, and ultra-easy monetary policy thus exacerbates the inequality, which, as Chapter 7 discusses, is itself one of the drivers of credit-intensive growth.

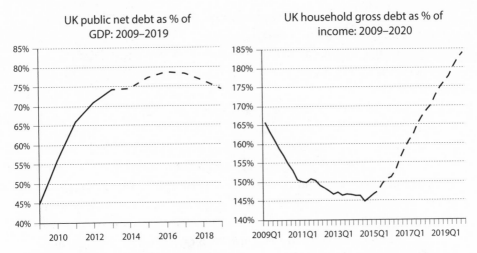

UK public net debt as % of GDP: 2009–2019

UK household gross debt as % of income: 2009–2020

Figure 5.4. UK leverage: Back to private again

Source: Office of Budget Responsibility, Economic and Fiscal Outlook, December 2014.

Moreover, low interest rates only work by restimulating that excessive credit growth. The UK economy is now recovering, and latest forecasts from the Office for Budget Responsibility suggest that public debt to GDP will cease rising in 2017 and slowly fall thereafter. But the Office for Budget Responsibility forecasts also show private-sector leverage returning to its upward path, with household debt as a percentage of income, having fallen by 22 percentage points between 2010 and 2014, predicted to rise 40 percentage points by 2020 and with total economy leverage, public and private combined, by then higher than ever before (Figure 5.4).[24]

Meanwhile, the longer interest rates stay very low, the greater will be the incentives for investors and companies to seek profit from high leverage and for the financial system to innovate complex new ways to support leveraged position taking. Given the purposes for which bank credit is actually used in advanced economies, ultra-low interest rates are likely to stimulate speculation in existing assets more than they stimulate new business investment.

Ultra-easy monetary policy has undoubtedly been better than a no-action alternative, and if I had been on the Bank of England's Monetary

Policy Committee between 2009 and 2012, I would have supported all of their stimulus initiatives. But as a cure for the debt hangover, ultra-easy monetary policy is essentially a stiff drink.

OUT OF AMMUNITION?

Once high leverage exists, all policy levers seem imperfect. We appear out of useful ammunition, the policy magazine bereft of options that do not cause as much harm as good. In fact, I argue in Chapter 14 that governments and central banks together never run out of ammunition to counter the effects of debt overhang and deflation as long as they are willing to consider the full range of available policy options.

But the severe difficulties that debt overhang creates, and the huge economic cost of the post-2008 recession and weak recovery, certainly make it vital to achieve future growth without excessive credit creation. We must therefore understand why it seemed before the crisis that adequate economic growth required yet faster credit growth: Chapter 7 considers that issue. But we also need to understand the role played by the second dimension of finance's remarkable growth—the huge growth of intrafinancial system complexity and financial innovation.

That growth made it easier for the financial system to create excessive debt, made it more difficult for regulators and central banks to identify emerging problems, and made the financial system itself more fragile and vulnerable to crisis. Shadow banking, financial innovation, and intense trading among financial institutions hardwired instability into the financial system, gave us the credit cycle on steroids, and made a severe debt overhang more likely. Chapter 6 tells that story.

SIX

LIBERALIZATION, INNOVATION, AND THE CREDIT CYCLE ON STEROIDS

There is growing recognition that the dispersal of credit risk by banks to a broader and more diverse group of investors ... has helped to make the banking and overall financial system more resilient. The improved resilience may be seen in fewer bank failures and more consistent credit provision. Consequently the commercial banks may be less vulnerable today to credit or economic shocks.

—IMF Global Financial Stability Report, April 2006[1]

Securitisation is a good thing. If everything was on banks' balance sheets there wouldn't be enough credit.

—Quoted from a senior American regulator, in "Playing with fire,"
The Economist, Feb 25th, 2012 © The Economist Newspaper
Limited, London (2012)[2]

FINANCIAL CRISES HAVE OCCURRED ever since societies were complex enough to have money and debt. But they have been far more frequent over the past 30–40 years; they were considerably less frequent for the 30 years before that, the decades from 1945 to 1975.

Carmen Reinhart and Kenneth Rogoff's book *This Time Is Different: Eight Centuries of Financial Folly* describes 153 banking crises in the period 1980–2010, compared with two from 1945 to 1970 and nine from 1970 to 1980.[3] Moritz Schularick and Alan Taylor's analysis in *Credit Booms Gone Bust* reveals that "the frequency of crises in the 1945–71 period was virtually zero ... but since 1971, crises became more frequent, occurring with a four percent annual probability."[4] Charles Kindleberger's analysis suggests that "despite the lack of perfect comparability across different time periods, the conclusion is unmistakable that financial failure has been more extensive and pervasive in the last 30 years than in any previous period."[5] And he wrote that in 2000, well before the global financial crisis of 2007–2008.

The past 30–40 years were also the period in which finance grew much bigger relative to the real economy. Finance accounted for an increasing share of GDP, finance sector pay soared, and financial sector innovations proliferated. As Chapter 1 describes, that growth partly reflected increasing real economy use of financial services: households and companies borrowed more, and their leverage grew. But in part it reflected still faster increase in intrafinancial system activity. Foreign-exchange trading grew far more rapidly than did real trade, gross capital flows grew more rapidly than did foreign direct investment, derivative market volumes soared, and major bank balance sheets came to be dominated not by deposits from and loans to real economy households and companies but by claims on and obligations to other financial institutions.

The strong consensus before the crisis was that this increasing intrafinancial activity had both improved capital allocation and made the financial system and economy more stable. Not surprisingly, the financial industry itself was happy to praise the impact of its increasingly complex activities. The article by Dudley and Hubbard, referred to in Chapter 1, which concluded that financial innovation had "improved the allocation of capital and risk throughout the US economy" was published by Goldman Sachs.[6] But the IMF was equally confident that credit structuring and derivatives had made the global financial system more stable.

That confidence turned out to be utterly mistaken. There is no evidence that advanced economies have become overall more efficient as result of the post-1970 increase in financial intensity: growth rates did not increase. And the development of a much bigger and more innovative financial system led to the crisis of 2007–2008 and to a severe post-crisis recession.

As in previous episodes, the root cause of both crisis and post-crisis recession was the credit cycle. But this time the credit cycle was on steroids. For the very developments that were supposed to ensure stable and useful credit supply in fact produced greater instability and waste. The innovations of securitization, credit structuring, and derivatives turbocharged the cycle, increasing the danger of too much of the wrong sort of debt.

This chapter therefore assesses the impact of increasing activity and complexity inside the financial system. It begins with the interrelated factors that unleashed increasing financial intensity—globalization, domestic liberalization, and the multifaceted phenomenon of shadow banking. It describes how supposedly sophisticated techniques for managing risks in fact exacerbated them. It concludes by identifying two adverse consequences for the real economy—wasteful credit extension and a search for yield that, while rational for individual market participants, at the aggregate level adds cost but no additional return.

Globalization and the Loosening of Constraints

The 1950s and 1960s were marked by a striking absence of financial crises and by robust growth in all advanced economies. In part, financial stability reflected tight domestic regulation. But it also reflected an international monetary system that limited global capital flows.

From the late 1940s until 1971, the major advanced economies operated within the Bretton Woods system of fixed but adjustable exchange rates. Such currencies as the pound sterling, the Deutsche Mark, and French franc maintained (or at least sought to maintain) a fixed parity against the U.S. dollar, and the U.S. dollar was, at least in some respects, convertible to gold at the fixed price of $35 per ounce. Countries unable to maintain a specific fixed exchange rate might (like the United Kingdom in 1967) devalue against the dollar but would then adopt a new fixed parity.

The system aimed to deliver enough fixity of exchange rates to facilitate international trade while allowing adjustment when necessary, avoiding the rigidities that resulted in the collapse of the gold standard in the interwar years. But it was a system that could only work if capital flows between countries were restricted: if UK citizens and companies had been free to invest in dollars or Deutsche Mark, their investments could have produced a drain on official foreign-exchange reserves, which would make the defense of the fixed exchange rate impossible. Across many advanced economies, freedom of capital movement was therefore tightly restricted.

Restrictions on domestic credit creation were a natural corollary of these international constraints.[7] Rapid domestic credit creation could undermine a fixed exchange rate by generating increased imports and an unsustainable current-account deficit; conversely, if foreign banks were free to lend money to domestic markets, domestic credit constraints would be undermined. As Chapter 8 describes, such countries as Japan, which used directed credit and financial repression to drive high investment and growth rates, had to impose capital flow constraints, both in and out, to protect those domestic policy objectives. And countries like the United Kingdom, which had a tendency to run current-account deficits, restricted domestic consumer credit through numerous regulatory devices. For the United States, concerns about the balance of payments were less important because of the dollar's role as the system's reserve currency. But constrained global financial markets made it easier to maintain the domestic restrictions put in place in the 1920s and 1930s. Regulation Q placed limits on interest rates on bank deposits: the McFadden Act of 1927 prevented banks from extending across state boundaries, and investment and commercial banking activity remained separated by the Glass-Steagall act of 1933.

The Bretton Woods system collapsed in the early 1970s. One of the very benefits of capital controls—freedom for a time to pursue expansionary domestic policies—fostered inflationary policies in some countries, which threatened the sustainability of fixed exchange rates. The U.S. dollar's reserve currency status made it easier for the United States to run fiscal and current-account deficits, but increasing U.S. deficits raised doubts about America's long-term commitment to the anchor of a fixed dollar / gold parity. And in a world of rapidly increasing international trade and free exchange between currencies for current trading purposes, effective capital controls became increasingly difficult to enforce. The relative importance of these different factors is debated. But by the early 1970s, it was clear that the system could no longer be sustained.[8]

The floating exchange rate system that replaced it made constraints on capital flow apparently unnecessary: with no fixed exchange parity to be defended, the danger of destabilizing speculation seemed to have been removed. And free capital flows were seen by many economists as positively beneficial: they ensured that capital was allocated in a globally efficient fashion, moving investment resources to areas of highest potential productivity. During the 1970s and 1980s, advanced economies removed almost all controls on cross-border capital flows, and an increasing number of emerging economies, strongly encouraged by the World Bank and the IMF, moved in the same direction.

In fact, as Chapter 9 discusses, the impact of free capital flows has not been the undiluted good that free-market theory anticipated. But their impact on the size of the financial system is clear. One reason financial balance sheets have grown relative to national income—and now entail far more intrafinancial sector assets and liabilities—is that major international banks are now extensively involved in global capital flows and trading activity, and in cross-border relationships with other banks.

That growth was greatly magnified by liberalization of domestic financial markets.

Domestic Liberalization

Freely floating exchange rates made domestic credit controls appear unneeded: the free movement of capital rendered them increasingly ineffective. If a company or household can hold or borrow money abroad, domestic constraints lose traction. But the case for domestic liberalization was seen as not simply pragmatic but as strongly positive.

The 1970s–1990s saw liberalization of financial markets in almost all advanced and many emerging economies. In the United States restrictions on interstate banking were progressively dismantled: Regulation Q constraints on interest rates were removed, and the Glass-Steagall division between commercial and investment banks was first eroded and then in 1999 entirely abandoned. In the United Kingdom, the 1971 Act on Competition and Credit Control jettisoned previous quantitative constraints on credit extension. The major commercial (or in UK parlance "clearing") banks became increasingly aggressive competitors in residential mortgage markets previously dominated by the mutual building societies: and these societies in turn were freed to compete in commercial real estate and to convert into banks. The "Big Bang" of 1986 removed divisions between different categories of firm active in London's wholesale capital markets. Constraints on Spanish banking competition were liberalized in the early 1980s; banks in several Scandinavian countries were freed from quantitative controls at around the same time. And in the same decade the Bank of Japan ceased providing "guidance" to the commercial banks on the sectoral allocation of their lending. Financial liberalization measures were also introduced in several Latin American countries and in emerging Asian economies.

The precise pattern of reforms reflected different initial positions: some countries started with publicly owned banks, others with predominantly private systems that were nevertheless subject to strong regulatory control. But the destination was characterized by three common factors

First, restrictions were removed on the quantity of lending in the economy, either in total or in specific sectors. Both the total quantity and the allocation of credit in the economy should, it was now believed, be determined by free market forces. The consequence was the relentless rise in the share of credit extended to finance real estate (which Chapter 4 describes).

Second, the distinctions were eroded between different types of financial institutions, with banks increasingly free to combine retail, corporate, and investment banking, and with firms free to combine bank and nonbank activities.

Third, short-term interest rates were increasingly relied on as the only policy lever required to manage the economic cycle, and increasingly the focus was on a low and stable rate of inflation as the sole or primary objective of central bank policy. Since the free market could be trusted to ensure the optimal level of debt in the economy, the fact that free-market choice drove a relentless increase in private-sector leverage was of no concern as long as inflation remained low.

Indeed, financial markets increasingly were treated as markets like any other, and credit as a product like any other, best provided at lowest cost and in optimal quantities in a freely competitive market.

Both internationally and domestically, the 1970s to 2000s thus witnessed the triumph of a new philosophy of financial liberalization, underpinned by the self-confident body of economic theory that Chapters 1 and 2 describe.

That confidence survived the uncomfortable truth that the early stages of financial liberalization were often followed by financial crisis. In the United States, interest-rate liberalization led directly to the savings and loan crisis of the late 1980s. In the Scandinavian countries, banks were freed from lending constraints in the 1980s and went on a commercial real estate lending spree that ended in crisis in the 1990s. Japanese banks freed to compete aggressively without bureaucratic direction produced the real estate lending boom and bust of the late 1980s and early 1990s. The collapse of the hedge fund Long Term Capital Management in 1998 illustrated the dangers inherent in derivatives trading. But it was always possible to attribute blame not to financial liberalization but to the fact that liberalization was incomplete or had been executed in an imperfect fashion.

And as the 1990s and 2000s progressed, policymakers became increasingly convinced that any initial problems generated by financial liberalization had been contained by the development of the new "technology" of securitized credit intermediation and by the application of new and sophisticated risk management techniques.

Securitization, Structuring, and Derivatives: Shadow Banking and Interbank Markets

Traded credit securities had always existed alongside bank loans. Until the 1970s most were issued by governments or large companies and were simple in form—promises made by one issuer to pay a defined stream of interest and capital repayments. But from the 1970s on, the innovation of "securitization" made it possible to take multiple smaller loans extended by banks or nonbanks and pool them together into composite credit securities. The role of traded credit securities was thus extended to new credit categories, such as household mortgages, auto finance loans, and student loans. Increasingly, the securities were also "structured" into different slices to provide alternative combinations of risk and return. The alphabet soup of CDOs, CLOs, and CDO squareds was born. By 2006, 60% of all residential mortgages in the United States were being packaged into tradable credit securities.[9] As a result, as Figure 6.1 shows, steady growth in bank balance sheets as a percentage of GDP was ac-

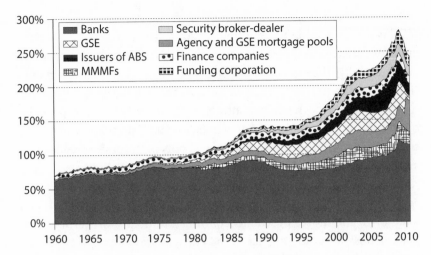

Figure 6.1. U.S. financial sector assets as percentage of GDP

Note: ABS, asset backed securities; GSE, government sponsored enterprise; MMMFs, money market mutual funds.

companied by far faster growth of the many nonbank financial institutions now involved in originating, trading, or holding credit securities.

Changes on the liability side of the financial system were equally important, with money market mutual funds emerging in the 1980s to offer instant access cash accounts paying higher interest rates than traditional banks. Credit extended to U.S. households could now be intermediated entirely outside the banking system: it could be originated by specialist mortgage sales companies; pooled and packaged into credit securities; and then distributed through complex chains of institutions and legal entities, which were often ultimately funded by money market mutual funds.

And even where banks did remain involved on the lending side, they increasingly did so as one link in multistep chains. Some bank deposits moved to money market mutual funds, but the money often flowed back to banks through wholesale funding markets.

The derivatives markets also boomed. Interest-rate swaps and options were developed in the early 1980s, enabling investors, traders, and banks to manage and hedge risks, for instance by converting floating-rate liabilities into fixed-rate or vice versa. By 2007 contracts with a notional value of almost $400 trillion were outstanding.

Credit default swaps (CDS) emerged in the 1990s and grew to $60 trillion notional value outstanding by 2007. These provided a form of credit insurance, paying out in the event of the default of a specified credit security. They therefore enabled banks and other financial institutions or traders to lay off credit risk without selling the underlying loans or bonds to which the CDS contract referred. But they also provided opportunities for market participants to take speculative positions, seeking to profit from anticipated movements in the price of underlying credit securities.

The United States was the epicenter of the developments: in Europe and Japan most credit continued to be extended in a traditional bank loan form, and most households continued to hold short-term cash in bank deposits. But the impact of the changes was global. The German Landesbanks were major investors in U.S. mortgage credit securities; other European banks drew short-term funding from U.S. money market funds. Major European banks—such as Deutsche Bank, Barclays, UBS, or Société Générale—were major players in U.S. dollar as well as in sterling or euro credit securities and derivatives markets. A huge amount of trading in U.S. dollar credit securities and derivatives was conducted in London by U.S., UK, and European banks, as well as in New York. Italian municipal governments could borrow loans from Italian banks, but hedge the interest rate risk by buying derivatives from U.S. investment banks.

Combined with globalization and facilitated by liberalization, these developments produced a profound change in the role of bank treasury and trading functions. In the 1970s bank treasury departments performed a largely passive function. The bank's real economy business, its loans to and deposits from customers and the balance of customer payments occurring through clearing houses, would leave the bank with either a funding need or surplus funds, and the treasury would either borrow in the interbank market to fund the deficit or place its surplus with other banks. The activity required neither screens with price information from across the world, nor armies of highly paid traders, nor powerful computers. It was a service function supporting the bank's customer business rather than being a profit-making activity in itself. But by the 1990s, treasury functions across the world had been collocated with trading functions, the combination becoming major profit centers staffed by hundreds of dealers seeking to profit from a complex mix of market-making, arbitrage, and pure position-taking activities.

The vast majority of this activity involved deals with other financial institutions, such as other banks, nonbank dealers, hedge funds, asset managers, or insurance companies. As a result, bank balance sheets came to be dominated by intrafinancial system assets and liabilities.

The Dream and the Reality

The years from 1980 to 2007 thus saw both a profound change in the global credit intermediation system and a huge increase in the complexity of markets that connected banks and nonbank financial institutions across the advanced economies. Most economists and policymakers, as well as the industry itself, believed this increased complexity had made economies more efficient and more robust.

Securitization, structuring, and derivatives, it was explained, enabled investors to hold their precisely desired combinations of risk and return, making possible both valuable credit creation and an improved distribution of risks. "Financial derivatives," wrote Rajan and Zingales in 2004, "can slice and dice risk precisely, placing it on those who can best bear it, and making risky ventures even easier to finance."[10] A securitized credit system, it was also assumed, would make credit supply less volatile, since it would be less dependent on variations in bank capital adequacy. Dudley and Hubbard noted approvingly that "'credit crunches' of the sort that periodically shut off the supply of loans to home buyers ... are a thing of the past."[11] Alan Greenspan noted that the "growing array of derivatives" was one of the "key factors underlying the remarkable resilience of the banking system."[12]

In theory, indeed, a system of securitized credit provision could have some advantages over a purely bank-based system. It could enable banks with particular concentrations of customers (by geography or sector) to distribute some of their loans to investors holding more balanced portfolios. And it could reduce the risks created by maturity transformation: while medium or long-term loans on bank balance sheets are partly funded by short-term deposits, long-term debt securities could be held by long-term investors, such as pension funds and insurance companies.

But the model of securitized credit that actually developed differed from this ideal world in four crucial respects. First, many of the credit risks apparently moved off bank balance sheets were not transferred to natural end investors but were held within the trading books of the same or other banks. When the market turned sour in 2007–2008, the largest losses on securitized credit were suffered by the large commercial banks and by broker dealer investment banks rather than by long-term institutional investors.

Second, even when credit risks were moved off balance sheets, maturity transformation risk was not removed from the system. A 30-year mortgage security could end up in the portfolio of a "Special Investment Vehicle," funded in part by asset-backed commercial paper, which was bought by a money market mutual fund, whose investors believed that they held an instantly available cash investment. The system that emerged was therefore appropriately labeled "shadow banking," since it replicated the maturity transformation risks of banks but did so outside the regulatory constraints of bank liquidity and capital requirements. And just as a formal banking system can create new credit and private money that did not previously exist, this shadow banking system created new credit and new forms of "near money" equivalents, such as balances at money market mutual funds.

Third, the system fatally undermined incentives for good credit analysis. If bank loans had been directly distributed to long-term investors intending to hold the credit securities to maturity, credit analysis might conceivably have been enhanced. But since in fact credit securities were distributed through multistep chains, each player in the chain needed only to think about how sentiment and prices would change before they sold the security on. Mortgage salespersons made loans to subprime borrowers who had little hope of repaying, confident that the securities packaged from those loans would be sold to investors far away, and many investment bankers sold credit securities whose value they doubted to investors whose judgement they disparaged—"stupid Germans in Düsseldorf" in one telling phrase.[13]

Fourth, derivatives were used not only to hedge risks but also to generate them on a huge scale. Chapter 2 discusses the paradox of market-making and liquidity—that some pure betting can provide useful market liquidity, which enables other market participants to hedge risks, but that betting can also create risks that did not previously exist. In the case of credit default swaps, the bets placed were an enormous multiple of the underlying real economy credit supposedly being "insured." Indeed, so great was the demand for betting opportunities that entirely new but fictional credit exposures—synthetic CDOs—were created to provide something to bet against. Long and short credit exposures unrelated to real economic activity thus multiplied counterparty risk in the financial system.

The Market Completion Delusion

Because of these features, the new technologies of securitization, structuring, and derivatives produced not the utopia of smoothly operating perfect markets that its proponents lauded, but the crisis of 2007–2008. They helped generate even more wasteful credit than a pure banking system would have produced, and a cats-cradle of intrafinancial system claims, which increased the danger of self-reinforcing domino effects if ever confidence was undermined.

Indeed, what the pre-crisis orthodoxy illustrates is the market completion delusion described in Chapter 2. If all markets could be made perfect, and all human beings made rational, then more financial contracts, more trading, more liquidity, and more price discovery would indeed bring us closer to an efficient competitive equilibrium in which all resources would be allocated as efficiently as possible. But in the real world of inherently imperfect markets, imperfect information, and of human beings part rational and part not, market completion and increased liquidity can have negative effects. More-liquid markets for residential mortgage securities made it easier to fund poor quality mortgage loans.

Market completion in the real world—and in particular financial market completion—is a double-edged sword. Applied to the world's debt markets, it turbocharged the credit cycle and helped produce the disaster of 2007–2008.

But the pre-crisis optimists were still convinced that the system was safe because its increased complexity had been matched by the development of sophisticated risk management tools.

Risk Management Delusions and the Doomsday Machine

When Alan Greenspan praised the contribution of the "growing array of derivatives" to improved resilience, he also stressed the importance of "the related application of more sophisticated methods for measuring and managing risks." He noted moreover that these techniques were not just applicable to the world of securitized credit and derivatives, but also more generally across the financial system, including in traditional banks. "Partly because of the proposed Basel II capital requirements" he noted, "the sophisticated risk management approaches that derivatives have facilitated are being employed more widely and systematically in the banking and financial services industries."[14]

Central to these sophisticated approaches were four ideas. First, market participants could glean useful information about risk from observation of the market price for risk. Second, if exposures and profits were continually recalculated on a mark-to-market basis, firms would be better placed to manage risks. Third, risk could be limited by securing financial contracts against collateral and by using "haircuts" and margin calls to ensure that exposures were more than covered by the value of the collateral that could be claimed in the event of counterparty default. Fourth, that Value at Risk models could be used to estimate how risky any given set of positions was (whether in loans, securities, or derivatives), and therefore how large the risk-absorbing buffers needed to be, whether in the form of haircuts at the level of the individual contract or capital at the level of the overall firm. These tools were assumed to make the system less risky: in fact they made it more unstable.

The idea that observed market prices for credit could be used to infer the appropriate price of credit risk, and thus the pricing of new loan commitments, was officially endorsed by the IMF. "By enhancing the transparency of the market's collective view of credit risks, credit derivatives," it noted approvingly in April 2006, "provide valuable information about broad credit conditions and increasingly set the marginal price of credit."[15] And seen from an individual market participant's viewpoint, market reference pricing could indeed make sense: if new loans were priced in line with current market prices for comparable credit securities, it was more likely that they could be sold down without loss. If the EMH holds, moreover, the observed market price is by defini-

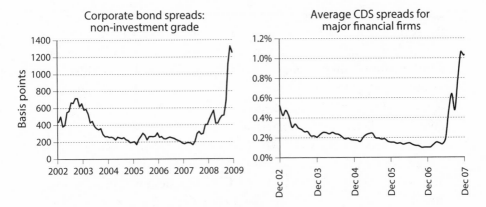

Figure 6.2.   Market perception of private credit risk

Note: (right) Firms included: Ambac, Aviva, Banco Santander, Barclays, Berkshire Hathaway, Bradford & Bingley, Citigroup, Deutsche Bank, Fortis, HBOS, Lehman Brothers, Merrill Lynch, Morgan Stanley, National Australia Bank, Royal Bank of Scotland, and UBS. CDS series peaks at 6.54% in September 2008. CDS, credit default swaps.

Source: (left) Merrill Lynch; (right) Moody's KMV; Financial Services Authority calculations.

tion correct, since it reflects the collective wisdom of the efficient market. Pricing in line with the market is thus bound to produce more efficient capital allocation.

But real life markets, as Chapter 2 describes, can be driven by self-referential cycles of irrational exuberance and despair, and the more that market players derive their own judgments simply from the judgments of others, the greater the danger of such self-reinforcing cycles. Figure 6.2 shows CDS spreads for major international banks and corporate bond yields from 2002 to 2008. Both reached historic lows in spring 2007 before soaring to previously never-observed levels. Ahead of the crisis the wisdom of the market thus provided no forewarning of impending disaster but instead drove first a credit boom and then a bust. CDS prices did indeed help bring the marginal price of credit in line with the collective judgement of the market. But the market's collective judgement was utterly wrong.

The potential inefficiency and instability of market prices in turn had implications for the impact of mark-to-market accounting and the use of collateral. In trading operations there is no alternative to mark-to-market accounting: the value of positions on the books is the value at which they can be sold, and the best (though imperfect) measure of that is the current market price. But if mark-to-market prices are used to determine continually changing collateral requirements against numerous secured transactions, movements in prices can become strongly self-reinforcing. If Bank A lends $9 million to Bank B secured against $10 million of collateral, with the haircut set at 10%, and if the price per unit of collateral falls, then Bank B has to post more collateral. But to do so it may have to sell other assets or curtail trading activities, which may drive yet further falls in asset prices. Chapter 4 describes how banking systems can produce credit and asset price cycles: mark-to-market accounting and the increasing use of collateral hardwired such cycles into the core of the financial system.

The use of Value at Risk models in turn further magnified the potential for hardwired instability. Their logic appeared clear: the size of buffers needed to absorb risks had to reflect how volatile prices might be: and observations of past price volatility seemed to provide information relevant to the future. Value at Risk models appeared therefore to tell management what was the maximum possible loss at any given "confidence interval" (for example, 95%, or 99%, or 99.9% of the time). Developed in the 1990s, these models were hailed as a major step forward in scientific risk management and were applied first to trading book control systems and then, under the Basel II capital standard, to the assessment of risks in traditional bank loans.

But Value at Risk models were doubly flawed, wrong in both their precise design and their fundamental assumption. They were usually based on past records of price movements too short to capture the full historic experience of price volatility. And they were typically built, for reasons of mathematical ease, on the assumption that the probability distribution of price movements followed a "normal distribution," ignoring the extensive evidence of more extreme price movements, documented for instance by the mathematician Benoit Mandelbrot.[16]

But more fundamentally still, they were based on the flawed assumption that the probability of future developments in financial markets can be inferred from observation of the past. Effectively they assume that past price movements represent a random sample from a universe of possible patterns, and that future price movements will also be samples drawn from that unchanging universe. They thus fail to recognize that the future is governed not by quantifiable probabilistic risk but by inherent uncertainty.

Because of both their technical deficiencies and their fundamental philosophical flaw, Value at Risk models therefore excluded the possibility of the extreme events that are central to financial crises.[17] They failed utterly to protect financial institutions from the market turbulence of late September 2008, when price movements that the models suggested were close to impossible occurred multiple days in a row.

Value at Risk models are irrelevant in extreme crisis: but even in more normal times, they have pernicious procyclical effects. If traders become less risk averse and volatility declines, these models suggest that smaller haircuts are acceptable: they therefore allow traders to take bigger positions, which leads to price rises, rising confidence, and reduced volatility in a self-reinforcing cycle. When risk aversion and volatility rise, conversely, they give a further twist to the cycle of falling market activity and declining asset prices.

Mark-to-market accounting, contracts secured against collateral, margin calls, and Value at Risk models can thus, as economists such as Marcus Brunnermeier and Hyun Shin have illustrated, combine to create a dangerously procyclical financial system, in which initial changes in sentiment and prices are magnified by financial contract terms and risk control rules.[18] The sophisticated risk management systems tools that Greenspan and others lauded hardwired instability into the system. And in autumn 2008 they became a financial doomsday machine, which once switched on, drove self-reinforcing cycles of declining prices, confidence, and market activity. Haircuts demanded on some repo market transactions increased from 1% to 15% between July 2007 and June 2008, before soaring to 45% by October that year.[19] Repo market volumes collapsed by 38% between July and October 2008.[20] Bank funding markets seized up not because of traditional deposit runs, but because wholesale secured funding markets went into a meltdown driven by the very risk management tools that were supposed to make them safe.

But seen from a purely individual point of view, and if each individual assumed that overall market developments were a given, their use was totally rational. The banks or dealers who were more rigorous in applying mark-to-market disciplines did indeed spot emerging price trends earlier and got out of potential loss-making positions a little ahead of the laggards.[21] But individually rational actions to improve relative positions produced collectively destabilizing results.

The summary scorecard on three decades of financial innovations is therefore simple; whatever their theoretical advantages, their actual impact was a disaster. But one assertion made by the pre-crisis optimists was undoubtedly true: the new technology facilitated more credit creation.

The Credit Cycle on Steroids—Even More of the Wrong Sort of Debt

Chapter 1 describes the dominant pre-crisis assumption that financial deepening must be beneficial. One of the pillars of that orthodoxy was that more credit was a good thing, spurring investment, consumption, and growth. The new technologies of securitization, structuring, and derivatives were therefore beneficial, because increased liquidity of credit markets resulted in increased credit supply. Dudley and Hubbard welcomed the fact that "a revolution in housing finance" had made mortgages more available and that "at times homeowners can obtain 100% financing to purchase a home."[22]

But more credit is not necessarily a good thing: there can be too much and of the wrong sort. Shadow banking certainly enabled faster credit growth, but as a result it drove private-sector leverage to still higher levels and made the post-crisis debt overhang more severe.

It also accentuated the bias of credit creation toward real estate and consumption finance and away from the textbook function of providing finance for business investment. Banking systems have become primarily real estate lenders, and securitized credit markets have primarily financed residential mortgages, commercial real estate, and increased consumer expenditure through, for instance, auto loans.[23]

The amount of credit created and its allocation is too important to be left to bankers; nor can it be left to free markets in securitized credit.

Searching for Yield: A Zero-Sum but Costly Game?

Increasing intrafinancial activity thus in part reflected a more complex system of credit intermediation. But as Chapter 1 notes, increasing debts owed by real economy companies and households must be matched by an increase in financial assets held in debt or money form. And increasing intrafinancial intensity was also in part driven by asset management activities, as market participants attempted to achieve additional return without apparent additional risk.[24] Moreover, achieving such yield uplift appeared to be vital in an environment where the real return on risk-free investments—government indexed linked bonds—had fallen from more than 3% in the late 1980s to less than 1.5% on the eve of the crisis.

A report by the Financial Stability Board in 2012 described the complex intrafinancial links that this search for yield generates.[25] Secured funding from prime brokers enables hedge funds to trade with borrowed money: long-term institutional investors earn fees from lending securities to hedge funds or other traders, who can use them to take short positions or as collateral to raise money to be used in other trading activities. Collateral swaps are used to provide trading firms with higher quality collateral than they initially hold, enabling them in turn to borrow more money with which to trade. Collateral received as security against funding provided to other market players can in turn be rehypothecated to raise funds with which to trade, generating chains of contracts all underpinned by the same collateral. Asset management–focused activities, as well as new ways to fund real economy credit, thus played a major role in generating the complex mesh of contractual relationships captured in the New York Federal Reserve's 3 feet × 4 feet map of the shadow banking system.

For each individual participant—whether bank, broker-dealer, hedge fund, insurance company, or asset manager—this activity appears to earn additional return without additional risk. And in some specific cases it clearly does: an asset manager holding a portfolio of securities can earn additional return for its clients by lending securities in return for a fee, and successful trading strategies may for a time beat returns from passive investment.

But financial innovation cannot magically produce additional return for all investors together unless it increases the size of the real economic cake available. At the level of the whole system, indeed, all this trading, securities lending, swapping, and funding, can only generate additional return for end clients if it results in a more efficient allocation of capital in the real economy. True believers in the EMH believe that such benefits must flow from the increased liquidity and price discovery generated, but for the reasons discussed in Chapter 2, their argument is unconvincing.

Much of this activity is therefore inevitably a zero-sum game, privately beneficial for the most adept players but making society as a whole no better off, while absorbing real economic resources of capital, technology, and skilled labor for which the ultimate investor clients must in some way pay. In addition, some of it may only appear to promote superior returns because of imperfectly understood risks, which often crystallize long after the private participants have been handsomely rewarded for apparently superior performance.[26]

The policy issues that this raises are beyond the scope of this book. While value for money in asset management is very important, my focus is on the still bigger issue of the harmful effects of excessive credit creation. But if some trading activity in the financial system is in aggregate socially useless, that carries implications for the policies that aim to contain instability risks. As Chapter 10 describes, some possible policies are attacked because they might reduce trading activity and liquidity in secured funding markets. But if that activity is of no social value, reduced activity and liquidity is of no concern.

Fundamental Drivers of Credit Growth and the Search for Yield

The social scorecard for increasing intrafinancial intensity is negative. The more complex credit intermediation system made the financial system more unstable and a major financial crisis more likely, and by facilitating more credit creation it made the post-crisis debt overhang more severe. The ever more intense pursuit of yield uplift without additional risk, meanwhile, was in aggregate an impossible objective, but it generated additional cost and risky complexity.

But seen from the point of view of the bank, asset manager, broker, or dealer, all the activities involved could appear rational and in their clients' interest. Securitization responded to an apparently increasing "demand" for credit from individuals and a "need" for credit in the economy, and asset managers aware of their fiduciary duties must search for all opportunities to achieve yield uplift in a world where risk-free returns have fallen to low levels.

To understand the underlying factors that drove financial system developments, we therefore need to ask why the demand or need for credit appeared so strong, and why long-term risk-free rates have fallen so far. Chapter 7 turns to those questions.

||||||||||||||||||||||||||||||||||||||||||||||||||||||||||||||||||||||||||||||||||||||||||||||||||||||||||||||||||||||||||||||||||||||||||||||||||||||||||||||||

SEVEN

SPECULATION, INEQUALITY, AND
UNNECESSARY CREDIT

Demonstrating that an exchange economy is coherent and stable
does not demonstrate that the same is true of an economy with
capitalist financial institutions.

—*Hyman P. Minsky,* Stabilising an Unstable Economy[1]

A giant suction pump had by 1929 to 1930 drawn into a few hands
an increasing proportion of currently produced wealth. This served
them as capital accumulations. But by taking purchasing power
out of the hands of mass consumers, the savers denied themselves
the kind of effective demand for their products which would justify
reinvestment of the capital accumulation in new plants. In consequence as in a poker game where the chips were concentrated in
fewer and fewer hands, the other fellows could stay in the game
only by borrowing. When the credit ran out, the game stopped.

—*Mariner Eccles (Chairman of the Federal Reserve, 1951),* Beckoning Frontiers[2]

FOR SEVERAL DECADES BEFORE the 2007–2008 financial crisis, private
credit in advanced economies grew faster than nominal GDP, and
leverage therefore increased. Excessive leverage in turn made the economy more fragile and produced crisis, post-crisis debt overhang, and
recession.

But that poses the question: did we *need* that rapid credit growth to
achieve reasonable economic growth? At first sight it seems we did. From
the mid-1990s on, major central banks in Europe and North America
were remarkably successful in delivering low and stable inflation. They

did so by varying interest rates to influence the growth of nominal demand. The result was nominal GDP growth averaging about 5%, with real growth of 2–3% and inflation near 1–3%. But this was accompanied by private credit growth on average of about 10–15% per year. If central banks had set higher interest rates that would have produced slower credit growth, but also slower growth in nominal GDP: either real growth or inflation, or most likely both, would have been lower.

So we seem to need credit growth of about 10–15% per year to ensure inflation of about 2% and real growth in line with potential. But if so, we face a severe dilemma: we need credit growth faster than GDP to achieve adequate growth, but the resulting rise in leverage leads to crisis and post-crisis recession. It seems we face an unavoidable choice between either financial and macroeconomic instability, or suboptimally slow growth. We will suffer either periodic financial crisis or secular stagnation.

So is that really the case? Did we in fact need the rapid credit growth that led to eventual crisis? The answer is no for two reasons. First, because much of the credit growth played no necessary role in stimulating nominal demand growth, but it still contributed to excessive leverage and debt overhang. And second, because if necessary we can stimulate nominal demand without relying on private credit creation.

We could therefore achieve a more stable and sustainable growth path. But to do so we need to address three fundamental drivers of unnecessary credit growth—real estate, rising inequality, and global current-account imbalances. We need to reject the idea that the quantity and allocation of private credit can be left to free market forces. And we need to accept that government money creation can sometimes be less dangerous than private creation.

To understand why such radical changes in theory and policy are required, we must begin with a basic question: why do we need nominal demand growth, and what are the alternative ways to deliver it?

The Need for and Potential Sources of Increasing Nominal Demand

In principle, economies do not need increasing nominal demand to grow in real terms. An economy could in theory grow at, say, 2% in real terms per year, but with prices falling on average by 2% per year and nominal

GDP therefore flat. For much of the nineteenth century, for instance, the British economy saw gentle price decline.

But there are strong arguments for believing that continuous deflation would be harmful in modern economies. Real wage rates for different categories of skill need to adjust in light of changing consumer demands and productivity potential, and these adjustments are easier to achieve if the average level of wages is rising, reducing the need for actual cuts in nominal wages. A mildly positive rate of inflation can also make it easier to service already accumulated debts: if prices fall, the real value of existing debt increases. And central bank ability to stimulate the economy with low real interest rates can be constrained if inflation is very low or negative. If prices fall by 2% per year, a nominal interest rate of zero means a real interest rate of +2%. If that is too high to ensure growth in line with capacity, negative nominal rates will be required. But there are limits to how negative interest rates can be without inducing conversion of deposit money into zero interest-bearing notes and coins. The "zero lower bound" for interest rates is a serious potential impediment to optimal policy.[3]

A strong consensus has therefore emerged that inflation rates should ideally be low but positive—say about 2%. Combined with real growth in line with potential, this will require nominal GDP growth rates in advanced economies that average about 4–5% per year.

That growth in turn can be achieved in three conceptually distinct (though in practice sometimes overlapping) ways: increases in metallic money, government "fiat" money creation, and private credit and money creation. Under some, but not all, circumstances, it might also be stimulated by fiscal deficits even if these are financed by the issue of public debt. But that stimulation is only likely to be permanently effective if it is underpinned by or ultimately produces either private or fiat money creation.

Metallic Money

In a pure metallic money system, in which all payments take the form of payments in gold or other metal and in which no system of credit has developed, spending power in nominal terms would be constrained by the amount of the chosen metal available and by the pace at which it circulated.[4]

In reality no major economy has ever relied solely on metallic money, since all human societies advanced enough to need money have created forms of credit as well. Even before there were formal banking systems, individuals and businesses extended credit between one another to finance transactions that did not need to be immediately settled in metallic money. In his book *Money: The Unauthorised Biography*, Felix Martin describes how a significant proportion of late medieval trade was financed by means of the exchange and then clearing of various forms of promissory note.[5] And while nineteenth-century Britain used a gold standard, even then a significant proportion of purchasing power was created through credit extension by commercial banks.

But the supply of the relevant metal could still be a constraint if commercial banks chose to—or were required to—hold a given proportion of their liabilities in reserves at the central bank, and if the central bank in turn followed rules requiring a given proportion of its liabilities to be backed by gold. Aggregate spending power in the economy was therefore at least to a degree influenced by the quantities of gold (or other metal treated as money), which were being discovered and mined. Limited increases in global gold supply in the 1870s and 1880s resulted in deflationary pressures, with major economic and in some cases political consequences: over the subsequent 20 years large increases in global gold production generated or at least facilitated significant inflation. Purchasing power was somewhat dependent on the vagaries of new resource discovery.

Government Fiat Money Creation

Purchasing power can also be created through the government issue of "fiat" money (that is, of money that is accepted as valuable because government fiat makes it so). Governments can print paper money, and if it is accepted as having money value, it creates effective purchasing power. But purchasing power can also be created by governments in a modern electronic deposit form. Chapter 12 discusses the concept of 100% reserve banks—savings banks all the deposits of which are backed by reserves at the central bank. If a government ran a deficit equal to say 1% of GDP and paid for it by simply crediting private customers' accounts at the 100% reserve banks, matched in turn by increased reserves held by those banks at the central bank, then increased purchasing power equal to 1% of GDP would enter the expenditure flows in the economy, and the money supply would increase by the same amount.[6]

Throughout history, money and purchasing power have often been created by government fiat. Marco Polo recorded with surprise and admiration the fact that Kublai Khan was able to create sovereign spending power with paper money. "With this currency" Polo noted, "he orders all payments to be made throughout every province and kingdom and region of his empire," and "of this money the Khan has such a quantity made that with it he could buy all the treasure in the world."[7] And even before paper was invented Chinese emperors had created fiat money in the form of coins made from nonprecious metals.

Fiat money can create purchasing power and thus aggregate nominal demand. And provided that capacity is used responsibly, it could in theory meet the requirements of an advanced economy growing nominal GDP at say 5% per year and achieving a stable and low rate of inflation, such as 2%. In 1948 Milton Friedman argued that such fiat money creation, financing small public deficits with government created money, would be a better and more certain way to achieve stability and low inflation than relying on private bank credit and money creation.[8]

History records several examples of the successful and responsible use of fiat money creation to stimulate demand. The colony of Pennsylvania successfully stimulated its economy with paper money creation in the 1720s.[9] Japanese finance minister Takahashi Korekiyo used money-financed fiscal deficits to pull the Japanese economy out of severe recession between 1931 and 1936 and did so without excessive inflation.[10] The U.S. Union government paid for a significant proportion of its Civil War expenditures with "greenbacks"—dollar bills simply printed by the government. The result was significant inflation (about 80% in total over the five years of the war) but not hyperinflation.[11]

But at the same time, the Confederacy was printing money to pay its soldiers in such large quantities that inflation reached 9,000% by the end of the war. The impact of fiat money creation thus depends crucially on its scale. As Adam Smith noted of the Pennsylvania colony, the success of its printed money system was dependent "upon the moderation with which it was used," whereas "the same expedient … was … adopted by several other American colonies, but from want of this moderation …

produced ... much more disorder than conveniency."[12] The hyperinflations of Zimbabwe in recent years and of Weimar Germany in the 1920s illustrate the political economy risks in fiat money creation.[13] If governments are free to create money, they may do so in excessive quantities.

For that reason, all advanced economies and most emerging ones constrain governments' ability to finance public deficits with fiat money. Overt money finance of fiscal deficits is treated as taboo: acquiescing in it is seen as a breach of central bank duty, and many central bank mandates, in particular the European Central Bank's, expressly forbid it.

But by elimination that means we have to rely on private bank credit and money creation to achieve adequate growth in nominal demand.

PRIVATE CREDIT AND MONEY CREATION

In advanced economies the primary source of additional purchasing power and thus of aggregate nominal demand is private credit and money creation. This did not result from overt public policy choice—it evolved over time. Goldsmiths who provided safekeeping services found that they could loan out the gold, or notes which proved ownership of the gold, and thus turned gradually into fractional reserve banks—holding gold reserves equal to only a small fraction of their total liabilities. Initially in many cases these liabilities took the form of actual bank notes: in the United Kingdom private banks could issue their own notes up until 1844; in the United States until 1863. But the subsequent restriction of this right made no difference to the banks' ability to create credit, money, and purchasing power: a deposit in a commercial bank is as much money as a banknote issued by a commercial bank.

As a result, the development of private banking helped expand purchasing power in line with output potential. But from the very start, the process was unstable. In all the leading economies the nineteenth century was punctuated by banking crises in which purchasing power was first rapidly created and then destroyed in bank failures, with private bank notes and deposits becoming worthless. Between 1921 and 1929, the U.S. banking system extended credit that enabled the money stock to increase 40%: between 1929 and 1933; all of that increase was reversed.[14] Viewing the resultant economic destruction, the Chicago economist Henry Simons concluded that "in the very nature of the system, banks will flood the economy with money substitutes during booms and pre-cipitate futile efforts at general liquidation thereafter."[15]

Over time central banks and regulators therefore increasingly sought to constrain the instability or offset its consequences. Central bank li-quidity facilities aimed to ensure that total money creation was in line with business needs and to counter the danger that bank failures could trigger self-reinforcing destruction of purchasing power. Bank capital regulations aimed to limit the danger of individual banks going bank-rupt. And many central banks required commercial banks to hold a defined fraction of deposits or loans in reserves at the central bank, thus limiting the amount of private credit and money that they could create.[16]

But over the past 30 years, central banks in advanced economies have largely abandoned any explicit focus on the total amount or the alloca-tion of private credit created. They continued to worry about the sol-vency and stability of the banking system itself. But they gravitated to the belief, in line with Knut Wicksell's theory, that as long as inflation was held at a low and stable level, the amount of private credit and money being created was bound to be appropriate. And policy based on that belief appeared to deliver a remarkable Great Moderation, with nominal demand growing at a pace compatible with low inflation and steady real growth. But the Great Moderation of steady nominal demand growth and low inflation ended in disaster, because rapid credit growth pro-duced excessive leverage, financial crisis, and post-crisis debt overhang.

FUNDED FISCAL DEFICITS

Fiat money creation has been considered taboo, and free markets in private credit creation produced disaster. But some economists would argue that there is another route to stimulate nominal demand—without any creation of private or public fiat money—through fiscal deficits funded by public debt issue. Funded fiscal deficits are indeed seen as the classic "Keynesian" response to deficient demand.[17]

So do they work and if so, how? The answer is yes under some specific circumstances, but that for a funded fiscal stimulus to be permanently effective, it will almost certainly need to be underpinned by one or an-other category of money creation.

If the government runs a fiscal deficit funded by the issue of interest-bearing bonds, no new money is initially created: instead some households or companies are persuaded to give up money in return for bonds, and that money is then spent to support government expenditure in excess of taxation revenues. The money supply does not directly increase, but private financial assets increase, because in addition to unchanged money stock, the private sector now holds the government bonds.

Whether this will stimulate nominal demand has been debated by economists and depends on specific circumstances. The argument that it will be ineffective rests on two potential effects. The first is "crowding out," with reduced private-sector investment or consumption offsetting the stimulative effect of increased public expenditure or reduced taxes. This could occur if interest rates have to rise to induce the private sector to buy government bonds, or if central banks raise policy interest rates to prevent the fiscal stimulus from producing inflation above target. The second is the potential "Ricardian equivalence" effect, in which the direct stimulative impact of fiscal deficits is offset because households and companies rationally anticipate that current deficits imply future increased tax burdens, and therefore they cut investments or consumption to save resources so they can pay those future taxes.

Given these two potential effects, the predominant assumption of modern economics has been that funded fiscal deficits will in most circumstances be ineffective in stimulating nominal demand.[18] But they could be effective if either or both effects are absent. Crowding out may not occur if interest rates are already close to zero and if central banks are constrained from reducing them further by the zero lower bound:[19] as Chapter 14 discusses, this may mean that funded fiscal deficits can stimulate demand in the specific circumstances that emerged after 2008. And individuals or companies receiving the direct benefits of fiscal stimulus may not be as rational as Ricardian equivalence assumes and may ignore (at least for a time) the future taxation consequences of public debt accumulation.

Thus in some circumstances funded fiscal deficits may stimulate nominal demand growth, even though no new money is directly and immediately created. But that effect is unlikely to be permanent unless at some time money creation results. For even if people initially ignore the consequences of public debt accumulation, at some future time it may become essential to run fiscal surpluses to contain public debt levels. And those surpluses will then have a depressive effect on nominal demand, offsetting the initial stimulus.

It is therefore likely that a permanent increase in nominal demand will only result if one of two things occurs: the initial fiscal stimulus produces an increase in private credit and money creation that proves permanent; or the public debt accumulated is at some future date monetized, with public interest-bearing debt replaced by non-interest-bearing fiat money.[20]

So in modern economies we have essentially two ways to produce permanent increases in nominal demand: either government fiat money creation or private credit and money creation. And if we treat money finance as taboo, we inevitably rely on private credit. In 2008 that reliance produced disaster. But this poses two key questions for economic theory and policy. First why did the rapid credit growth not produce an excessive increase in nominal GDP to which inflation-targeting central banks would have had to respond? And second, did adequate nominal GDP growth *require* the rapid credit growth that led eventually to crisis and post-crisis recession? The clue to the answers lies in the fact that most credit in modern economies is unnecessary for economic growth. Instead part of it supports "speculation," part results from rising inequality, and part reflects unsustainable global imbalances.

Credit-Financed Speculation

In advanced economies most credit is used to finance the purchase of existing assets, in particular real estate. Such credit does not have a necessary and proportional impact on demand for the current goods and services that form national income. As a result it can grow to excessive levels that cause eventual crisis without that growth ever producing an increase in inflation and without it being necessary to economic growth.

John Maynard Keynes discussed this possibility in his *Treatise on Money*.[21] His focus was alternative uses of "money," but since most money derives from private credit creation, his insights apply equally to the impact of alternative types of credit.[22] He distinguished two types of transactions: first, those involving the purchase of current goods and services, whose value therefore "will be a fairly stable function of the money-value of current output" (that is, of nominal GDP). Second, those involving "speculative transactions in capital goods or commodities" or which are pure "financial transactions." The value of these transactions, he noted, "bears no definite relation to the rate of current production" and "the price level of the capital goods thus exchanged may vary quite differently from that of consumption goods." Credit to finance the purchase of existing capital goods can thus grow in a fashion unrelated to current nominal demand, and the price of capital goods, driven by credit supply, can diverge massively from the prices of current goods and services.

Keynes described this phenomenon in terms of the activities of "financiers, speculators and investors." But as Chapter 4 describes, in today's economy most wealth resides in real estate and land; for most people their most important investment is their house; and most bank credit is extended to finance the purchase of already existing houses. Keynes's insight into the potential disconnect between capital goods speculation and current nominal demand is therefore central to understanding the dynamics and implications of real estate credit and asset price cycles.

Those dynamics can be understood by first considering the direct impact of credit used exclusively to finance existing asset purchase. Suppose people borrow more money from banks to finance the purchase of already existing houses: the price of houses rises in response, and people who have sold houses now hold larger money balances in banks. Aggregate credit, wealth, and money balances have all increased, but there is no necessary increase in nominal demand for any current goods and services.

But in the real world, we also need to consider indirect effects. Rising house prices will make people feel richer, and some home owners as a result may consume more and save less. And some home sellers, having initially seen their money balances increase, may subsequently redeploy them into other financial investments, potentially stimulating, through a variety of indirect routes, increased real investment in the economy.

But while these impacts are possible, there is no reason for them to be fully proportional to the initial value of the new credit created. Thus, for example, from 2000 to 2007, mortgage credit in the United Kingdom increased by 97%; household deposits in banks increased by 79%; gross housing wealth increased by 105%, but nominal GDP grew by 44%, and thus at an annual average of 5.3% broadly compatible with the Bank of England's 2% inflation target.[23]

Moreover, the importance of wealth effects may be influenced by wealth distribution and may be asymmetric over time: in the upswing of the cycle wealthy people observing a still further increase in their housing wealth may leave their consumption expenditure largely unchanged; but in the downswing poorer people who are highly leveraged may cut expenditure significantly in the face of falling net worth, as Mian and Sufi describe.

Credit creation that finances the purchase of existing assets does not therefore stimulate nominal GDP to the same extent as credit extended directly to finance new real investment or consumption. Richard Werner's book *Princes of the Yen*[24] provides empirical evidence of the difference in Japan in the 1980s. He divides bank credit stocks and flows into the element that financed real estate and the element that financed new investment or consumption. The former grew at annual rates of between 20–45% between 1982 and 1987, and so too did real estate and land prices: the latter grew at around 7–8% per year and so too did nominal GDP.[25] But while rapid growth of real estate credit produced neither an acceleration of nominal GDP growth nor an increase in current inflation, it was the fundamental reason that Japan suffered a sustained postcrisis balance-sheet recession.

Keynes called transactions in already existing assets "speculation," and I have used the same word in my title to this section. But purchasing existing assets often does not feel like speculation to the individuals concerned: it entails ordinary families borrowing money to purchase a decent family home. And we should certainly not assume that mortgage lending to finance existing assets is socially valueless, simply because it is unrelated to the mobilization and allocation of capital. As Chapter 4 stresses, the rising importance of real estate in modern economies is inevitable: actual new investment in real estate is likely to account for a large proportion of all new investment, and mortgage loans perform a useful social function, enabling people to smooth consumption across the life cycle and lubricating the exchange of homes between and within generations.

But mortgage loans that in each specific instance serve a useful social purpose, can in aggregate generate credit and asset price cycles ending in recession, crisis, and post-crisis recession. To achieve a less credit-intensive and more stable economy, we must therefore deliberately manage and constrain lending against real estate assets.

Inequality, Credit, and More Inequality

Inequality has grown dramatically in advanced economies over the past 30 years. Since 1980 the bottom quintile of U.S. earners has received no increase in real wages; the incomes of the top 1% have tripled (Figure 7.1). The root causes are widely debated. Globalization of product and capital markets has certainly played a significant role; the impact of new technology may be even more profound.[26] And the growth of finance has itself produced rapidly increasing earnings at the top of the distribution.

This increasing divergence is an important social issue in itself. But it is also another reason economic growth has been so credit intensive. Rising inequality can make unsustainable credit growth essential to

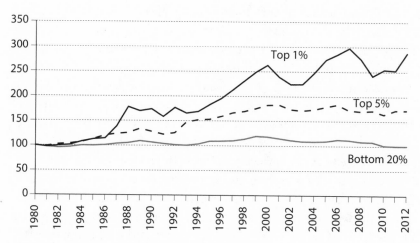

Figure 7.1.   Average income increases in the United States (1980 = 100)

Source: U.S. Census Bureau; World Top Incomes Database.

maintain economic growth. But the increasing use of credit can foster yet further inequality.

"Let Them Eat Credit"

Keynes was concerned that advanced economies might face secular stagnation. He believed that it was "a fundamental psychological truth ... that men are disposed, as a rule and on the average, to increase their consumption as their income increases, but not by as much as the increase in their income."[27] He therefore worried that as societies grew richer, aggregate desired savings would run ahead of required / desired investment, producing a deficiency of aggregate demand.

Experience has challenged Keynes's assumption: in a world where people care about relative status as well as absolute consumption levels, and in which advertising is used to stimulate demands, there is neither necessary reason nor empirical evidence that aggregate national savings rates increase over time.

But what is true is that within societies at any time, richer people are likely on average to save a higher proportion of their income. Rising inequality could therefore lead to a rising average desired savings rate and to a deflationary impact on aggregate demand, unless offset by other factors.

Credit can be that other factor. Richer people may save more, but their savings can be channeled through banks and other financial institutions to provide credit to poorer people attempting to maintain or increase consumption despite stagnant or falling real incomes.[28] But this credit flow need not produce excess demand; instead increased credit may be required to keep demand at a merely adequate level. If inequality had not increased the credit growth would have been unnecessary, but because of rising inequality we need credit to grow faster than GDP growth simply to keep demand growing in line with productive potential.

Rising credit to finance consumption might not cause subsequent financial instability if all of it performed the function described in economic theory—smoothing consumption over the borrower's life cycle on the basis of rational decisionmaking within the constraints of the individual's total lifetime income. People would borrow to finance consumption in excess of income during some periods and would have made rational plans to repay that borrowing at a later stage of life.

But if consumers borrow in an attempt to maintain consumption in the face of stagnant or falling income prospects, unsustainable debts will accumulate. And that risk is increased if consumption can be financed with mortgage credit secured against rising house values, which appear for a time to make increased borrowing affordable. The combination of rising inequality and the self-reinforcing dynamics of credit and asset price cycles can therefore result in unsustainable credit growth and rising leverage.

Well-informed observers argued that rising inequality was central to the credit-induced Great Depression of the 1930s. Mariner Eccles, chair of the U.S. Federal Reserve from 1934 to 1948 described in colorful terms how

a giant suction pump had by 1929 to 1930 drawn into a few hands an increasing proportion of currently produced wealth. This served them as capital accumulations. But by taking purchasing power out of the hands of mass consumers, the savers denied themselves the kind of effective demand for their products which would justify reinvestment of the capital accumulation in new plants. In consequence as in a poker game where the chips were concentrated in fewer and fewer hands, the other fellows could stay in the game only by borrowing. When the credit ran out, the game stopped.[29]

Raghuram Rajan, previously chief economist of the IMF and now governor of the Reserve Bank of India, has described a similar phenomenon in the years running up to 2008. The United States faced rising inequality but was unable or unwilling to fashion policies addressing the fundamental causes. Easy mortgage credit appeared a costless answer, enabling low-income people to finance consumption with credit secured against houses whose value kept rising. As Rajan puts it, the response to inequality was "let them eat credit." But it was an answer that led to crisis and post-crisis recession.[30]

Eccles's and Rajan's intuitions are supported by formal modeling and empirical analysis. Michael Kumhof and Roman Rancière have illustrated how the different marginal propensities to save and consume of richer and less rich people can drive increases in the credit intensity of growth.[31] And they provide empirical evidence that rising inequality stimulated rapid credit growth in both the 1920s and the decades running up to 2008. But growing credit dependency may in turn have stimulated yet further inequality.

LEVERAGE AND INEQUALITY: CREDIT ACCESS
AND CREDIT DEPENDENCE

Asset price fluctuations inevitably produce winners and losers. Leverage increases both the gains and the losses. Differences in access to credit, in the price paid for credit, and in the capacity to survive asset price downswings and benefit from the subsequent upswing can therefore play a major role in exacerbating inequality.

Superior access to credit in volatile economic circumstances has often been crucial to the accumulation of large fortunes. Many of today's Russian oligarchs achieved massive wealth because the moderate wealth they had already accumulated by the mid-1990s enabled them to borrow to buy natural resource assets cheap in a society where most people had no wealth at all. Indeed, several established their own banks, giving them access to newly created credit, money, and purchasing power.

Conversely, at the lower end of the income distribution excessive borrowing can often lead to falling wealth. In residential mortgage markets, for instance, poorer people, with lower initial wealth endowments are likely to face higher interest rates and may need to be more highly leveraged to afford a home. In addition they are usually more vulnerable to unemployment and income loss during recessions. As a result they are more likely, in the downswing of the cycle, to fall into negative equity and to suffer repossession, losing the opportunity of recouping losses in the subsequent upswing.

Mian and Sufi illustrate this effect in the United States. Falling equity and house prices between 2007 and 2010 cut the accumulated wealth of many Americans. But while the average net worth of the top 20% of households fell from $3.2 million to $2.9 million, the bottom 20% saw their average net worth fall from $30,000 to almost zero. Between 1992 and 2007 the top 10% of U.S. households saw their share of total wealth grow from 66% to 71%: in the subsequent 3 years it increased further to

74%. As Mian and Sufi put it "this is a fundamental feature of debt: it imposes enormous losses on exactly the households that have the least."[32]

Similarly in the United Kingdom, the credit-driven housing boom and bust between 2003 and 2013 increased inequality of wealth ownership. In the upswing of the cycle, potential first-time buyers with small initial wealth were either unable to buy at all in the face of rising prices or borrowed at high LTVs and loan to income ratios (LTIs), which increased the danger of subsequent repayment difficulties. In contrast, buy-to-let investors with significant already accumulated wealth were able to use finely priced credit to buy ever more houses. Between 2003 and 2013, owner-occupied households with mortgage borrowing outstanding suffered a net loss of £59 billion, while buy-to-let landlords gained £434 billion.[33] Buy-to-let now accounts for 14% of the U.K. housing stock versus zero in 1990: the owner occupation rate has fallen from a peak of 70% to 65%, and the average age at which people purchase their first house or apartment has steadily risen.

Thus while in both the United Kingdom and the United States rapidly growing mortgage credit markets have been traditionally lauded as a means to "spread wealth more widely" and while in the initial stages of their growth they may have helped do so, the impact of mortgage credit growth beyond some point can produce increasing wealth inequality.

Meanwhile, in economies facing both increasing inequality and only slow recovery from the post-crisis recession, the increasing reliance of poorer people on high-interest credit, for instance from the United Kingdom's growing "payday lenders," is likely to exacerbate the inequality of which it is also the consequence. The supposed benefit of consumer credit is that it enables smoothing of consumption across the life cycle within a total lifetime income constraint. But if people borrow at very high interest rates, their lifetime resources available for consumption are significantly reduced.

Indeed throughout history, debt contracts have played a role in exacerbating initial inequalities. As David Graeber describes in *Debt: The First 5000 Years*,[34] lending at high interest rates to people facing either temporary or permanent deficiencies of income relative to consumption needs or aspirations has often played a major role in trapping people in poverty. Small initial variations in economic fortune—for instance, in the quality of the harvest and in the resources available to different farmers to withstand short-term financial pressures—resulted in loan contracts between rich and poor that could produce long-term dependency and even debt bondage. Awareness of this danger lay behind Islamic and Christian strictures against "usury."

Those strictures were subsequently rejected as impediments to economic progress. It was rightly argued that debt contracts can play a useful role in mobilizing and allocating capital investment. But public policy toward debt also needs to recognize that most credit extension in modern economies is unrelated to capital investment.

Global Imbalances

Lending to finance existing real estate or to support consumption in the face of rising inequality are thus two reasons advanced economies experienced rapid credit growth without excessive growth in nominal GDP. The third is large capital flows unrelated to capital investment.

Between 1998 and 2008 the total of all current-account surpluses grew from 0.5% to 2.0% of global GDP, and so necessarily did the total of all the deficits. The flipside of those surpluses and deficits were capital exports and imports. And just as modern finance theory has told an optimistic story about the beneficial impact of increasing leverage, so too it has lauded the benefits of capital flows. Free capital flows, it is said, facilitate a globally efficient allocation of scarce capital, with resources flowing from countries that have savings in excess of investment needs to those with investment needs unmatched by domestic savings.

But most capital flows in today's global economy do not fund high investment rates in the recipient country. Instead they have predominantly financed increased consumption and given further stimulus to domestic credit and asset price booms. And where they have been associated with increased investment, it has often entailed excessive investment in residential and commercial real estate, with Chinese and German surpluses, for instance, helping finance wasteful U.S., Spanish, and Irish construction.

As a result, the capital flows that mirrored current-account imbalances typically did not contribute to productivity and income growth and therefore did not help generate the additional cash flows required to make the debts repayable.[35] Instead they contributed—in the peripheral eurozone countries, the United States, and some emerging economies—to the growth in excessive debts, which produced the debt overhang effect.

Indeed, many international capital flows have simply accentuated the problems of "too much of the wrong sort of debt" discussed in Chapters 4 and 5. As Chapter 9 discusses, the problems created by such debt are particularly severe when the debt flows are international.

But as with the other drivers of "unnecessary" credit, the credit extended to finance global imbalances did not generate excessive nominal demand growth to which central banks felt required to respond. Within increasingly unequal societies, credit-financed consumption by the less well-off was matched by high savings among the rich; and across the world, credit-financed booms in real estate prices and consumption in countries such as the United States, the United Kingdom, Spain, and Ireland, were offset by high savings rates in China, Germany, and Japan. Current-account imbalances thus contributed to the phenomenon of rapid credit growth without high inflation, which has left us with the debt overhang effect.

Secular Stagnation and Chronic Deficient Demand?

We do not need credit growth as rapid as that before the crisis to achieve adequate economic growth. Three of the main drivers of that rapid growth—real estate speculation, rising inequality, and current-account imbalances—entail the creation of credit that is not inherently essential either to the mobilization and allocation of capital or to the stimulation of adequate nominal demand. But that credit growth leads to crisis and post-crisis recession. Policies addressing these fundamental drivers of credit-intensive growth are therefore as important to future financial and macroeconomic stability as the technicalities of bank capital ratios, bank resolution, or derivatives risk control.

One additional question we need to address, however, is whether rapid credit growth was in part simply a response to a deeper underlying problem: whether advanced economies face the challenge of potential "secular stagnation."[36]

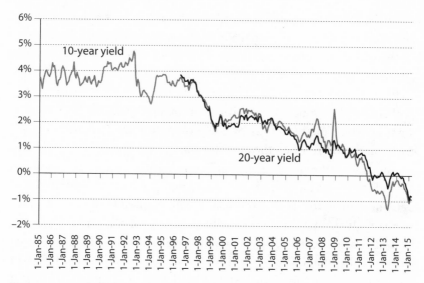

Figure 7.2.   Real yields to maturity on UK indexed-linked gilts

Source: Bank of England Statistics, zero coupon real yields.

Over the two decades before 2008 there was a dramatic fall in real risk-free interest rates, as measured by the real yield to maturity on government index-linked bonds. In the late 1980s and early 1990s, as Figure 7.2 shows, a UK investor could buy 10-year index-linked gilts providing over 3% real yield to maturity: by 2007 that yield had fallen to 1.8%; it subsequently fell to reach –1.0% in January 2015.[37] The trend in U.S. real yields was very similar. The final step in this fall, after the crisis in 2007–2008, is explained by the specific conditions of post-crisis debt overhang. But even before the crisis, real yields had fallen to levels almost certainly lower than throughout the entire previous history of modern capitalism.[38]

These very low real interest rates played a major role in the origins of the crisis. They encouraged homeowners and investors to borrow money to purchase real estate or finance consumption, and they stimulated the intense search for yield that underlay the explosion of financial innovation and intrafinancial system activity described in Chapter 6.

Why did this dramatic fall occur? Theory suggests that it must have been because desired savings (or as economists call it, "ex ante" desired savings) rose relative to ex ante desired investment. This could have been either because desired savings rose or desired investment fell.

The savings explanation often focuses on China and other large current-account surplus countries. Ben Bernanke argued in 2005 that high Chinese savings rates, in excess even of China's high investment rate, had generated increased demand for U.S. government bonds, depressing yields.[39] The ex ante desired global savings rate had thus risen relative to desired global investment. This may be part of the explanation, and rebalancing of the Chinese economy to reduce its extremely high savings rate is certainly an important priority for global macrostability. But Chinese surpluses large enough to have a big impact on the global savings/investment balance only arose in the 5 years or so before the 2007–2008 financial crisis, whereas the fall in real yields began some 15 years before that.

Changes in demography and wealth distribution in advanced economies may also have had an important effect on both desired savings and desired or needed investment. Societies are on average ageing for two distinct reasons—because average life expectancy is increasing and because fertility rates have fallen, reducing the ratio of younger people in the population. Increasing longevity would have no necessary impact on aggregate desired savings rates if retirement ages rose to keep stable the proportions of adult life spent in work and in retirement. But if retirement ages do not rise proportionately, people may attempt to increase savings rates during working life to secure adequate income during longer retirements, but with no natural or offsetting increase in aggregate investment needs. And lower fertility rates reduce the need for societies to accumulate capital stock for use by succeeding generations, but they may produce no offsetting reduction in desired savings rates.

Meanwhile, by concentrating an increasing percentage of wealth in the hands of people rich enough to bequeath substantial wealth to their inheritors, rather than needing to liquidate savings during retirement, rising inequality may drive an increase in desired savings unmatched by investment requirements, as Thomas Piketty has suggested.

This complex combination of factors could change the balance between desired savings and desired or required investment—and thus the equilibrium real interest rate—without the impact being apparent in actual resulting levels of saving and investment, which by definition must be equal. Higher desired savings could thus be playing a role, even though aggregate actual saving rates in most advanced economies have not increased.

But the available data suggest that falling investment needs may be even more important to the changing balance than any attempted increase in savings. Business investment as a percentage of GDP has been on a downward trend in many advanced economies.[40] Many big corporations are sitting on large cash balances. Many indeed have become net holders of financial assets, rather than net borrowers from the financial system. In the United Kingdom, borrowing by businesses outside the commercial real estate sector has fallen as a percentage of GDP over the past 25 years. The entire manufacturing sector has at times been a net depositor into the banking system.[41]

These falling rates of capital investment may in turn be explained by the falling cost of capital equipment goods relative to current goods and services, down 33% from 1990 to 2014, according to IMF figures.[42] In many business sectors, each dollar of investment spent is increasingly buying "more bang per buck" as the dramatic progress of information technology drives down hardware and software prices. The result is the phenomenon of massive wealth creation from minimal investment— Facebook worth $150 billion after only 5,000 personyears of investment— which was highlighted in Chapter 5.

Declining aggregate investment needs relative to desired savings may thus have driven a large fall in equilibrium real interest rates. Separate from the adverse impact of the debt overhang effect, we may face what Martin Wolf has labeled a chronic deficiency of aggregate nominal demand.[43] Very low interest rates may therefore be needed for many years or even in perpetuity, if economies are to grow in line with their potential.

But that would leave us facing two problems. First, if the required interest rate is actually negative, the zero bound will constrain us from setting rates low enough to ensure optimal growth. Second, very low interest rates maintained over many years are bound to create strong incentives for private credit growth focused not on the finance of new investment but on the speculative purchase of existing assets.

The less we need actual new investment relative to desired saving, the more the private credit system will finance competition for the ownership of irreproducible assets, such as desirable real estate, together with complex and risky financial engineering.[44] If we need ultralow interest rates forever to avoid secular stagnation, we seem doomed to economic instability.

Whether we really face a serious secular stagnation threat—and if we do, what has caused it—is still unclear and debated. The good news is that if the danger is real, two effective responses would still be possible. But they would require us to reject key tenets of pre-crisis orthodoxy— the commitment to free market allocation of credit and the absolute ban on fiat money creation.

The relative price of capital equipment assets bought by private businesses is falling, but it is not clear that total investment needs in advanced economies have declined. Tackling climate change requires very large investments in new energy systems, and in many countries, such as the United States, the quality of transport infrastructure—whether highways or mass transportation systems—is seriously deficient. Business "machines" may be getting cheaper due to Moore's law and the zero cost of software replication, but long-term investments in necessary social infrastructure are not.

But adequate investment in infrastructure often depends not just on private business decisions but also on public-private partnerships and risk sharing, or on the effective design of regulatory regimes to create appropriate private incentives. In some cases, indeed, infrastructure investment may be most efficiently delivered by direct public capital expenditure.

So alongside "unnecessary" credit unrelated to growth-enhancing investment, we may also face investment needs that free markets alone will not adequately finance. In response public policy may need not only to constrain some categories of credit creation but also deliberately foster others or compensate for their deficiency.

Unmet investment needs could be financed by public debt issue, and such economists as Larry Summers and Paul Krugman have argued that if public investment that enhances growth potential can be funded at rock-bottom interest rates, any fears about the resulting public "debt burden" are misplaced.[45] But even if those fears were justified, we would still not be out of policy ammunition. For it is always possible for governments to finance deficits with fiat money creation, and if the alternative is slow growth and deflation, or perpetually low interest rates that generate financial instability, money-financed public investment could be the lowest risk strategy.

Indeed, money-financed deficits could be a feasible answer to secular stagnation even if we did not face a problem of unmet investment needs. For if we truly do face a situation where privately chosen desired savings rates exceed investment needs, and where nominal demand is as a result chronically deficient, fiat money could be used to stimulate additional consumption rather than additional investment.

The essential point is simple: there are very few problems in economics to which there is always a potential answer. But deficient nominal demand is one of them. If necessary, it can always be stimulated by printing money. Doing so would of course involve major risks: but so too does relying on private credit creation to deliver adequate demand. Pre-crisis orthodoxy was too relaxed about private credit creation and too absolute in its prohibition of fiat money finance.

The implications for policy are considered in Parts IV and V. The underlying principle is that we cannot rely on free market credit creation to produce either an optimal allocation of capital or an adequate and stable level of nominal demand. That contradicts the orthodox belief that any attempt to influence credit allocation would result in inefficiency and waste. But as the history of economic development reveals, credit direction has played a crucial role in some of the most remarkable growth stories of the past 60 years. Chapter 8 considers the lessons from those stories.

PART III

Debt, Development, and Capital Flows

||||||||||||||||||||||||||||||||||||||||||||||||||||||||||||||||||||||||||||||||||||||||||||||||||||||||||||

FREE MARKETS IN CREDIT CREATION can produce severe economic harm in advanced economies and could do so even in a closed economy unaffected by international capital flows. But effective control of credit creation is even more important in the early stages of economic development and is greatly complicated by capital flows among nations.

As Chapter 8 describes, successful developing nations in the past, such as Korea and Japan, got rich by means of financial repression—using credit direction rather than free markets to foster rapid and productive capital accumulation. But credit direction is no more a panacea than is financial market liberalization, and it led in other countries to corruption and waste. We face a choice of dangers. How well China navigates that choice, after the past 6 years of dramatic credit boom, will have huge consequences for global financial stability over the next decade.

Chapter 9 explores how international debt capital flows can be even more unstable and disruptive than domestic credit and asset price cycles. As a result, some fragmentation of the global financial system would be a positively good thing. In the eurozone, free market credit creation and capital flows have interacted with a flawed political design to produce a severe debt overhang from which there is no clear escape. Unless the eurozone can agree to the radical reforms required to support adequate nominal demand growth, breakup may be inevitable and preferable to continued slow growth and deflation.

||||||||||||||||||||||||||||||||||||||||||||||||||||||||||||||||||||||||||||||||||||||||||||||||||||||||||||||||||||||||||||||||||||||||||||||||||||||||||||||||||||||||||||||||

EIGHT

DEBT AND DEVELOPMENT

The Merits and Dangers of Financial Repression

There can be no doubt at all that the development of the capitalist economy over the last 100 years would not have been possible without the "forced savings" effected by the extension of additional bank credit.

—*Friedrich von Hayek,* Money,
    Capital and Fluctuations[1]

The case for deregulating, and liberating, finance so that it seeks out the most immediately profitable opportunities is not strong in the early stages of economic development. Far better to keep the financial system on a short leash.

—*Joe Studwell,* How Asia Works[2]

A KEY THEME OF THIS BOOK is the danger of too much debt. Beyond a certain level, increasing leverage makes the economy more fragile. But debt can also play a positive role. The Industrial Revolution would probably not have been possible without debt contracts. The apparent certainty of debt contracts facilitates capital commitments that would not be made if all investments had to be equity financed. But it is not just debt contracts that can play a vital role, but also banks.

Banks do not just intermediate existing savings—they also create credit, money, and purchasing power. So it matters a lot to whom that purchasing power is allocated. In advanced economies most of it is not devoted to the textbook function of financing capital investment. But the finance of investment is certainly one possible use. Bank credit creation can therefore be directed to skew demand in an economy toward investment rather than consumption.

High investment fueled by bank credit creation was central to the high growth rates achieved by the most successful developing economies—Japan and Korea in the 1950s and 1980s and China over the past 30 years. Moreover, their success depended on the deliberate repression of free financial markets. Neither in Japan and Korea in the 1950s to 1980s nor in China over the past 30 years was the quantity and allocation of bank credit creation left to free market forces.

But directed bank credit is no panacea: in other countries, such as the Philippines, it caused harm. But so too did the liberalization of bank credit markets implemented in many East Asian economies in the 1980s and 1990s.

This chapter therefore considers the role of credit creation in economic development, particularly in the most successful East Asian countries. Their story illustrates that neither political direction nor free market forces ensure an optimal quantity or allocation of credit; we face a choice of dangers. It also illustrates that countries that have used credit-funded high investment to drive economic growth need to transition away from that model at some stage, but that the transition is extremely difficult and should not entail switching to an entirely free market approach. China's success in managing that difficult transition will be the most important determinant of global financial stability or instability over the next decade.

Successful Catch Up by Breaking the Rules

The years 1800 and 1950 saw a great divergence in living standards across the world. First in Britain, and then in a widening number of European countries and their colonial offshoots—particularly in North America—the Industrial Revolution took us from a world of zero or glacial growth to one in which the leading industrial nations grew at around 1.5–2% per capita per year, doubling living standards every 30–50 years.

Initially other regions saw little growth, and their living standards fell far behind the industrial leaders. In 1820 the difference in prosperity between richest and poorest regions of the world was no more than 3 to 1; by 1950 U.S. living standards were 15 times higher than in Asia (excluding Japan) and more than 10 times higher than in Africa.[3]

The past half century has seen significant catch up, and the attainable pace of catch up is now far higher than in the nineteenth century. When Germany was catching up to British living standards in the late nineteenth century, that meant growing at 1.9% per capita while the United Kingdom grew at 1.4%. But after the Second World War far faster convergence has been achieved. The Western European countries grew per capita incomes at 3–6% per year in the 1950s to 1970s, as they caught up with U.S. productivity levels. Brazil achieved per capita growth rates of more than 5% in the 1950s and 1970s; Japan and Korea grew at about 7%; and over the past 30 years, China has achieved three decades of 7.5% per capita growth.

The fundamental drivers of this rapid catch up are clear. In a world where technology can be copied across the world, where capital flows can supplement domestic savings, and where the import demand of the already rich can make possible export-driven growth, attainable growth rates in catch up countries are far higher than possible in countries already at the leading edge of technology and prosperity.

Catch up may therefore seem inevitable. But in fact it is striking how few countries have achieved catch up to advanced economy living standards. Most Latin American countries have been stuck at about 20–30% of U.S. standards of living for the past 40 years. Most African countries fell further behind the advanced economies from 1950 to 2000; since then there has been significant recovery but from a very low base. Many East Asian countries, such as Thailand and Indonesia, are still at less than 25% of Western prosperity levels despite occasional periods of very rapid growth. India has grown, but only from about 6% of Western per capita income in 1950 to 10% today. China's growth is startling but it still needs to quadruple income to reach advanced economy per capita income.[4]

Only a handful of countries have achieved full convergence from far behind in 1950. They include some small population but resource-rich countries, such as Qatar or Abu Dhabi. They also include Hong Kong and Singapore: but the paths to prosperity of these small population city-states tell us little about what large population countries must do to get rich.

There are indeed only three large population countries that have achieved catch up to living standards equal to or at least at 70% of Western levels—Japan, Korea, and Taiwan. And these countries did not get rich with free financial systems, free capital flows, or even free trade. The precise policy mix differed by country, but in all it involved a significant role for industrial tariffs, financial repression, and directed credit. Indeed, they got rich by rejecting almost all the precepts of the subsequently dominant "Washington consensus" and of the neoclassical theories of economic efficiency on which that consensus was built.

That consensus of course, had not yet even developed when these countries launched their periods of rapid catch up. That was their good fortune. If the Washington consensus had been fully developed by 1950, and if Japan, Korea, and Taiwan had decided to follow its precepts, they would not have achieved such rapid growth.[5]

Joe Studwell's book *How Asia Works* identifies three crucial elements—present in different degrees in each country—in the Japanese, Korean, and Taiwanese success stories.[6] The first was land reform, and the creation of intensive small plot farming, creating employment for rapidly growing populations and achieving high productivity per hectare. This part of the story itself had a financial element: land reform freed tenant farmers from debt-based reliance on landlords, and the supply of small scale credit to farmers and agricultural businesses financed improvements in technique and productivity.

The second was industrial policy to encourage the development of world class manufacturing. This combined protection against foreign competition in the domestic market with strong encouragement to companies to enter export markets. Particularly in Korea, it also involved an overt strategy to achieve world class performance in specific heavy industries, such as steel, chemicals, and shipbuilding.

The third element, in particular in Japan and Korea, though less so in Taiwan, entailed a highly directive approach to the financial system and in particular to banks, driven by two objectives: ensuring a high level of investment and ensuring that investment was allocated to productive ends.

Financial Repression, "Forced Saving," and the Quantity of Investment

Investment is essential to economic growth. We get more productive by investing in "machines" that enable us to automate existing economic activities or to perform functions not previously possible at all.[7] That remains true even for advanced economies operating at the frontier of technological progress.[8] In the catch up phase, investment is even more important, and the higher the rate of investment, the higher the attainable rate of growth will be.[9]

Catch-up countries do not need to innovate at the frontier of technology: they can invest in capital stock that embeds already developed technologies. And they start with capital stocks per capita far below advanced country levels. Sheer brute investment, provided the investment is not very badly misallocated, can drive a lot of catch up growth. In 1995, the economist Alwyn Young produced an oft-quoted analysis of Asian growth. It used "growth accounting" techniques to decompose country growth rates into increases in labor input, increases in capital input, and the residual increase in total factor productivity. Young illustrated that there was nothing magic about Asian growth: it mainly reflected rapid capital accumulation.[10]

High rates of investment necessarily imply some sacrifice of current consumption with resources transferred to the production of capital goods. Countries can achieve the required transfer in several ways. The Soviet Union in its early decades did so in the most straightforward and brutal fashion—by forcing the peasants to give up grain to feed an industrial workforce building state-owned capital assets. Alternatively, states can directly finance or subsidize investments even in a partially capitalist economy, gaining the financial resources for such investments in one of three ways—taxation, government bond issuance, or the printing of fiat money. Each will, in different ways, reduce real consumption to make the increase in real investment possible.[11]

But additional nominal demand can also be delivered by bank credit creation. And that credit creation can also be used to skew demand toward investment. Banks create purchasing power: by lending newly created money to businesses to fund capital investment projects, they can therefore increase the rate of investment. Recently dominant neoclassical economics has paid little attention to this fact, but early twentieth-century economists, such as Friedrich Hayek and Joseph Schumpeter, correctly identified it as central to economic development, as well as to the instability inherent in monetary economies. Bank lending to businesses for investment effectively achieves "forced savings," which as Hayek put it, "consists in an increase in capital creation at the cost of consumption, through the granting of additional credit, without voluntary action on the part of the individuals who forgo consumption and without their deriving any immediate benefit."[12]

The precise mechanism by which this "forced savings" effect works was debated by the early economists. Several argued that it must involve inflation, as additional investment demand drove up wages and thus attracted workers from consumption goods– to capital goods–producing industries. But a variant of forced savings is possible without inflation if when new credit is extended to businesses, households are required or strongly encouraged to hold increased money balances. And households may increase savings and money balances if the interest rate they receive is so low that they need to save more to ensure adequate resources for future retirement and other needs.[13] Policies that require banks to lend to business, that prevent them from lending to consumers and that ensure that consumers receive a low rate of return on money savings, can thus be used to achieve higher rates of savings and investment than would otherwise occur.

Korea and Japan both followed precisely these policies during their periods of most rapid growth. Korea's nationalized banks lent to businesses, not consumers. Japan's private banks were required to do so by guidance from the Bank of Japan and Ministry of Finance. And in both countries, household savers received negative real interest rates, while business borrowers were able to borrow cheaply. Investment was effectively subsidized by a large net transfer of resources from household savers to business investors: but the result was high investment, which drove economic growth.

Of course, the system only worked if savers were sufficiently conservative in their savings decisions to prefer bank deposits to alternative higher return investments, or if their access to other options was constrained by regulation. Directed and subsidized credit policies were therefore underpinned by constraints on retail financial competition and by capital controls that prevented savers from investing overseas.

Capital controls also helped prevent inward flows of lending, which might have undermined the real economy's industrial investment focus, for instance, by funding real estate development or consumer lending. They therefore buttressed the other objective of directive policy—ensuring that the credit extended went to productive investment.

Credit Allocation and the Quality of Investment

Chapter 7 discusses the alternative ways to increase nominal demand. One potential advantage of relying on private credit creation, rather than government fiat money creation, is that it might depoliticize the allocation decision, reducing the danger that new spending power would be allocated to wasteful ends.

But in fact neither Korean nor Japanese authorities left bank credit allocation to private decisionmaking driven by profit-maximizing objectives. Instead, they deliberately directed credit toward what they judged to be desirable investments with greatest potential to drive economic growth. Credit was made available to manufacturing industry, not real estate development; to export industry, not importers or traders; and to support strategic priorities, such as Korea's heavy industrial developments.

This direction was achieved by guidance or instructions to the banks, and by the criteria that defined whether loans could be "rediscounted" at the central bank and thus effectively funded by it.

The practice of rediscounting private-sector loans by the central bank illustrates that the dividing line between private credit–financed investment and fiat money finance is sometimes not absolute. If the central bank stands ready permanently to expand its balance sheet to fund growing private-sector loans, this is very close to money finance, but with the resources lent to the private sector, rather than given to the government. In the case of Korea, the investment boom of 1960–1980 could be described as in a sense financed by fiat money: its commercial banks had been nationalized by President Park Chung Hee, and its central bank, operating under direct government control, stood ready to provide them with almost limitless resources for on-lending to exporters at negative real interest rates.

But from the point of view of economic development the crucial issue was not how precisely the spending power was created, but whether it was well used. In Japan and Korea enough of it was well used to drive dramatic economic catch up.

In the history of catch up, indeed, the effective allocation of additional purchasing power has been far more important than more conventional measures of "good policy," such as control of inflation. Park Chung Hee's Korea was in macroeconomic terms highly unstable, with inflation running at up to 25% and with soaring foreign debts. But enough of the rapidly expanding nominal demand ended up in useful investments to drive strong and sustainable growth. Other countries (such as Thailand), which pursued more conventional and internationally approved macroeconomic policies, were less successful.

But while Japan and Korea both illustrate that encouraged and directed credit creation can deliver successful catch up, two caveats are important. First, although this approach can work, it doesn't always. Second, countries need to devise a path out of credit-intensive and investment-led growth, and that transition has proved extremely difficult.

Credit-Financed Waste

Credit creates purchasing power, which can fund productive investment. But it can also be used to fund wasteful investment, or the purchase of existing assets (such as real estate and the land on which it sits), driving self-reinforcing cycles of asset price appreciation and further credit extension.

Direction of credit, if done well, can increase the proportion of credit put to good productive use. But government or central bank direction of credit, favoring one potential borrower over another, can also drive corrupt or inept misallocation of credit to favored cronies or to unsuccessful white elephant projects. Korea under Park Chung Hee managed to direct credit in ways that were on balance favorable: the same tools used in Suharto's Indonesia and Marcos's Philippines gave preferential credit access to political supporters and financed less successful development projects.

So there is a case for depoliticizing the credit decision. That case indeed formed a key element of the Washington consensus. Across East Asia the 1980s and 1990s, internationally trained advisers, whether from the World Bank or IMF or working in governments, argued for independent central banks, the removal of credit and capital controls, and greater competition in banking sectors. They aimed to bring the discipline of free markets to bear, reducing the potential for cronyism and ensuring that capital was allocated to efficient ends.[14]

But the cure was as harmful as the disease, and the financial liberalization urged on East Asian countries as the cure to cronyism contributed directly to the real estate booms and short-term capital flows that led to the Asian financial crisis of 1997. Private credit allocation produced wasteful real estate developments in Jakarta, Kuala Lumpur, and Bangkok, quite as much as directed credit allocation had funded Marcos's and Suharto's cronies.

The Challenge of Transition

Korea suffered in the Asian financial crisis of 1997, and Japan had suffered a severe shock in the early 1990s and by 1997 was stuck in a balance sheet recession. Their experience illustrates that transitioning out of a credit-fueled high investment model is very difficult.

High investment rates are essential to drive rapid growth during economic catch up. But the closer countries get to advanced economy levels of prosperity and per capita capital stock, the less need there is for such investment, and the greater the danger becomes that investment will be wasted. Countries therefore need to transition to less investment and more consumption-intensive growth: the subsidies from household savers to business borrowers need to be wound down, and consumer credit may have a useful role to play. And as people get richer, there is a natural tendency for more expenditure to be focused on buying or renting desirable real estate. Some shift of the financial system toward real estate lending is inevitable.

But achieving a smooth transition without excessive consumption or real estate booms has proved extremely difficult. The reasons are partly inherent—the processes of liberalization cannot be precisely controlled. But they are also partly political and ideological—interest groups lobby, and policymakers find all-encompassing theories attractive.

If banking systems are tightly controlled, alternative shadow banking systems will develop: consumers will seek opportunities for higher returns on savings, and nonfavored businesses will seek alternative sources of funds. In Korea this led from the 1960s on to the extensive development of nonbank financial institutions, imperfectly regulated by the authorities. Globalization meanwhile opens financing opportunities for larger companies whether the authorities desire it or not. Increasingly from the 1970s on, large Japanese companies with export revenues and factories abroad were able to issue Eurobonds, leaving the Japanese banks with spare credit capacity.

Those banks in turn lobbied to be allowed into new business areas, such as real estate and consumer finance. And as it became apparent that the Japanese economic model needed to move away from directed credit and high investment, policymakers were attracted to the idea that the new model should be rigorously free market, maximizing the potential gains from liberalization.[15]

But liberalization was followed by the biggest real estate credit and price bubble the world has ever seen and by the continued balance sheet recession of deleveraging, deflation, and slow growth, in which Japan has been trapped for two decades. As Chapter 5 describes, excessive private debt creation, not directed by the government to productive ends, created a debt overhang from which there is no apparent escape.

A Choice of Dangers

The story of East Asian development thus illustrates the fundamental problem—neither government direction nor market allocation are certain to produce optimal results. We face a choice of dangers.

High investment rates can be achieved by direct state expenditure, whether tax, bond, or money financed. History has many examples of successful state-sponsored industry development—but also many disasters. Governments can also use bank credit creation to achieve developmental aims: Korea and Japan did so successfully; the Philippines used the same tools badly. But if decisions on bank credit creation are left entirely to private decisionmaking, driven by profit objectives, the result can be equally harmful—with a skew toward real estate lending, driving harmful credit and asset price cycles.

The Washington consensus of the 1980s and 1990s sought to prevent government misallocation of credit by depoliticizing credit markets, but financial liberalization simply swapped one danger for another.

The transition away from a high investment and credit driven model therefore needs to be handled with great care, wary of the dangers of free financial systems as much as the dangers of state direction. How well China handles that transition will be one of the most important determinants of global financial stability over the next 10 years.

China: Transition without Crisis?

Neither Korea nor Japan managed transition from financial repression and high investment rates without financial crisis. Whether China can do so in the next 10 years is hugely important. China's sheer size means that if it does suffer a financial crisis similar to Japan's in the early 1990s or Korea's in 1997, the shock will be felt around the world.

From 1980 to 2007 China achieved an average GDP growth rate of 10%. That required high investment, which averaged 38% of GDP over that period.[16] In part that investment was funded out of very high business profits, with workers' wages suppressed by rapid labor force growth.

But it was also in part funded by the credit system, with the ratio of bank credit to GDP reaching about 120% by 2002 and staying at that level until 2008 as credit grew in line with nominal GDP. Interest rates were regulated to keep both deposit and loan rates below free market levels. The banking system, as in Korea and Japan in the 1950s to 1980s, transferred resources from household savers to business investors.

By 2008 there was a strong consensus, shared by economists inside and outside China and by the Chinese authorities, that China needed to shift away from its investment- and also export-led economic model.[17] Capital stock per capita remained well below advanced economy levels, making a reasonably high investment rate still appropriate. But it was clear that more domestic consumption and somewhat less investment was essential to avoid increasing waste, overcapacity, and financial stress. Premier Wen Jiabao commented in 2007 that the Chinese economy had become "unbalanced, uncoordinated, and ultimately unstable."[18]

But in fact over the subsequent 5 years, the Chinese economy moved in precisely the other direction, with the investment rate increasing from 42% in 2008 to 49% in 2012, well above the maximum rates observed in Japan and Korea during their periods of rapid catch up. The root cause of this investment spurt was the global financial crisis. The advanced economies contracted: export demand for Chinese goods fell precipitately, and employment fell. Concerned about the potential social and political consequences, the Chinese government sought a rapid economic stimulus, and the easiest and most direct way to stimulate was by means of a massive boost to investment.

The investment was credit financed. The desired investment level exceeded the internal resources of either state-owned enterprises or local government, and while the government could have used fiscal resources (borrowed or printed) to finance the stimulus, they chose instead to use bank credit creation. The state-owned banks were directed to "open your wallets wide" to finance big increases in investment in urban real estate, infrastructure, and heavy industry. Bank lending grew far faster than nominal GDP, but so too did multiple variants of shadow bank credit creation. The stock of "total social finance" (a Chinese official measure that captures multiple forms of financing to non–central government entities) grew from 124% to more than 200% of GDP. Figure 8.1 shows the trend over time.[19]

This massive credit-fueled stimulus has played a valuable role in China, offsetting the impact of the advanced economy financial crisis of 2007–2008. It has also usefully contributed to global demand in the face of advanced economy deleveraging. But the huge increase in Chinese leverage creates severe financial and economic vulnerability.

The particular nature of the vulnerabilities reflects the hybrid nature of the Chinese economy. In part it is a market economy with intense competition among companies, but it is also one dominated by state-owned companies enjoying privileged relationships with state-owned banks. It is to a degree state controlled but is also decentralized, with

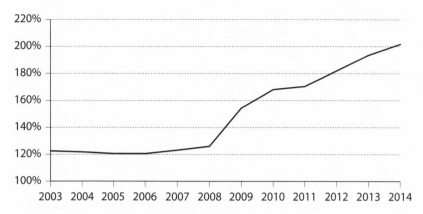

Figure 8.1.   China: Total social finance to GDP

Source: People's Bank of China

significant autonomy enjoyed by local provincial and city governments, who pursue economic development in competition with one another. Like Japan and Korea, China is industrializing, but government policy objectives also defines "urbanization" as an objective in itself; this was not the case for the earlier catch up countries, where urbanization was seen simply as the likely result of industrialization. Credit meanwhile is not allocated by an entirely free market, but its allocation is not subject to as much central control as was the case in Japan and Korea.

As a result, China faces two different vulnerabilities. One lies in heavy industry sectors, with state-owned enterprises in steel, coal, cement, and other capital-intensive industries now facing credit financed overcapacity, in a classic example of the sort of overinvestment cycle described by both Friedrich Hayek and Hyman Minsky.

The second vulnerability lies in real estate and infrastructure investment, where huge investments have been financed by second- and third-tier as well as leading cities—in airports, roads and railways, apartment blocks, industrial parks, convention centers, sports stadiums, and museums—in a competitive rush to urbanize. Much of this investment may be valuable, but much will prove to have been wasted. And the financing model used could not have been better designed to hardwire and turbocharge the credit and real estate cycle. Local governments borrow money to fund urban infrastructure projects in the hope that economic development will drive land price increases, enabling them to raise money from land sales to repay loans. The very structure increases the dangers of self-reinforcing credit and real estate / land price cycles, fostering excessive exuberance in the upswing, but threatening debt overhang and default on the way down.

China, although still a lower middle income country, has thus become exposed both to the dangers of the directed credit model (excessive investment in heavy industry) and of a liberalized banking system (excessive investment in real estate).

During 2014–2015 the risks crystallized, and China suffered a major economic slowdown with falling property prices in many cities; increasing bad debt problems in local government; and falls in heavy industry output, which drove reduced global commodity demand and major falls in commodity prices. So while China's credit boom after 2008 helped offset the deflationary impact of debt overhang and deleveraging in advanced economies, its slowdown in 2014–2015 has had a powerful deflationary effect. When debt simply shifts around the global economy, from private to public sectors, or from one country to another, the deflationary consequences of debt overhang are delayed but cannot be permanently avoided.

China now faces the same two challenges faced by advanced economies—how to build a less credit-intensive economic growth model and how to manage the problems of high debt stocks created by past credit-intensive growth.

Achieving the first will, in China as elsewhere, require policy changes that go far beyond the details of the financial system. Wage rises faster than nominal GDP are required and may occur naturally as the Chinese labor market tightens in the face of falling numbers of young adults. But reduced household savings are also desirable and will only occur if the government establishes better social security and healthcare systems, reducing the need for high precautionary savings. In the financial sector itself, China, like other countries, needs strong policy tools to constrain real estate lending. But it also needs to address land pricing and purchase rules: the current ability of local governments to take land from peasants in return for little compensation creates huge incentives for excessive real estate development.

As for the problem of existing debt, China faces a difficult choice between three risky policies. It could "let the market work" as companies and local governments deleverage where they can and default where they cannot. But that could produce a bigger economic downturn than the authorities are willing to accept. The second would be to "let the credit boom run," with yet more credit extended to highly indebted companies and local governments. But that route would delay the desirable transition to a less investment focused economy and build up bigger financial problems for the future. The third choice would be explicitly to socialize some of the debt—writing off bad loans in the banking sector and bailing out banks, state-owned companies, and overextended local governments—financing the operation with central government debt. With Chinese total government debt still only about 39% of GDP, the potential for such socialization is significant, but it is not limitless.[20] Beyond some level, concerns about Chinese public debt sustainability might emerge. That problem in turn could in theory be dealt with by monetization—by printing rather than borrowing money—but at the risk, potentially, of inflation.

China thus illustrates again the problem of the debt overhang. Private credit creation can be used to achieve both aggregate demand growth and a high investment rate. And it seems to have advantages over more direct mechanisms, such as bond- or money-financed government expenditure. But private credit creation left to itself may produce too much unsustainable debt, even when it does not produce excessive demand to which inflation-targeting central banks feel the need to respond. And once excessive debt has been created, while it can be shifted from private to public sectors, actually reducing it turns out to be much more difficult. In some countries, as Chapter 14 discusses, escape without monetization may be impossible.

In China's case the chances of a successful transition without monetization are far higher than in some advanced economies. This reflects China's potential for further rapid growth, reducing the ratio of debt to GDP by growing the denominator. With appropriate policies China can grow for several more decades at 5% per year or more. In contrast, Japan's sustainable growth rate is unlikely to exceed 1%.[21] Provided China can shift to a less credit-intensive growth for the future, its existing debt stock could still, at least at this stage, be manageable.

Achieving that shift is essential. For if China continued to grow in its recent credit-intensive fashion, its debt stock would become daunting, not only in relation to China but also with respect to the whole world. By the early 2020s, China could have a nominal GDP of $20 trillion. If by then it had a nongovernment debt to GDP of 250% that would be $50 trillion of debt, 3.5 times the size of the U.S. mortgage markets which played such a major role in the origins of the 2007–2008 financial crisis. And while China's debt mountain is today owed almost entirely within China—and largely by banks, companies, and local governments all ultimately controlled or owned by the state—the more that China progresses toward a more normal market economy and the more that it liberalizes its capital account flows, the greater will be the danger that instability in the Chinese financial system is transmitted to the rest of the world.

China's decisions on capital account liberalization will therefore, alongside its domestic policy choices, have major global implications. As Chapter 9 describes, they should reflect the fact that volatile capital flows can make domestic credit cycles even more unstable.

‖‖‖

NINE

TOO MUCH OF THE WRONG
SORT OF CAPITAL FLOW

Global and Eurozone Delusions

On both the empirical side and on the calibration side, it has so
far proved hard to find robust support for large quantifiable
benefits of international financial integration.
  —*Hélène Rey, "Dilemma not Trilemma: The Global Financial Cycle
  and Monetary Policy Independence"[1]*

Despite the numerous cross-country attempts to analyse the effects
of capital account liberalisation, there appears to be only limited
evidence that supports the notion that liberalisation enhances
growth.
  —*Committee on the Global Financial System,* Capital Flows and
  Emerging Market Economies[2]

C HAPTER 2 DESCRIBES THE favorable assessment of financial liberalization and deepening that dominated pre-crisis thinking. Financial
innovation was beneficial because it had enabled better risk management: increased market liquidity supported capital mobilization, price
discovery, and the efficient allocation of capital to its most productive
use. Debt contracts played an essential role. As a result a larger financial
sector was in general beneficial, and higher private-sector credit as a
percentage of GDP helped deliver faster growth.

Those propositions were believed to hold in advanced economies. But they also seemed to justify international financial integration and suggested that emerging economies would gain major benefits if they opened their economies to free global capital flows.

The Washington consensus therefore urged on emerging economies both domestic financial market liberalization and capital account liberalization: many IMF programs made financial support conditional on such policies, and in Hong Kong in 1997 the IMF proposed making capital account liberalization a requirement for IMF membership.

But just as financial deepening within countries is not limitlessly or in all respects beneficial, so too with international financial integration. Some types of capital flows can help foster growth, but excessive quantities of other types can cause harm. In domestic markets, free financial markets will inevitably create too much of the wrong sort of debt. Free global capital markets will tend to create too much of the wrong sort of capital flows. Global debt capital flows can destabilize emerging economies, and in the eurozone, unstable debt capital flows played an important role in the origins of the crisis which developed after 2008.

Global Financial Integration: The Elusive Benefits

Chapter 7 describes the growth of global current-account imbalances in the decade running up to the 2007–2008 financial crisis. The total current-account surpluses grew from 0.5% to 2.0% of global GDP, and so necessarily did total deficits.[3] The flipside of those current-account balances were capital flows, with surplus countries accumulating large financial claims against deficit countries.

Such large surpluses and capital flows are not unique in economic history. The United Kingdom ran large current-account surpluses before the First World War: in 1911–1913 they amounted to almost 10% of UK GDP, and the country accumulated huge overseas assets.[4] But today's capital flows are different in two crucial respects. Just as most modern credit creation does not fund new capital investment, the same is true of most net capital flows. And just as the modern financial system overall has witnessed an explosive growth of intrafinancial system trading and claims—with gross financial assets and liabilities growing far faster than real economy loans and deposits—so too, gross two-way capital flows have grown far more rapidly than have net flows.[5]

Both features help explain why the theoretically possible benefits of global capital flows have in practice proved elusive.

Net Capital Flows Unmatched by Useful Capital Investment

The origin and economic function of pre–First World War capital flows was clear. Britain was then one of the world's richest countries and generated domestic savings in excess of domestic investment needs. In its own colonies and in other emerging economies (for instance, in Latin America), there were major investment opportunities but limited domestic savings resources. Capital flowed, largely in the form of long-term debt or equity, to finance capital investment. That investment then generated return with which to repay the debt and reward the equity investors.

Some modern capital flows take this form. Foreign direct investment in China has brought the transfer of technology and skills that has helped stimulate rapid economic growth. But most modern capital flows neither flow from richer to poorer countries nor finance sustainable capital investment. Instead they are often from poorer to richer countries, or, for instance in the eurozone, between countries of similar income level. And they have predominantly funded a mix of unsustainable consumption, wasteful investment, and booms in the price of existing real estate assets.

In most deficit countries capital inflows have not resulted in increased productive investment. In the United States ahead of the 2007–2008 crisis, they helped fund a mortgage borrowing boom that temporarily enabled middle- and lower-income Americans to increase consumption despite stagnant real earnings. In Spain and Ireland they helped fund investment booms in excessive real estate construction, repeating a pattern observed in countries like Thailand and Indonesia ahead of the 1997 Asian financial crash.

Those construction booms were also usually accompanied by rapid increases in the price of existing real estate, which both reflected and induced an expansion of domestic credit. Capital inflows and domestic credit expansion thus interacted to produce an increase in leverage far greater than would have resulted from the net capital flows alone.

Many modern capital flows do not therefore play the positive role described by economic theory, allocating capital across the world to its most efficient use. Instead they increase the scale of unsustainable debt creation and post-crisis debt overhang effects.

Debt overhang, resulting from excessive leverage growth, can produce a deflationary bias even in a closed economy. Overleveraged net debtors cut investment and consumption, while net creditors in the same economy feel no offsetting need to increase expenditure. But an overhang of unsustainable debt *between* countries can be particularly harmful because of current-account financing constraints.

Those constraints are irrelevant to the largest deficit country of all, the United States, which enjoys reserve currency status: neither the financial markets nor the U.S. government pay much attention to the U.S. current-account deficit. But in emerging economies the deflationary impact of debt overhang effects can be exacerbated by unavoidable public policy responses. Even when current-account deficits and resulting debts arose entirely as a result private borrowing, if markets decide that these deficits have become unsustainable, governments may be compelled to tighten fiscal and monetary policy to prevent excessive exchange rate depreciation. As a result, their actions may magnify the deflationary impact of private deleveraging. Creditor nations are however under no equivalent pressure to stimulate their demand.

In an entirely closed economy, indeed, the government might be able to offset the deflationary impact of private-sector deleveraging with fiscal or monetary stimulus. But at the international level, there is no global government or central bank to perform this role.[6]

Too much of the wrong sort of debt can produce crisis and post-crisis deflation even in a closed one-currency economy. But when the debt claims are international, the potential for harm is still further increased.

Destabilizing Gross Flows

Net capital flows not matched by valuable long-term investment have therefore played an important role in the origins of several financial crises.

But another striking feature of modern capital flows is that their gross value is much higher than their net value—capital does not simply flow to finance current-account deficits, it flows back and forth among countries in massive quantities. Gross flows in and out of high income countries increased from 9.5 times GDP in the 1970s to 37 times in the 2000s; for medium income countries they grew from 2 times in the 1980s to 15 times in the 2000s. They have grown far more rapidly than net flows and are far more volatile.[7]

Such large gross capital flows might of course be socially useful and beneficial. Optimal investor portfolios in country A might require investments in country B, even while country B investors choose to invest in A. In an efficient global capital market, a continual search for optimal combinations of risk and return could in theory deliver improved price discovery and capital allocation. And that search will generate continual readjustment of portfolios and trading activity, and thus it will generate gross flows greatly in excess of the net flows that finance current-account deficits.

The possible benefits of large gross two-way flows are therefore a subset of the wider benefits of market completion and increased market liquidity. But as Chapter 2 describes, there are reasons for doubting whether those benefits always exist.

Even in a closed economy, market completion and increased liquidity can facilitate trading activity that at best absorbs additional resources to no net social benefit and at worst generates instability. Gross two-way capital flows represent a subset of increasing intrafinancial system activity and can have the same adverse economic effects. It is, for instance, unclear what economic benefit—at the social rather than the private level—can possibly result from carry trade activities that seek to exploit interest rate differentials and expectations of future exchange-rate movements. At very least, they employ the talents of skilled individuals in activities that are zero-sum at the social level.

But as with increased financial intensity in general, so too with gross two-way capital flows: the most important issue is not whether they result in some unnecessary activity, but whether they can have actually negative effects. In many circumstances they almost certainly do.

If all markets can be made perfect, then market completion and more liquid markets must bring us closer to maximum attainable efficiency. But if all are to a degree imperfect, increased interactions among them can make the whole system less stable. In the case of global capital flows, the inherent instability of domestic credit cycles can be further magnified by expectations of exchange-rate movements. Large gross capital inflows can produce increases in both domestic asset prices and in exchange rates, generating for a time self-fulfilling expectations of further rises in both. Once confidence breaks, capital outflows can both exacerbate domestic asset price falls and produce overshooting depreciation. As a result, volatile short-term capital flows can undermine the effectiveness of domestic monetary policy; using interest rates to slow down domestic credit and asset price booms can have the perverse effect of stimulating more capital inflows and more asset price rises.

The dangers are moreover magnified by partially informed investors acting in ways that are individually rational but collectively destabilizing. Even more than in domestic markets, investment analysis may focus on the anticipation of other investors' anticipations or may be driven by broad asset categories ("BRICS," "fragile five," "emerging markets") rather than by more fundamental analysis. And a high premium may be placed on holding short-term liquid positions that can be exited rapidly. But the collective effect is that when confidence breaks, the rush for the exit creates self-reinforcing price changes.

Bonanzas and sudden stops in credit supply are observed in domestic markets and could exist even in a "one nation" global economy. But they are inherently more likely and more disruptive when they operate at the international level.

EMPIRICAL EVIDENCE AND FAITH-BASED BELIEFS

So net capital flows often have little to do with efficient capital allocation, and gross two-way capital flows sometimes produce harmful volatility. Unsurprisingly, therefore, empirical analysis finds little evidence that short-term capital flows deliver positive benefits. A report by the Committee on the Global Financial System in 2009 concluded that "despite the numerous cross-country attempts to analyse the effects of capital account liberalisation, there appears to be only limited evidence that supports the notion that liberalisation enhances growth." And it noted the danger that "large swings, over a very short period of time, complicate the conduct of monetary policy and liquidity management in the emerging markets economies."[8] An important recent paper by economist Hélène Rey reaches the same conclusion: "it has so far proved hard to find robust support for large quantifiable benefits of international financial integration."[9]

The evidence instead suggests that any benefits of capital flows depend on their type and tenor. Foreign direct investment is the least volatile and most beneficial, because it results in incremental capital investment often accompanied by technology transfer. Equity portfolio investments, while liquid for the investors, at least represent a permanent commitment of funds to the issuing company. But short-term debt flows are more volatile, and short-term bank-intermediated capital flows are the most volatile of all.

A striking feature of the debate on capital flows, however, is the extent to which faith in the benefits of global financial integration survives the lack of evidence. There is indeed a strong tendency among true believers to describe the empirical findings as "ambiguous" rather than "negative" and to hold out the hope that more subtle analysis will reveal the benefits that complete markets theory tells us must be there. But better theory tells us why they might not exist, and empirical evidence suggests they do not.

The implication is that fragmentation of the international financial system, far from being in all respects dangerous, can in some specific ways be positively desirable. Specific policy implications of that conclusion are discussed in Chapter 13.

One Market, One Money—The Eurozone Delusion

People often lay the blame for adverse events according to their ideological predilections. When the 2007–2008 financial crisis first broke, many continental Europeans blamed it on the excesses of Anglo-Saxon financial markets. Many Anglo-Saxon commentators, conversely, saw the eurozone's subsequent travails as the inevitable result of a political project pursued without respect for financial market realities.

In fact the eurozone crisis has been driven by the interaction between inefficient and unstable financial markets and a profoundly flawed political design.

UNSTABLE PRIVATE CREDIT CREATION AND CAPITAL FLOWS

European Monetary Union was always partly a political project. But its proponents also saw it as a valuable next step in "completing" the single market and unleashing the benefits of increased international capital flows. A European Commission document, *One Market, One Money*, published in 1990, set out the argument.[10] A single currency would remove exchange-rate risk in the eurozone, making surpluses and deficits of individual nations as irrelevant as the imbalances of U.S. states. It would create more liquid European capital markets and facilitate capital flows previously constrained by exchange-rate risk. Larger capital flows in turn would ensure a more efficient allocation of capital: capital would flow to regions of lower productivity, speeding the process of economic convergence.

In one respect this narrative came true. In the 9 years between the launch of the euro and the 2007–2008 crisis, private capital flows across the eurozone soared. Current-account deficits grew from 3% to 9.6% of GDP in Spain, and in Ireland from zero to 5.6%.[11] Italy switched from a current-account surplus of 1% of GDP to a deficit of 2.9% (see Figure 9.1). These deficits were financed by private capital flows, with foreign investors and banks willing to invest in peripheral country debt securities or to lend money to their banks, companies, and households.

But the capital flows were not the sort that *One Market, One Money* had envisaged and largely did not finance investments that could drive increases in productivity and spur economic convergence. Instead they took several unsustainable forms. In the case of Greece they financed unsustainable public deficits. In Spain and Ireland they financed increased private consumption and excessive real estate investment, and they gave additional impetus to domestic credit and asset price cycles in existing real estate.

International financial integration in the eurozone thus caused economic harm. Increased market liquidity in Greek government bonds made it easier for the Greek government to increase public debt to unsustainable levels, and market completion through the removal of exchange-rate risk facilitated harmful private borrowing. The free market misallocated capital.

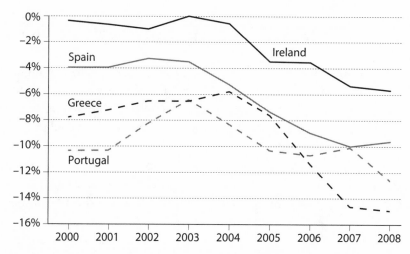

Figure 9.1. Eurozone current account deficits as percentage of GDP

Source: International Monetary Fund World Economic Outlook Database, October 2012.

In 2010 private capital flows in the eurozone abruptly stopped. Private-sector investors who had previously ignored many risks suddenly became risk averse.[12] But by the time the party stopped, the bonanza of pre-crisis capital flows and domestic credit creation had left the eurozone peripheral countries with a particularly severe debt overhang problem.

FLAWED AND INCOMPLETE CURRENCY UNION

The eurozone crisis thus in part reflects a free market vision gone awry, a particular variant of overconfidence in the benefits of free capital flows. But the eurozone's ability to escape from post-crisis debt overhang has been stymied by the flaws in its institutional design.

The fundamental problem is that all public debt in the eurozone is issued not at the federal eurozone level, but at what Charles Goodhart has rightly labeled the "sub-sovereign" level of nation states, who no longer issue their own currency and therefore no longer have the capacity if necessary to repay public debt with sovereign fiat money. Eurozone nations with large accumulated debts are therefore perceived by financial markets to face a potential default risk that does not apply to the debt of fully sovereign debt issuers, such as the United States, the United Kingdom, or Japan.

As a result, eurozone countries on average have had to pay higher interest rates on their debt than, for instance, Japan, even though the eurozone's average public indebtedness—at 74% of GDP—is far below Japan's 138%.[13] And as a result, the eurozone has felt compelled to keep fiscal deficits in the aftermath of the crisis far smaller, at about 2% of eurozone GDP on average, than the 6–7% allowed in Japan, the United States, and the United Kingdom. The large fiscal deficits in those latter countries may pose future fiscal challenges, but in the short term they have helped offset the contractionary effect of private deleveraging. In the eurozone, in contrast, fiscal consolidation has added to that contractionary effect. While in 2014 domestic nominal demand in both the United Kingdom and the United States was about 16% above the 2008 level, in the eurozone it was only 2% higher than in 2008.[14]

The macroeconomic risks created by large amounts of sub-sovereign debt have moreover been exacerbated by the fact that banks in each eurozone country hold as their supposedly safe liquid assets large portfolios of the debt of their local sub-sovereign nation state. It is as if banks in Illinois or California held their liquid assets not in U.S. federal Treasury bonds but in large and undiversified portfolios of Illinois and California state bonds.

The inevitable result, particularly troublesome during 2010–2013, was a self-reinforcing cycle of increasing risk and falling demand. Simultaneous private deleveraging and fiscal consolidation in eurozone periphery countries produced inadequate demand and recession. Government bond yields rose, and prices fell. That in turn raised questions about the value of the banks' government bond holdings, exacerbating concerns about bank solvency, increasing bank funding costs, and increasing the price and reducing the quantity of private credit extended to the real economy. And that in turn made escape from recession still more difficult.

The eurozone's flawed design has thus made it more difficult to offset the debt overhang problem created by private-sector excess. Policy failures and market failures have compounded one another and threaten to trap the eurozone in a prolonged period of slow growth, very low inflation, and unresolved debt burdens.

Radical reform is needed if the eurozone is to succeed. Public debts held at sub-sovereign level need to be radically reduced, with some public debt issued instead at the eurozone federal level: some capacity to run countercyclical fiscal deficits at eurozone rather than sub-sovereign levels must be created, and some monetization of accumulated public debt will be required. The link between bank and sub-sovereign risk needs to be broken, with banks no longer allowed to hold sub-sovereign debt, but instead holding eurozone level debt as their safe liquid asset.

In sum, the eurozone needs to become a complete currency union and therefore a political union, since only if it does so can it deal effectively with the problems that irrational and inefficient financial markets can leave behind. In fact, as Chapter 15 describes, it may well be impossible to forge an agreement to such radical reform. But if it cannot be done, eurozone breakup is likely to be inevitable and is preferable to sustained stagnation.

But whatever the choice in the eurozone, the general point is clear. In domestic economies both the quantity and the category mix of credit creation must be actively managed, and countries (or currency unions) need domestic policy tools that can offset the depressive effects of debt overhang resulting from past policy errors. Among countries, meanwhile, the wrong sort of capital flows must sometimes be constrained. The idea that international financial integration is always and in all respects beneficial is a delusion.

PART IV

Fixing the System

IIIIIIIIIIIIIIIIIIIIIIIIIIIIIIIIIIIIIIIIIIIIIIIIIIIIIII

B ANKS AND SHADOW BANKING systems left to themselves are bound
to create too much of the wrong sort of debt and leave economies
facing severe debt overhangs. Two questions follow: how to fix the system to prevent excessive credit creation, and how to escape the debt
overhang created by past policy mistakes. Part V answers the second
question. This Part answers the first.

Following the 2007–2008 crisis, major reforms have sought to make
the financial system itself more stable, ensuring better run banks and
fixing the problem of "too big to fail." But as Chapter 10 describes, they
are insufficient to create a more stable economy. Lending that looks good
from a private perspective can have bad economic effects, and better
risk management tools can make the overall financial system more unstable. We need to manage credit creation, not just fix the banks. Chapters 11–13 describe the policies required.

Chapter 11 argues that without action to address the three fundamental drivers of unnecessary credit growth—real estate, rising inequality,
and global imbalances—financial reform alone cannot be effective. So
policies relating to urban design and property taxation, to minimum
wages and social benefits, or to the dividend policies of Chinese state-
owned enterprises, are as important to long-term financial stability as
are the technical details of prudential regulation.

Chapter 12 considers structural solutions: abolishing banks, taxing
debt, and encouraging new equity contracts. None provides a silver bullet, but the reforms we do introduce should reflect the arguments for
these radical proposals.

Chapter 13 proposes major changes to financial regulation. Bank capital requirements should be four or five times their current levels, and capital to support real estate lending should be set far higher than private risk assessments suggest is appropriate. Short-term debt capital flows should be constrained by some fragmentation of the international financial system.

And a new policy philosophy is required: central banks cannot focus solely on low and stable inflation nor financial regulation only on the solvency and liquidity of individual institutions. Public policy needs quite explicitly to manage the quantity and to influence the allocation of credit creation: it cannot rely on free markets in credit to produce optimal social results.

||||||||||||||||||||||||||||||||||||||||||||||||||||||||||||||||||||||||||||||||||||||||||||||||||||||||||||||||||||||||||||||||||||||||||||||||||||||||||||||||||||||||||||||||||||||

TEN

IRRELEVANT BANKERS IN AN UNSTABLE SYSTEM

After a crisis it will always be possible to construct plausible
arguments—by emphasizing the triggering events or institutional
flaws—that accidents, mistakes, or easily corrected shortcomings
were responsible for the disaster.

—*Hyman Minsky,* Financial Instability Revisited: The Economics of
Disaster[1]

[H]ow nonsensical it is to formulate the question of the causation
of cyclical fluctuations in terms of "guilt" and to single out e.g. the
banks as those "guilty." ... Nobody has ever asked them to pursue
a policy other than that which ... gives rise to cyclical fluctuations;
and it is not within their power to do away with such fluctuations,
seeing that the latter originate not from their policy but from the
very nature of the modern organization of credit.

—*Friedrich von Hayek,* Monetary Theory and the Trade Cycle"[2]

T HE TITLE OF THIS CHAPTER may offend some people. Many who
played no role in the origins of the 2007–2008 crisis have lost jobs
and homes or have seen their income decline. Many who worked in finance were hugely well paid. There is a strong desire to "name the guilty
persons" and punish them. So how can the bankers be irrelevant?

But I have chosen the title to make a point. Yes, many individual financiers were greedy or incompetent, and we should punish fraud severely and increase the penalties for reckless behavior. But if we think
the crisis occurred because of individual "bad apples" who corrupted the
system, or because of badly designed incentives and inadequate sanctions, we will fail to make adequately radical reforms.[3]

The 2007–2008 crisis was the worst since the crash of 1929 and the Great Depression that followed. One of the best books on that earlier crisis is Liaquat Ahamed's *Lords of Finance*.[4] In the run-up to it many unscrupulous financiers made huge profits out of socially useless activities. But in *Lords of Finance* unscrupulous financiers are footnotes at best. Instead the focus is on the finance ministries and central banks that designed and executed policy, and on the economic theories that underpinned that policy. It was mistakes in policy, economic theory, and in the overall design of the financial system that led to the crisis of 1929. The same is true of our latest crisis.

This chapter therefore focuses on the ideas and principles that should guide radical reform. It explains why better run banks will never be an adequate answer. It identifies three elements of the pre-crisis orthodoxy that we must discard if we are to design an effective response. And it argues that our objective cannot be simply to make the financial system itself more stable, or to fix "too big to fail," but must be to manage the quantity and influence the allocation of credit in the real economy

Irrelevant Bankers

"After a crisis," Hyman Minsky observed, "it is always possible to construct plausible arguments … that accidents, mistakes, or easily corrected shortcomings were responsible for the disaster." In the wake of our latest crisis, numerous mistakes and shortcomings have been identified. Bad lending, poor risk management, and misaligned incentives played a major role. But adequately radical reform must reflect the paradox that good lending can be bad and good risk management can make the system more unstable. And while bad incentives mattered, delusions and mistaken ideas were more important still.

GOOD LENDING CAN BE BAD—THE SOCIAL EXTERNALITY OF DEBT POLLUTION

There was lots of bad lending before the crisis. In the U.S. subprime mortgage market, lenders made loans to borrowers who could not possibly repay out of income. For the borrowers the loans only made sense if house prices rose and loans could be refinanced. For lenders, the loans worked because they could sell them on to other investors, through the multistep distribution chains described in Chapter 6. Some bankers got rich by selling securities whose value they doubted to investors whose judgement they mocked. The U.S. authorities have rightly brought poor conduct cases against several major banks, with large fines and restitution payments. A new agency—the Consumer Financial Protection Bureau—will in the future regulate selling practices for mortgages and other consumer credit.

In the United Kingdom some commercial real estate lending was conducted with such poor controls that the Financial Services Authority was able to bring successful regulatory cases against both a bank and an individual banker.[5] The Spanish and Irish real estate booms were driven by some lending that was clearly reckless. Bad lending drove some banks to the verge of bankruptcy and made taxpayer bailouts essential to prevent an even worse depression than actually occurred.

Extensive bad lending before the crisis justifies a regulatory response. Bank supervisors must demand high standards in loan underwriting, and bank executives and directors should be more accountable for reckless decisions. But policy priorities must also reflect two facts. First, the direct costs of taxpayer bailout were the small change of the economic harm wrought by the crisis. Second, lending that is "good" from a private perspective could cause harm even if no bank ever went bankrupt and no taxpayer capital injection were ever required.

By "good lending" I mean loans where there is a high probability that the loan can be repaid, and where the likely loan losses suffered by the lender over the economic cycle are more than covered by the interest rate charged and can be absorbed by the bank's capital without any need for taxpayer bailout.

Most lending before the crisis was on this definition "good." In most countries the vast majority of residential mortgage borrowers will meet their loan obligations. Indeed, in the United Kingdom, mortgage losses in the years following the 2007–2008 crisis have turned out to be very low; much lower, for instance, than in the early 1990s recession.

But the debt overhang effect described in Chapter 5 can be driven as much by borrowers who *do* pay off their loans as by those who do not. Most of the Japanese companies whose deleveraging drove the balance sheet recession described by Richard Koo did not default on their loans.[6] But their determination to pay down debt still drove the Japanese economy into deflation and slow growth. Most of the U.S. householders described in Mian and Sufi's *House of Debt* will at the end of the day have paid off their mortgages in full, but their sudden switch from exuberant confidence before the crisis to concern about debt burdens post-crisis produced cuts in consumer expenditure that drove the United States into recession.

"Good lending" can generate bad aggregate effects, just as carbon emissions from the most efficient car or power plant still contribute to global warming. Lending, even when good, can impose a negative social effect—what economists label a negative externality—which private lenders do not and cannot be expected to take into account. Debt can be dangerous, even if all bankers are as honest, responsible, and professional as possible, and even if each individual loan seems in itself socially useful and economically sustainable. We therefore need strong public policies to constrain the total quantity of credit created and not solely to ensure solvent and better run banks.

SOPHISTICATED RISK MANAGEMENT MADE THE SYSTEM MORE UNSTABLE

All advanced economy banks suffered big share price falls in 2008, but most survived without taxpayer support. Lessons can be learned from the relative winners. Simple caution—a banker's gut intuition that markets were too exuberant and that it was time to let others take market share—was often as important as any sophisticated risk management techniques.

But some banks were also better at using risk management tools to spot market trends early and exited trading positions to avoid loss. The less capable suffered disproportionate losses. The UK Financial Services Authority's report into the failure of the Royal Bank of Scotland noted that the bank lacked best-practice systems to monitor rapidly changing risks, and that its mark-to-market valuations of trading positions were toward the less prudent end of the acceptable spectrum.[7] It was left holding securities that more competent banks had sold.

But that does not mean that if all banks had had excellent risk management systems, disaster would have been averted. For as Chapter 6 describes, the sophisticated risk management techniques deployed—secured lending against collateral, mark-to-market accounting, the calling of margin, and Value at Risk models—hardwired the system's tendency to produce self-reinforcing credit and asset price cycles. Better risk management could advantage one bank relative to others, but moving every bank to best practice could paradoxically make the *overall* system more unstable.

The economist Hyun Shin has likened instability in secured funding markets to the alarming and self-reinforcing wobble that afflicted London's new Millennium Bridge when it first opened.[8] Initially random patterns of pedestrian weight distribution could produce small initial wobbles that disoriented people. But the way in which people then responded, moving weight between their feet to stabilize themselves, had the collective effect of making the wobble worse. Some people in such an environment will be more adept than others, better able to move their weight and keep their balance. Others may actually fall over. But the movements of the successful contribute as much to the collective instability as those of the unsuccessful.

The banks that proved most adept at risk management in credit securities and derivatives trading—and as a result managed to offload their positions on to others before large losses were suffered—contributed to the instability of the whole system quite as much as those who came close to bankruptcy and were bailed out by taxpayers. Better risk management systems alone thus cannot make the whole system more stable.

Put Options, Incentives, and Delusions

People are justifiably angry that bankers were highly paid for activities that led to economic disaster. There seem to be private gains and public losses. Before the crisis many traders were paid huge cash bonuses for trading activity that left behind a trail of toxic assets and losses; but the bonuses could not be clawed back. Highly paid bankers enjoyed a "put option" on to their shareholders: they took the upside, and the shareholders took the downside. But beyond a certain level of losses, shareholders had a put option on to the state—once the losses eroded bank capital, the taxpayer took the hit.

New rules on remuneration were therefore needed. Regulations now in force in Europe, though sadly not elsewhere, require bonuses to be deferred, subject to potential clawback, and to be paid primarily in non-cash form.[9] Ideally these regulations should be strengthened. Deferral periods should increase, and deferred bonuses should be paid not in equity but in subordinated debt whose value entirely disappears if a bank fails or has to be rescued by the state.

But we must not overstate the importance of bad incentives. There certainly were individual traders cynically aware of huge risks but hoping to get big bonuses before the bubble burst. But there is no evidence that such cynical awareness was common among chief executives. Dick Fuld, the head of Lehman Bros, owned Lehman shares worth close to $1 billion in 2007, all of which was lost in Lehman's failure. Fred Goodwin, the chief executive of Royal Bank of Scotland, owned £5.7 million worth of the bank's stock and options in 2007, the value of which fell 97% by the end of 2008.

Bad decisions in the run-up to the crisis primarily reflected not cynicism but delusion. The decisionmakers at banks that made big mistakes did not consciously seek to take risks, get paid, and get out: they honestly but wrongly believed that they were serving their shareholders' interests.

In summer 2007, Citicorp's Chief Executive Chuck Prince made a subsequently infamous comment. "As long as the music is playing," he said, "you've got to get up and dance. We're still dancing."[10] He meant that Citicorp would keep trading credit securities even if there were growing risks. He thought it in the best interests of shareholders to make current profits and maintain market position even if this meant some losses in the medium term. Neither he nor the Citicorp board remotely envisaged how large those later losses would be. And if the losses had been in line with their mistaken expectations, keeping dancing might well have been in shareholders' interest.

Those mistaken expectations in turn reflected beliefs about the stability of the financial system that turned out to be utterly wrong but were endorsed by trusted public authorities. If the IMF honestly believed and told the market that financial innovation had made the global financial system safer, it is not surprising that bank senior executives thought the same. Fixing remuneration structures is important, but it is far less important than implementing reforms that address the fundamental drivers of financial instability.

Mistaken Ideas

Chapter 1 describes three ideas that seemed to justify pre-crisis confidence in the benefits of increased financial activity. Market completion and increased market liquidity improved allocative efficiency, low and stable inflation was sufficient to ensure financial and economic stability, and credit growth was vital for economic growth. Effective reform requires rejecting all three.

Less Liquid and Less Complete Markets Can Be Good

Economic theory tells us that if all markets are complete, maximum possible efficiency will be achieved. In fact all economists recognize that this bliss point of perfect efficiency is unattainable in the real world. But the idea of market completion still had a pervasive influence on pre-crisis policy. Derivatives were said to enhance economic efficiency, because they made possible new forms of risk transfer. Increased market liquidity was beneficial because it enabled better price discovery. And regulators, such as the UK Financial Services Authority, felt compelled to avoid actions that might have a "chilling" effect on financial innovation or reduce liquidity in traded markets.

Faith in the virtues of market completion and liquidity became a belief system so obviously true that it could hardly be questioned, and it was justified by proofs that were essentially circular. Alan Greenspan in 2005 proposed that "the clearest evidence of the perceived benefits that derivatives have provided is their continued spectacular growth."[11] Derivatives were good, because they made markets more liquid and complete, and the proof for that was that liquidity in derivative markets had grown. Greenspan indeed was effectively the high priest of the faith, and heretics were aggressively dismissed. When in 2005 Raghuram Rajan presented to the Jackson Hole conference of central bankers and economists a paper titled "Has Financial Development Made the World Riskier?" his insightful analysis was attacked as "misguided," "problematic," and "Luddite" and as a contravention of "the Greenspan doctrine."[12]

In fact as Chapter 2 describes, market completion in financial markets can be a double-edged sword, and the impact of increased financial trading is ambivalent and depends on specific circumstances. Market completion, which makes hedging possible, also enables pure betting: and while some betting (that is, position taking) can support useful market liquidity, large-scale betting can generate harmful instability. Price discovery in reasonably liquid equity markets is useful, but at the millisecond by millisecond level is of no social value. And when financial innovation plus increased trading and liquidity were applied to the credit markets, they gave us the credit cycle on steroids (see Chapter 6). Free capital flows meanwhile, as Chapter 9 describes, can sometimes do more harm than good.

While recognizing the potential benefits of a reasonable level of market liquidity, financial regulation should not therefore be constrained by the pre-crisis belief that ever more trading, liquidity, and financial innovation is by definition good. Less complete markets can sometimes be better markets, and regulations limiting the range of financial contracts available are sometimes justified. Less trading and less liquidity could in some markets be a good thing. And some fragmentation of global capital markets could be desirable.

Inflation Targeting Is Insufficient—Bank Balance Sheets Matter

Pre-crisis monetary theory and central bank practice gravitated to the belief that provided low and stable inflation was achieved, financial and macroeconomic stability would follow. As Olivier Blanchard, chief economist of the IMF, said in 2012 "we had assumed that we could ignore much of the details of the financial system."[13] Banks were therefore almost entirely missing from central bank models—so-called Dynamic Stochastic General Equilibrium models—in which "representative households" contracted directly with "representative firms." Any focus on banks as autonomous creators of credit and purchasing power—which had been central to the thinking of such earlier economists as Wicksell, Hayek, Fisher, and Keynes—largely disappeared.

The Epilogue explores the roots of this strange amnesia of modern economics. One important factor was that that economists and policymakers drew the wrong conclusion from the observation that the growth of private bank money had no necessary and proportionate implications for price inflation. In the 1960s and 1970s monetarist theories reiterated long-familiar arguments that prices must be driven by the total amount of money in circulation, since if the supply of money exceeded individuals' or companies' "demand for money" for transactions purposes, they would increase spending and thus stimulate nominal demand. As a result, it was assumed that the velocity of circulation of money (the ratio of nominal GDP to the money stock) would be somewhat stable.

In fact velocity declined in most economies in the 1980s and 1990s, as both credit and money increased more rapidly than nominal GDP. Declining velocity (nominal GDP divided by money) was indeed the inevitable consequence of rising leverage (credit divided by nominal GDP), given that credit creation results in money. And as Chapter 7 describes, the increase in leverage (and thus falling velocity) was no mystery but followed inevitably from the fact that most credit is not devoted to financing new capital investment but to funding the purchase of already existing assets. Most "money" in advanced economies, moreover, is not held for transactions purposes but arises as a by-product of credit creation and is held as an interest-bearing store of value. The aggregate value of money balances, or of other similar bank liabilities, can therefore increase as a proportion of GDP without stimulating any necessary increase in current expenditure.[14]

As a result, stocks of credit and money (or other bank liabilities) can grow more rapidly than GDP without ever producing high inflation to which an inflation-targeting central bank will feel compelled to respond, but the growth can lead eventually to crisis and post-crisis debt overhang.

Facing declining velocity, mainstream economics wrongly concluded that if money supply and inflation were not highly correlated, aggregate levels of credit and money did not matter at all. The correct conclusion should have been that while money is not a good forward indicator of inflation, the stock of *credit* matters because of potential implications for financial stability, debt overhang effects, and deflation. In the future we need to constrain the growth of that stock.

Much Credit Growth Is Unnecessary but Potentially Harmful

The stock of private credit matters, and too much private leverage can cause economic harm. That goes against dominant pre-crisis assumptions. Credit growth was assumed essential to stimulate nominal demand,

and debt contracts enabled a mobilization of capital investment that would not occur if all investments had to be equity financed. Both narrative economic history and empirical research suggested that financial deepening—in the specific form of increased private credit to GDP— was positively correlated with growth.

As Part II argues, however, most credit in advanced economies is not needed either to spur nominal demand growth or to ensure adequate investment. But excessive credit growth, particularly when it finances existing asset purchase or consumption, can create financial instability and debt overhang.

Whereas pre-crisis theory tended to assume a positive, linear, and limitless relationship between financial deepening and economic performance, we should instead recognize an "inverted U" relationship, with increasing private leverage potentially positive for growth over some range, but becoming negative beyond some turning point. As Ross Levine and others have argued, India might well benefit if private debt to GDP were higher than today's 54% level,[15] but beyond some threshold, rising private debt to GDP can cause harm.[16]

We therefore need policy levers that can constrain excessive credit growth. But we must also address the underlying factors—real estate finance, rising inequality, and global imbalances—which left to themselves generate credit growth faster than nominal GDP growth and drive relentlessly rising leverage.

Managing Credit Creation, Not Just Fixing the Banks

Major reforms are now being implemented. Bank capital requirements have been increased, and liquidity standards imposed. Bank resolution procedures have been improved, and requirements for so-called bail-in-able debt introduced. Central clearing for derivatives seeks to reduce the dangers created by the complex mesh of contracts struck between different financial institutions. Rules on remuneration structure have been imposed, at least in Europe.

These reforms aim to make the financial system more stable, reducing the probability of a major bank failure and the danger that taxpayers will need to rescue insolvent banks. They reflect the belief that to make the system more stable, we must improve risk management and fix the bad incentives that allowed private gains and public losses.

Those objectives are important, and bad incentives certainly need fixing. Focus on the too-big-to-fail problem has in particular been justified. The root of that problem is excellently described by Anat Admati and Martin Hellwig in *The Bankers' New Clothes*.[17] Bank shareholders enjoy limited liability and thus cannot lose more than their equity stake: depositors are covered by insurance up to some level and need not worry about the risks that banks take. So it is rational for banks to maximize their own leverage, increasing returns on equity but also the probability of failure. But if public authorities simply allow large banks to fail, their collapse may produce further collapses and a harmful contraction in credit supply. Rescuing banks with public money is sometimes therefore the least bad option, but expectations of rescue mean that even uninsured depositors need not care about excessive risk taking. Left to themselves, banks inevitably choose higher leverage than is good for society as a whole.

Fixing this problem has rightly been a priority, and even if avoiding taxpayer rescue costs were the only objective, still more radical changes than those introduced would be justified. New bank resolution procedures will make it easier for public authorities to impose losses on shareholders and bondholders while ensuring that essential deposit taking and lending functions are maintained. And banks will in the future be required to issue bonds that can be "bailed in" (that is, written off or converted to equity) if needed, increasing the likelihood that banks can be kept solvent without taxpayer support. But if multiple banks were simultaneously in trouble, enforcing large losses on numerous bondholders could produce self-reinforcing shocks to confidence, which themselves generate financial instability. As Admati and Hellwig argue, it would be better simply to set much higher equity capital requirements, ensuring that equity buffers are already in place when problems arise, rather than having to be created by "bail-in."

But even that more radical solution to the too-big-to-fail problem would be insufficient to ensure more stable economies. For even banks that never fail and never need to be rescued with public money can cause economic harm if, along with all the other banks in the system, they create excessive quantities of debt. As Chapter 5 describes, a debt overhang effect could cause harm even without financial crisis, and as Mian and Sufi stress, excessive debt has been a more important driver of slow and weak recovery from the 2007–2008 crisis than impaired banks.

In the depth of the Great Depression several eminent economists presented a truly radical plan—the Chicago Plan—to President Roosevelt. That plan said nothing about punishing bankers, limiting their bonuses, ensuring good risk control, or fixing misaligned incentives. Instead it proposed abolishing fractional reserve banks. In Chapter 12 I argue that that proposal is too radical. But it certainly addressed the fundamental problem—the inevitability that a free market in banking, left to itself, will create credit in excessive and unstable amounts.

We need to build economies that do not rely on rapid credit growth to achieve adequate demand. We need to manage the quantity and influence the allocation of credit that banks create. Chapters 11–13 describe the policies required to do this.

|||||||||||||||||||||||||||||||||||||||||||||||||||||||||||||||||||||||||||||||||||||||||||||||||||||||||||||||||||||||||||||||||||

ELEVEN

FIXING FUNDAMENTALS

CHAPTER 7 POSES A QUESTION—WHETHER we need rapid credit growth and rising leverage to grow our economies, but at the inevitable cost of crisis and post-crisis debt overhang. It identifies three reasons credit growth has been unnecessarily credit intensive—the increasing importance of real estate, rising inequality, and global imbalances. We cannot wholly eliminate the impact of these factors: they reflect inherent tendencies in modern economies. But unless we at least reduce their severity, reforms to financial regulation and monetary policy alone will not deliver financial and economic stability.

Real Estate and Instability

At the core of financial instability in advanced economies lies the interaction between the potentially limitless supply of bank credit and the highly inelastic supply of real estate and locationally specific land. Unless deliberately constrained, banks and shadow banking systems can create private credit, money, and purchasing power in limitless amounts. But the locationally specific real estate that people seek to own is limited in supply: the land on which it sits is an irreproducible asset. The interaction of elastic spending power and inelastic supply makes the price of urban land highly indeterminate: London property prices are some three times their 1990 levels;[1] land prices in Japan's largest cities are about a quarter of theirs.[2] Credit and real estate price cycles, as a result, have been not just part of the story of financial instability in advanced economies: they are close to the whole story.

We cannot entirely remove this source of instability, since modern economies are inevitably real estate intensive and likely to become more so. Consumer demand for desirable real estate is highly income elastic, and rising real estate and land prices have been the predominant and inevitable driver of the increase in wealth-to-income ratios that Thomas Piketty has documented. Real estate and urban infrastructure investment will inevitably account for an increasing share of all capital investment as the prices of capital goods that incorporate information and communication technology (ICT) continue to fall. And residential mortgages are bound to account for a large share of lending, since they play an important and socially useful role in lubricating the exchange of assets within and between generations.

But these inherent tendencies make economies less stable. Higher wealth to income ratios mean that any given percentage change in wealth is larger relative to income, and thus increase the extent to which consumption and investment expenditures may respond to asset price fluctuations. Economies with higher wealth to income ratios would therefore tend to be less stable, even if debt contracts and leverage were entirely absent. But high leverage against real estate exacerbates the danger given the implications of debt contracts described in Chapters 4 and 5.

So it is precisely because modern economics are inevitably more real estate intensive that we must manage the implications. The available tools include financial regulation: Chapter 13 argues that capital requirements for real estate lending should be significantly increased, and borrower constraints such as maximum loan to value and loan to income ratios (LTVs and LTIs, respectively) imposed. But policies to address the underlying drivers of real estate supply and demand are also crucial.

Real estate prices are driven up and made more volatile by inelastic supply: easing planning constraints on new real estate development might seem the obvious answer. But it is not that easy. Powerful economic and social forces seem to drive the growth of particular cities, which attract skilled workers and economic activity in self-reinforcing clustering effects. But as people get richer, they rationally place greater value on the quality of their urban environment and on the protection of countryside close to the cities where they live, creating powerful public opposition to unconstrained building in and around the cities that face the greatest pressure. Particularly in densely populated countries, constraints on new building supply are almost certain to drive rising real estate prices: but even in lightly populated countries, clustering in a leading city can produce similar effects: Stockholm in lightly populated Sweden is a case in point.

No public policies can make these pressures completely disappear, but they may at least mitigate them. Some countries, such as Germany, are notably less affected than others by the rising importance of real estate, with property prices lower relative to income and less volatile through the cycle.[3] Multiple factors help explain this phenomenon, but the fact that Germany, unlike France and the United Kingdom, does not have one strongly dominant leading city—but multiple mid-sized cities—may be important. Analysis by McKinsey Global Institute suggests that real estate prices by country tend to be higher when a larger percentage of the population lives in dominant conurbations.[4] Public policies that encourage regional dispersion of economic development might therefore (if successful) reduce the importance of scarce urban land supply. And if that proves impossible because of the strong force of clustering effects, urban design and development policies that deliver attractive living environments despite high density will be vital to reduce pressure on land prices.

Appropriate taxation also has an important role to play. The demand for desirably located housing is highly income elastic for inherent reasons, but many tax regimes add fuel to the fire by making housing a highly favored investment. Capital gains tax regimes often exempt family homes: implicit rents on owner-occupied homes are often not taxed, making housing a capital asset that delivers a tax-free return. In some countries interest expense on mortgage debt is tax deductible for owner occupiers: and in almost all it is tax deductible for investors in rented property. In the United Kingdom this has helped finance a "buy-to-let" boom that has driven house prices higher.

There is indeed, a strong case in principle for taxing either land values or the gain from their appreciation. Land value appreciation produces wealth accumulation unrelated to the processes of innovation or capital investment that drive economic growth, and rising urban land prices are a very major contributor to the rising wealth inequalities that Thomas

Piketty has described. But while the case for land taxation was first made by the economist Henry George more than 100 years ago, few tax regimes reflect its strength.[5]

The details of appropriate policy—on both urban development and taxation—are complex and vary among countries. But the overall conclusion and implication is clear. As economies get richer, real estate and urban land will become still more important. We must mitigate that tendency as best possible to reduce the resulting risks to financial and economic stability.

Rising Inequality

Inequality is rising rapidly in both advanced and emerging economies. Chapter 7 describes the impact on the credit intensity of growth. High income earners tend to have a higher marginal propensity to save; many middle and lower income earners borrow to maintain consumption either in absolute or relative terms. Credit therefore has to grow faster than GDP simply to maintain the demand growth which would have occurred, without growing credit intensity, if inequality had not increased.

Differential access to and pricing of credit can in turn give a further twist to increasing inequality. At the top end of the distribution, access to well-priced credit increases opportunities for capital gain. At lower and middle income levels, mortgage borrowing at high LTV or LTI can result in wealth losses in post-crisis recessions. And dependence on unsecured debt at high interest rates can generate self-reinforcing poverty.

Does this rising inequality matter? Some people argue that in already rich societies, where even low incomes are high compared with the rest of the world, it does not. Others suggest that inequality at the bottom of the income distribution (for instance the bottom decile falling further behind the middle) does matter, but that the soar-away income of the very rich does not. I personally think both trends are concerning, but that debate is beyond the scope of this book. The key issue here is the danger that an increasingly unequal society means an increasingly credit-intensive economy, and as a result a potentially unstable one.

One way to address the instability problem would be to limit the availability of credit. Chapter 15 proposes much higher bank capital requirements, maximum LTV or LTI limits on mortgage lending, tight mortgage underwriting standards, and limits on the advertising of very high interest credit. These measures will make the financial system itself more stable, and will protect many customers from entering unsustainable debt contracts.

But if these were the only policies pursued, two harmful consequences might result. First we might well then face a deficiency of nominal demand. Rapid pre-crisis credit growth was not in some absolute sense required for economic growth, but because of rising inequality we needed it to offset the deflationary implications of richer people's high propensity to save. So if we remove the credit growth but not the rising inequality, we may be left with a deflationary problem.

Second, the impact on consumer welfare and inequality would be ambivalent. Some lower and middle income borrowers would be protected from the wealth destroying effects of excessive debt. But others would be disadvantaged by more restricted credit access: maximum LTV restrictions, by increasing required deposits, bite on those who have limited initial wealth.

For financial stability as well as wider social reasons, we should therefore seek to reverse or at least halt the dramatic rise in inequality. Policies to do so must reflect the root causes. Globalization of trade and capital flows has reduced the relative position of less skilled workers in advanced economies. Information and technology is almost certainly driving an increasing divergence in the free market wage rates of low and high skilled workers, and is creating opportunities for massive and rapid wealth creation by successful entrepreneurs. Financialization has itself played a major role in driving inequality at the top end of the income distribution. And Thomas Piketty argues persuasively that inequality at the top end is also driven by changing social norms and incentives, with top executive remuneration set in markets where comparative benchmarks play a crucial but circular role.[6]

The precise balance of factors is debated. But whatever the conclusion, there are strong reasons for doubting whether one of the standard answers to the problem—"let's increase people's skills"—can be more than partially effective. For as Eric Brynjolfsson and Andrew McAfee argue, an ICT-intensive world may be one in which very large differences in the free market price of labor are driven by minor differences in relative skill or simply by luck, rather than by absolute skill levels.[7] And as Thomas Piketty describes, growing income divergence can generate still greater wealth inequalities, as wealthier people save more and enjoy superior rates of return than do poorer individuals.[8]

It is therefore highly likely that offsetting the rise in inequality or even preventing further increases will require more redistribution of income and wealth, whether achieved through the tax and public expenditure system or through labor market intervention. Brynjolfsonn and McAfee argue for a basic income guarantee paid to all citizens regardless of the labor market price for their skills: higher minimum wages may also have merit. Piketty argues for a globally agreed wealth tax to offset the self-reinforcing effects of rising income inequality and wealth accumulation.

Political support for such measures may well be lacking. One of the paradoxical effects of rising inequality at the pre-tax level is that it tends to reduce rather than increase support for offsetting redistribution. But we must recognize the role of rising inequality in driving the increasing credit intensity of growth. If we fail to tackle it, we will face not only its direct adverse implications for social cohesion and human welfare, but its consequences for financial instability as well.

Global Imbalances

Large current-account imbalances have been the third driver of unnecessarily credit-intensive growth. Total surpluses and deficits increased from 0.5% to 2.0% of global GDP in the decade running up to 2008, and the resulting capital flows from surplus to deficit countries did not fund higher levels of investments but rather consumption and real estate booms. At the aggregate global level, higher consumption in deficit countries was required to offset surplus country saving and thus ensure adequate nominal demand. But the credit that fueled it resulted in rising leverage, crisis, debt overhang, and post-crisis recession. Global growth was more credit intensive that it would have been if savings and investment had been better balanced in major economies. Reduced global imbalances would help build a more stable global economy.

After 2008 some rebalancing did indeed occur. China's very large surpluses initially fell as its credit-fueled investment boom sucked in commodity imports. Japan's surpluses shrank dramatically, because the shutdown of its nuclear plants after the Fukushima accident led to increased oil and coal imports. And oil exporter surpluses fell between 2014 and 2015 in the face of oil price reductions. But huge structural imbalances still remain and in some cases have grown. China's trade surpluses returned to record levels in early 2015. Korea is running a current account surplus of 6% of GDP, up from 2% in 2007. Germany's 7% surplus is now matched by surpluses in other eurozone countries as well. Conversely, the United States and the United Kingdom continue to run large deficits. If not reduced, large global imbalances will continue to make financial and economic instability inevitable.

Reducing them requires action by both deficit and surplus countries. In the deficit countries that means constraining real estate booms, reducing inequality, and limiting the financial system's creation of excessive debt. On the surplus country side, what happens in China and in the eurozone is crucial.

China's surplus as a percentage of Chinese GDP declined significantly after 2008, from 9% to 2% in 2013.[9] But it grew again during 2014 as China's domestic investment boom slowed down, and by early 2015 the trade surplus had returned to a running rate of about 5% of GDP, implying a current-account surplus of about 3%.[10] But it is China's surplus as a percentage of global GDP that determines its impact on the global economy. That fell from 0.7% in 2008 to 0.2% in 2013, but by early 2015 it had grown back to close to 0.5% as China's overall weight in the global economy increased.[11] We have returned a considerable way toward the scale of imbalances that helped provoke the crisis of 2007–2008.

In part China's surpluses derive from exchange rate policy, with the People's Bank intervening to prevent appreciation that might hurt competitiveness and employment: a gradual appreciation of the renminbi is almost certainly appropriate. But China also needs to achieve the rebalance away from savings and investments and toward consumption, which the country's officials have talked about for many years. Better social welfare nets covering basic pension and health provision would give Chinese people the confidence to reduce high precautionary savings. Corporate savings rates could be reduced if the state-owned enterprises were required to pay larger dividends to their nominal owner, the Chinese state. Successful rebalancing also requires action to remedy the underpricing of energy and land inputs, and to curtail the subsidy that flows from household savers (whose bank deposit rates are capped) to state-owned enterprises (which borrow at cheap rates). The Chinese government is publicly committed to many of these actions following the important policy statements made at the Third Plenum in November 2013. Its success in implementing them will be as important to global economic and financial stability as many of the details of financial regulatory reform.

Changed German and eurozone policies will also be vital, with the eurozone's aggregate contribution to global imbalances now greater than in 2007. Germany has continued to run large surpluses, but whereas before the crisis these were partially offset by unsustainable deficits in such countries as Spain and Italy, almost all eurozone countries now run surpluses, and the aggregate eurozone balance has gone from a small surplus of 0.4% of eurozone GDP in 2007 to more than 3% today.[12] Simultaneous private deleveraging and public austerity has driven real domestic demand down by 4% since 2008, with the eurozone attempting to grow solely on the basis of improved export performance.[13] But eurozone surpluses have to be matched by deficits somewhere else in the world, and those deficits, if continued for many years, will inevitably be based on excessive credit growth. Before the crisis German economic growth depended on a credit boom in other countries: in the wake of the crisis, the whole eurozone has become committed to the same unsustainable model.

The most important contributor to the aggregate eurozone surpluses continues to be Germany, however, which has run surpluses of more than 5% of GDP every year since 2006.[14] These surpluses are sometimes seen as more natural than China's, since explicit policy drivers are less immediately obvious. Germany does not run its own managed exchange-rate policy: nor does it regulate interest rates to shift resources from households to companies. But as Simon Tilford of the Centre for European reform has argued persuasively, Germany's imbalances are still the result of deliberately chosen domestic policies.[15] Labor market reforms introduced in the early 2000s deliberately reduced the bargaining power of labor. As a result, private-sector real wages are up just 4% since 1999, and public-sector real wages have actually fallen. Taxation policies favor corporate profits at the expense of consumption: taxes on the latter have risen sharply, while the former are more lightly taxed than in almost all other OECD countries. And the determination to balance the fiscal budget has magnified rather than offset the impact of gradual private-sector deleveraging.

Consumption demand has been depressed, and low corporate investment has in turn reflected low expectations of future consumption growth. So Germany has had to rely on overseas demand to achieve full employment, accumulating large financial claims against the rest of the world. But since these claims have been matched by unsustainable credit growth in other countries, large investment losses have been the inevitable result. German banks were among the biggest losers from exposure to poor quality U.S. mortgage securities, and Tilford estimates total investment losses since 1999 at a whopping €580 billion.

The current German and eurozone export-led growth model is therefore unsustainable, because it is inherently dependent on deficits and excessive credit growth in other economies. Policies that could stimulate eurozone domestic demand, considered in Chapter 15, are therefore essential not only to ensure eurozone output and employment growth but also for future global stability.

Most of the actions required to address global imbalances, in both the deficit and surplus countries, can be taken by individual nations acting independently. But some global reforms or at least coordination might play a useful role.

One reason current-account balances increased in the decade before 2008 was that several emerging nations—in particular, Asian countries that had suffered financial instability in 1997–1998—accumulated official foreign-exchange reserves for precautionary purposes. If they ever again faced sudden stops or reversals in private capital flows, they wanted sufficient reserves to prevent excessive exchange rate depreciation. That accumulation of reserves had to be offset by current-account deficits elsewhere in the world, and in particular in the United States, given the U.S. dollar's role as the dominant international reserve currency. The danger of imbalances could therefore be somewhat mitigated if we could agree reforms to the international monetary system entailing either (or both) more extensive and flexible international liquidity facilities or a move away from the dollar's dominant reserve currency role.

The importance of such reforms to the global imbalance problem should not be overstated. For while some countries have accumulated reserves for precautionary reasons, that motivation has not been important for the two biggest surplus countries—China and Germany. China's foreign exchange reserves are massively higher than required for precautionary reasons and have resulted as a by-product of domestic imbalances and exchange-rate policy, not because China has deliberately sought to accumulate reserves. And the precautionary accumulation of reserves has played no role at all in Germany's case. In both China and Germany the most important drivers of the surplus have been internal, and the solutions lie in domestic policy.

Global coordination could nevertheless in theory play a useful role, aiming to achieve commitment to simultaneous action by surplus and deficit countries. Guidelines for maximum acceptable imbalances as a percentage of GDP in both surplus and deficit countries, such as those put forward by U.S. Treasury Secretary Tim Geithner to the G20 group of major nations in 2010, are in principle highly desirable.[16] But so far, the real world policy impact of such proposals has been nil. Seven years after a crisis in part provoked by large global imbalances, the danger that they will produce future crisis remains great.

The Still Remaining Problem

Policies to mitigate the fundamental drivers of credit-intensive growth are essential: central banks and regulators alone cannot make the financial system and economies stable. But we will never be so successful in fixing the fundamentals that no other action is needed. Policies to tackle inequality will only be partially successful in the face of strong underlying trends: global imbalances may decline, but there is no certain global coordination mechanism that can eliminate them. And while we can design policies to lean against real estate price trends and volatility, modern economies will inevitably become more real estate–intensive as technology reduces the relative price of other forms of capital, and as richer people devote more of their income to competing for the ownership of desirable real estate.

Even if we achieve maximum imaginable success in addressing the fundamental drivers of credit-intensive growth, we will still be left with credit and asset price cycles arising from the interface between the in-

finitely elastic supply of private credit and money, and the inelastic supply of existing irreproducible assets (in particular, real estate).

We cannot therefore avoid the question that Hyman Minsky posed—
whether a monetary economy with debt contracts and capitalist financial institutions will ever be stable, and in particular whether stability is
possible as long as there are fractional reserve banks.

Chapter 12 therefore considers whether we should abolish banks or
by some other means radically reduce the role that debt contracts play in
our economies.

|||||||||||||||||||||||||||||||||||||||||||||||||||||||||||||||||||||||||||||||||||||||||||||||||||||||||||||||||||||||||||||||||||||||||||||||||||||||||||||||||

TWELVE

ABOLISHING BANKS, TAXING DEBT POLLUTION, AND ENCOURAGING EQUITY

Private initiative has been allowed too much freedom in determining the character of our financial structure and in directing
changes in the quantity of money and money substitutes ... in
the very nature of the system, banks will flood the economy with
money substitutes during booms and precipitate futile efforts at
general liquidation thereafter.
    —*Henry Simons,* Rules versus Authorities in Monetary Policy, *1936[1]*

If we are going to fix the financial system, we must address the key
problem: the inflexibility of debt contracts.
    —*Atif Mian and Amir Sufi,* House of Debt[2]

D EBT CONTRACTS AND BANKS make financial instability inevitable.
Left to itself, a free financial system will produce too much private
credit. Chapter 13 discusses how to manage the instability of the credit
creation cycle through monetary policy and financial regulation.

But shouldn't we fix the problem by structural reforms rather than
expecting central banks and regulators to manage an inherently unstable system? This chapter considers three possible approaches: abolishing
banks, taxing debt pollution, and encouraging equity contracts through
useful financial innovation. None provides a silver bullet, but the principles that underlie these radical proposals should guide actual policies.

Abolishing Banks: Outlawing Private Money Creation

Banks do not simply intermediate the flow of already existing money from savers to borrowers; they create credit and money, and thus generate purchasing power. Private credit creation is therefore one of two ways to increase nominal purchasing power; the other is money creation by government fiat. Fear of excessive government money creation has made it a taboo option, outlawed by many central bank legal regimes. But several economists who experienced the Great Depression concluded that private credit and money creation was the even more dangerous option. They therefore proposed to outlaw private money creation and to rely on fiat money to achieve growth in nominal demand. Effectively they wanted to abolish banks.

100% RESERVE BANKING—THE CHICAGO PLAN

Henry Simons was one of the founding fathers of the Chicago school of economics, a strong believer in the virtues of capitalism and competition and of sound money with low inflation. But in 1933 he joined other economists in proposing to President Roosevelt "the Chicago plan" which would require all banks to operate with 100% reserves."[3]

Under this plan, banks would hold money deposits for customers and make payments between accounts, but they would have no other economic function. All deposits in commercial banks would be matched by deposits at the central bank; the money supply would equal the monetary base; the "banking multiplier" through which banks create private money in addition to fiat money would be abolished. Debt contracts would still exist, but they would function outside the banking system, and lending would require the actual transfer of deposit money from the saver to the borrower. The ability of banks to create credit and money by simultaneously crediting and debiting a borrower's loan and deposit account would be eliminated.

In such a system, banks would no longer create new purchasing power. The question therefore arose, how (if at all) would an increase in nominal GDP be achieved? The answer proposed was through money creation by government fiat, with governments running each year small fiscal deficits funded not by bond issues but by the creation of pure fiat money.

Such fiat money creation was the only possible answer. But several of Chicago plan supporters believed it was also positively desirable. Irving Fisher believed that such an arrangement returned to the public authorities, and thus to the people in general, the economic benefit of new purchasing power creation, which under the fractional reserve system had been quite wrongly granted to private banks.[4] He also saw a positive benefit in the fact that the government would be able to run small fiscal deficits without incurring debt interest expense. Milton Friedman supported the same position in a 1948 article, arguing that money-financed fiscal deficits were the best way to stimulate economies in deflationary times, and that appropriate targets could ensure that the size of the unfunded deficits was compatible with a desirable slow expansion in the level of nominal GDP.[5]

Viewing the disaster of 1929–1933, economists who were strongly committed both to free markets and sound money thus supported the radical combination of 100% reserve banks and money-financed deficits. The 2007–2008 crisis has illustrated yet again what harm private credit and money creation can wreak. So is it time to return to the radicalism of Irving Fisher, Henry Simons, and the early Milton Friedman?

A recent IMF paper by Michael Kumhof and Jaromir Benes argues that we should, and sets out a detailed transition plan to achieve not only a 100% reserve system for the future but also a radical reduction in today's high level of private leverage.[6] A thoughtful book by Andrew Jackson and Ben Dyson, *Modernising Money. Why Our Monetary System Is Broken and How It Can Be Fixed*, argues the same case.[7]

RESERVATIONS

However there are three reasons for caution.

The first and most fundamental is that there may be some positive benefits to private rather than public creation of purchasing power. Wicksell's confidence that private credit creation would be optimal provided central banks set interest rates appropriately turned out to be seriously misplaced. But it could still be true that not only debt contracts but also banks can play a useful role in mobilizing capital investment that would not otherwise occur. Maturity-transforming banks enable long-term investments to be funded with short-term savings: that might seem like an illusion, a sort of confidence trick, but it may be a useful one. Inevitably it creates instability risks, but some instability may be the inevitable and reasonable price to pay to gain the benefits of investment mobilization and thus economic growth.

Moreover, any risks of private credit creation need to be balanced against the risks that would arise if we instead relied entirely, as the Chicago Plan proposed, on fiat money creation to increase nominal demand. For if we allow governments to run money-financed fiscal deficits, there is a danger that they will do so in excess or will allocate the spending power inefficiently for short-term political advantage. One of this book's messages is that we must not assume private credit creation is perfect nor treat fiat money creation as taboo, but neither should we iconize fiat money and demonize private credit. We face a choice of dangers, and the best policy is unlikely to lie at either extreme.

Second, we must certainly be clear that 100% reserve banking will not be sufficient to solve the problem of excessive private credit creation. A modern economy needs some private debt contracts both to support the mobilization of capital investment and to lubricate the exchange of existing real estate between and within generations. Proponents of 100% reserve banking argue that they can be provided outside the banking system, in ways that do not involve new money and purchasing power creation. But near-money equivalents and new credit and purchasing power can be created outside banks. If promissory notes are believed to be low risk, they can be used as a money equivalent; and as Chapter 6 describes, the development of shadow banking illustrates the remarkable ability of innovative financial systems to replicate banklike maturity transformation and thus the creation of near-money equivalents outside the formal banking system. The challenge of constraining credit and money creation would not be wholly resolved by requiring the formal banking sector to hold 100% reserves.

Third, the problems of transition from today's highly leveraged economies are significant. The plan outlined by Kumhof and Benes seeks not only to create 100% reserve banks but also to put right the problems of past excessive debt creation by writing off substantially all existing mortgage debt. Under this scheme the government would replace the mortgage debts currently sitting on bank balance sheets with newly created money reserves. But this huge benefit to one group of citizens cannot be achieved without some offsetting loss to others: in economics there are rarely free lunches, at least not on this scale. This objection might well be overcome by some different transition path in which existing bank mortgage debt ran off slowly over time, with all new bank business conducted on a 100% reserve basis. But the general point still stands: optimal social and economic policy can never focus simply on the ideal solution but is always dependent on the starting point. And for good or ill, we start with large fractional reserve banking systems and related debt contracts.

I am therefore unconvinced that it is desirable or feasible to go all the way to 100% reserve banking. But the reforms we do implement should reflect the underlying principles and insights that have motivated Chicago Plan supporters.

Money is different from other commodities, goods, or services, and neither the economic nor the political arguments in favor of free markets apply to money. Entrepreneurs should be free to innovate iPads and new restaurant formats and new car designs, and myriad goods and services we cannot yet imagine, both because that will deliver economic benefits and because the freedom to innovate is in and of itself desirable. But creating credit and money is different. It results in purchasing power, and as a result can have beneficial or harmful macroeconomic and distributional consequences.

Fisher and Simons were therefore convinced that to apply to banking the same free market principles which apply to goods and services markets was to make a category error. They were right. Credit markets raise issues of vital general public interest: free market approaches to them are simply not valid.

Even if we reject the radicalism of the Chicago Plan, we should still embrace its key conclusion. We have to constrain and manage the quantity and mix of credit that the banking or shadow banking systems create.

Taxing Debt Pollution

Debt contracts can deliver economic advantages, but they create economic risks. Those risks, however, are not apparent from a private perspective. Indeed, as Chapter 10 discusses, lending that looks good to an

individual banker or customer—loans that will be paid back in full—
can, when combined with multiple other loans simultaneously granted,
make the economy more vulnerable to crisis and post-crisis recession.
There is a negative social externality of debt creation: debt can be a form
of economic pollution.

Taxation is in principle an appropriate response. Optimal climate
change policy requires taxes on carbon emissions: so why not impose
taxes on credit intermediation? The Chicago economist John Cochrane
has made that case, arguing in particular that we should tax credit intermediation funded with short-term liabilities, since maturity transformation creates risk.[8] Any such taxes would increase the price of credit
to the real economy; but if the problem is too much debt, that could be
a good result.

In fact today most tax regimes, far from taxing credit intermediation,
favor debt contracts over equity. The overall impact of tax regimes results from the complex combined effect of corporation taxes, personal
income taxes, and capital gains taxes imposed on companies, institutional investors, and individuals. But in most countries the net effect is a
significant bias in favor of debt and in particular of leveraged real estate
investment. Almost all company tax regimes allow full tax deductibility
of interest expense: most do not treat dividend payments equally. Some
personal tax regimes allow partial or full tax deductibility of mortgage
interest payments. Even where these have been removed, as in the United
Kingdom, investment in owner-occupied property is favored over other
asset classes, since neither imputed rents nor capital gains are taxed.[9]

To different degrees in different countries, but significantly on average, tax regimes have thus effectively subsidized leveraged asset investment, both in real estate and in some other business activities. High
returns to private equity funds, for instance, often depend on leverage,
tax deductibility, and a rising market more than on superior management of the businesses in which the fund invests. Even in a taxless world,
free financial markets would have a bias to create debt in excessive quantities. But tax regimes throw more fuel on the fire.

The issue is not whether reform is desirable, but whether it can be
achieved. Economists have long argued for reducing the tax bias toward
debt, but most policymakers have concluded that significant reform is
too difficult. Almost any change would produce windfall gains and losses,

and the latter would inevitably generate political opposition. The global nature of finance also makes effective reform difficult. National governments jealously guard total autonomy in tax policy, and tax is subject to far less international coordination than is financial regulation. We have global capital standards for banks, but no global tax agreements. Cross-border lending would at least partially undermine national attempts to remove a pro-debt bias.

But despite the implementation difficulties, the desirable direction of change is clear, and national governments should make reforms that, even if imperfect, can still have some effect. Biases toward leveraged real estate investment in personal tax regimes could be reduced. Limits on the tax deductibility of interest if corporate leverage exceeds certain levels should be considered. And equity investment could be encouraged by more favorable treatment of dividend payments.

In addition we should recognize an important implication of today's pro-debt bias for optimal financial regulation. Chapter 13 proposes much higher bank capital requirements, particularly for real estate lending. Opponents will say that this amounts to a "tax on credit," increasing the cost of mortgage loans. And they will be right: since returns to equity are not tax deductible, while debt interest payments are, forcing banks to hold higher equity buffers will increase their average cost of funds. Requiring banks to hold large liquid asset reserves can have a similar effect.[10] But in a world where free markets left to themselves will produce too much debt, and where tax regimes magnify that bias, implicit taxes on credit creation can be a good thing.

Indeed, in principle the more that contracts take an equity and not a debt form, the more stable the economy will be. We should therefore also consider whether new types of equity contract could reduce our reliance on debt.

Equities and Hybrids: Socially Useful Financial Innovation?

Debt contracts are less flexible than equity contracts. That is indeed their economic advantage. It is because debt contracts give an apparently certain return that they help foster capital mobilization; if the only financial contracts were equity, the capital accumulation required to power the

Industrial Revolution and subsequent growth would have been far more difficult to achieve. But the fact that debt contracts give an apparently certain return also makes the economy unstable. It fosters the creation of excessive debt and means that debt overhang can have severe deflationary effects. As Atif Mian and Amir Sufi put it, "if we are going to fix the financial system, we must address the key problem: the inflexibility of debt contracts."

Much pre-crisis financial innovation was of little social value. But in principle financial innovation, by designing new products that overcome the inflexibility of pure debt, could help create a more stable system. Robert Shiller's book *Finance and the Good Society* explores many possibilities.[11] For instance, GDP-linked government bonds could reduce the danger that governments would have to tighten fiscal policy in the face of recession, since government debt-servicing payments would automatically fall if GDP declined.

If financial innovation is to make a major contribution to a more stable economy, it must address the largest debt category—lending against real estate. Mian and Sufi's *House of Debt* therefore concludes with a specific proposal for real estate finance reform—the innovation of "shared-risk mortgages." Under these contracts, lenders would receive not only a predefined interest payment, but also an element of return that moved with house prices in the relevant region: if prices rose, the lenders would share in the capital gain: if they fell, lenders would take some of the loss. The contract would become somewhat "contingent" on the borrower's economic circumstances. If enough people used the product, the danger of a severe debt overhang would be reduced, since household consumption would not fall as dramatically in the face of falling house prices.

The logic of this position is compelling. But it is important to understand the barriers to its acceptance and implementation and to recognize the risks as well as the advantages.

Shared-risk mortgages not only could reduce macroeconomic risks but also might seem in some senses "fairer." Islam prohibits debt contracts, because it seems unjust to hold someone to fixed interest payments if their circumstances have changed; under a shared-risk mortgage, people would no longer have to make unchanged payments despite falling housing wealth.[12] But despite these advantages, free market competition and consumer choice have not produced a major role for shared-risk mortgages. From the borrower's point of view they have one major disadvantage: if house prices rise, the borrower loses some of the upside and is less able to buy another house of equivalent price. In a world of rising house prices, individuals lose real economic opportunities if their housing equity does not rise in line with everyone else's. As a recent book on Islamic financed has noted, it has proved remarkably difficult to induce even devout Muslims to embrace Islamic-compliant mortgages.[13] Thus shared-risk mortgages may not take off without significant public policy support, for instance, through tax incentives.

And if they did take off, they might create some risks while mitigating others. Shared-risk mortgages entail someone other than the householder taking an equity position in house prices: a bank or an investor in mortgage securities shares in the upside and downside of house price movements. But while that helps hedge the borrower's risk, it would also create a new opportunity to place pure speculative bets, with investors buying house price–linked securities in the expectation of capital gain. Those speculative positions in turn could be financed by borrowing, market prices could be driven by self-reinforcing herd effects, and large-scale leveraged investment in housing equity securities could increase the volatility of house prices.

We are back to the conundrum discussed in Chapter 2: any financial innovation that completes markets, increases liquidity, and makes it easier to hedge risks simultaneously makes it easier to place bets that can increase the volatility against which people are hedging.

Financial innovation to ensure more risk sharing would certainly be desirable but is unlikely to prove a panacea.

• • •

There is no silver bullet: no single structural policy that will remove the risks created by debt contracts, private money creation, and price cycles in existing assets. We cannot therefore avoid a significant role for central banks and financial regulators in constraining and managing the quantity and the mix of debt. Chapter 13 sets out the specific policies required.

||||||||||||||||||||||||||||||||||||||||||||||||||||||||||||||||||||||||||||||||||||||||||||||||||||||||||||||||||||||||||||||||||||||||

THIRTEEN

MANAGING THE QUANTITY AND MIX OF DEBT

> The central question is whether central banks can contain the
> instability of credit and slow speculation to avoid its dangerous
> extension.
> —*Charles Kindleberger*, Manias, Panics and Crashes[1]

WE NEED TO LEAN AGAINST the tendency of a free financial system to create too much of the wrong sort of debt. Three things matter: the pace of credit growth, the level of private-sector leverage, and the mix of debt by category. Rapid credit growth is a strong indicator of potential financial crisis: but once financial crisis has occurred, the *level* of private-sector leverage determines the severity of the debt overhang problem. The mix of debt by category also matters: different types of debt perform different economic functions and create different risks.

What we lack is any precise science to tell us how much debt is too much and what mix of debt is optimal. Both the harmful level of private-sector leverage and the dangerous pace of credit growth will vary among countries and over time.[2] This chapter does not therefore propose a specific set of universally applicable rules. But it does propose a clear philosophy: we need to constrain the quantity and influence the mix of debt that banks and shadow banks create. That will require five sets of policies:

- Bank regulation designed not merely to make the banking system itself safe but also to constrain lending to the real economy, particularly against real estate;
- Constraints on risky non-bank credit intermediation (shadow banking), even if these are at the expense of reduced market liquidity;

- Constraints on borrowers' access to credit;
- Measures to put sand in the wheels of harmful short-term debt capital flows; and
- Actions to ensure that there is enough credit to fund required capital investment, for instance through the creation of banks with a dedicated focus on specific lending categories.

These proposals will provoke three objections: that they interfere too much with competitive markets, that constraining credit will constrain economic growth, and that they give too much discretion to central banks / regulators and burden them with responsibility for unattainable objectives.

I respond to these objections at the end of the chapter. The first two are entirely invalid. The third raises important and difficult issues. There are dangers in complexity and in granting too much discretion; ideally, great merit resides in setting simple, precisely defined objectives to be delivered by precisely defined tools.

But we must face reality. The pre-crisis orthodoxy that we could set one objective (low and stable inflation) and deploy one policy tool (the interest rate) produced an economic disaster. We face an inherently unstable financial system, and no simple set of rules can ever make it stable. Indeed, the chapter begins by explaining why the single rule that Wicksell proposed—to set the market interest rate in line with the natural rate of interest—will never be sufficient to contain harmful credit cycles or prevent excessive leverage.

Slowing Down Credit Booms with Interest Rates

Achieving low and stable inflation cannot be the sole objective of central bank policy; aggregate financial balance sheets matter not because rising money balances are good forward indicators of inflation, but because credit and leverage growth are forward indicators of crisis, post-crisis debt overhang, and potential deflation. But one could agree with that and yet still believe that the most effective way to lean against credit and asset price booms is by raising interest rates.

That argument has been made by William White, former chief economist at the Bank for International Settlements, and one of the few economists who warned of the dangers of increasing leverage before the crisis.[3] His analysis draws on Wicksell's theory. For many years before 2008, he argues, money interest rates were set below the "natural rate of interest," which must be somewhat close to the global growth rate. With the latter around 5% in real terms, but real interest rates substantially lower, there were strong incentives to borrow money, making rapid credit growth, rising leverage, and instability the inevitable result. In the future, central banks should, he argues, slow credit booms by raising interest rates even if inflation is at or below target.

Using interest rates certainly has one major advantage over quantitative controls: their impact is less easy to avoid. Quantitative levers apply to specific categories of contract or institution and as a result create opportunities for "regulatory arbitrage": if we impose higher bank capital on banks, credit extension will move to shadow bank forms. The financial system's search for profit opportunities will thus weaken the effectiveness of any quantitative policy. In contrast, when we use interest rates, profit-seeking and arbitrage ensure that the impact will spread to every nook and cranny of the financial system, influencing the price of credit in all contracts. As Federal Reserve Board member Jeremy Stein puts it, interest rate changes "get in all of the cracks;"[4] or as Claudio Borio and Mathias Drehmann of the Bank for International Settlements say, they "reach parts that other instruments cannot reach."[5]

But the interest rate tool also suffers from a major disadvantage: different categories of credit are likely to display very different elasticities of response to changing rates. If households or commercial real estate developers expect that real estate prices will increase over the medium-term by, say, 15% per year, varying the policy interest rates by a few percentage points is unlikely rapidly to change behavior, but varying it by more may cause severe harm to business investment long before it slows down the credit and asset price boom. Between 2011 and 2013, for instance, the Swedish Riksbank attempted to slow the Stockholm credit and property boom by raising interest rates despite inflation being below target: the boom continued, but Swedish growth slowed and inflation turned negative. The policy was abandoned in 2014.

Indeed, the essential problem is that when credit is used for different purposes, there is no one natural rate of interest, defined by the marginal productivity of new investment, that drives borrower and lender behavior. Both borrower demand and lender willingness to lend are instead driven by expectations of future return, which are volatile over time and variable by sector of the economy.[6] And especially when return derives from the rising value of existing assets, such as real estate, expectations are endogenous and self-reinforcing. In an advanced economy where existing real estate accounts for the majority of all assets and real estate lending the majority of all credit supply, there isn't one natural rate of interest, but instead several different and potentially unstable expected rates of return.

Thus while the pre-crisis orthodoxy believed that one of the great merits of relying on interest rates was their neutral impact on the allocation of credit, in the face of multiple private expectations of return, that neutrality is a serious disadvantage. Interest rates could certainly have a role to play in constraining credit booms and should sometimes be set higher than pure inflation targeting would suggest is appropriate. But we also need quantitative levers, including ones that discriminate among different categories of credit.

Constraining Bank Credit Creation

Regulations on required capital have for many decades placed some limitations on individual banks' ability to create credit, and post-crisis reforms have significantly increased minimum requirements. But reforms should go far beyond those introduced so far and should seek to achieve far wider objectives.

CAPITAL REQUIREMENTS

Capital requirements limit the quantity of loans or other assets that banks can hold as a multiple of their equity or other capital.[7] Post-crisis reforms have increased the absolute minimum equity requirement from 2% of "risk-weighted assets" to 4.5%, and the effective regulatory requirement for major banks is much higher still, in the 7–10% range.[8] But

Admati and Hellwig's *The Bankers' New Clothes* argues for far higher requirements. Banks should, they believe, hold equity capital equal to 20–25% of the gross unweighted value of their assets, increasing effective equity requirements by some four or five times.[9] They are right, but not only for the reasons they give.

Admati and Hellwig's case for much higher capital buffers focuses primarily on financial stability benefits, reducing the risks of bank failure, and fixing the too-big-to-fail problem. They aim to remove the put option implicit in high bank leverage rather than to constrain credit growth. Indeed, they stress that higher bank capital requirements will not necessarily constrain the growth of credit to the real economy or increase its cost. The equity required to back loans would increase, but investors who had previously held deposits or bank debt securities might invest instead in bank equity, so a higher dollar value of bank equity might offset the effect of a lower allowed multiple, leaving potential credit extension unchanged. The total cost of bank funding could also be unchanged, since the fact that equity is more expensive than debt would be offset by both equity and debt becoming less expensive because less risky.[10] As a result, they suggest, banking industry arguments that high equity requirements will constrain credit and thus economic growth are just another variant of "the bankers' new clothes."

Admati and Hellwig's argument that higher bank capital requirements have no impact on credit supply can be challenged. Investors do not switch between debt and equity investments in the rational and smooth fashion that economic theory suggests: imposing higher capital requirements, unless offset by other policy measures, could therefore curtail credit growth during transition to the higher standard. And because debt interest payments are tax-deductible while equity dividend payments are often not, higher equity requirements will increase the cost of bank-based credit intermediation. Implementing Admati and Hellwig's proposals would therefore mean a somewhat higher cost of credit to individuals and companies.

But this book's central argument is that we must constrain private credit growth. Much higher capital requirements would therefore be valuable both for financial stability reasons and for helping reduce the credit intensity of growth. In an ideal world, bank equity requirements would be much higher than agreed on in the Basel III negotiations, and

Admati and Hellwig's 20–25% is a reasonable target. The question, discussed in Chapter 14, is how to transition to much higher ratios without exacerbating the deflationary impact of deleveraging.

Countercyclical Capital

Much higher capital requirements would help constrain excessive credit creation over the long term. But even with much higher minimum requirements, a banking system could still generate harmful credit and asset price cycles. Banks that had to meet 20% minimum equity ratios could still fuel rapid credit growth and asset price increases in the upswing of the cycle and curtail credit supply to stay above the 20% minimum in the downswing.

So alongside higher minimum ratios applied throughout the economic cycle, we need policy levers that can lean against the cycle. The Basel III capital regime introduces for the first time a countercyclical capital buffer that can be increased in the face of rapid credit growth and removed if credit growth is anemic.

But the new regime suffers from two deficiencies. First, the guideline for applying the buffer defines excessive credit growth in terms of credit's own long-term trend.[11] On that basis, credit growth of 10% versus nominal GDP growth of 5% would be perpetually acceptable as long as credit growth was steady, even though leverage would be relentlessly rising. Second, the maximum envisaged buffer, set at 2.5%, will not be sufficient. Central banks should apply much larger countercyclical buffers if necessary to curtail credit booms, and they should consider applying them if leverage is already high and credit is growing faster than GDP, even if credit is growing in line with past trend.

Reserve Asset Ratios

Much stronger capital requirements are essential but will not be sufficient. For though the argument that higher capital requirements will not constrain credit may be overstated, it captures an important truth: capital requirements do not place an absolute constraint on credit growth, since bank equity can grow whether central banks / regulators want it to or not. Other policy levers are also needed.

One option is quantitative reserve requirements, which define the minimum reserves that commercial banks must hold at the central bank and therefore constrain the maximum quantity of bank loans (or total assets) that banks can extend.[12] Imposing them would constrain maximum bank loan growth more directly and more certainly than would equity requirements, since central banks themselves determine the quantity of reserves available.[13] Central banks can moreover choose whether to pay interest on reserves and at what rate. If they pay below-market interest rates, they essentially impose a tax on credit intermediation.

Reserve asset requirements represent a step along the road at the extreme end of which lies 100% reserve banking. The Chicago Plan would abolish fractional reserve banking: reserve requirements regulate what the allowable fraction can be. Many emerging economy central banks already use reserve asset requirements and variations in interest rates paid on them as policy tools to manage credit supply. Advanced economy central banks also did so in the past, but from the 1980s on increasingly rejected their use. Reserve asset requirements should return to the central bank toolkit.

But their implications and limitations must be recognized. Reserve asset requirements are in form a quantitative rather than a price tool, but they carry implications for interest rates. Central banks can ultimately control the quantity of reserve assets, but only if they are willing to let interest rates move to whatever level is required to constrain credit creation in line with the reserves available. So in essence reserve asset requirements achieve their effects through changes in the interest rate. As a result, the reserve asset policy tool, if applied as a proportion of all liabilities or assets, suffers from the same limitations as interest rates: different categories of credit will have very different elasticities of response.[14] We need in addition policy tools that can discriminate among different categories of credit extended.

RISK WEIGHTS TO REFLECT SOCIAL, NOT PRIVATE, RISK

Capital requirements against specific categories of lending should ideally reflect their different potential impact on financial and macroeconomic stability. Current international capital rules are designed around a completely different philosophy.

Under those rules "risk weights" are used to determine varying capital requirements by type of asset. But for the world's largest and most important banks, these "risk weights" reflect the bank's own assessment of potential loan losses on specific categories of loan.[15] Those assessments, drawing on past loss experience, usually suggest that loans to finance real estate are the safest form of lending. The resulting risk weights for prime real estate loans can be as low as 10% or even 5%, versus around 100% typical for lending to small and medium enterprises. Even if major banks hold equity equal to 10% of risk-weighted assets, equity divided by the total gross value of prime real estate loans can therefore be as low as 1% or even 0.5%.

Seen from the point of view of the individual bank, these assessments may be entirely rational and the resulting equity cushion sufficient to absorb losses. But they fail to allow for the fact that lending against real estate which is relatively safe for the individual bank can still contribute to aggregate instability through the asset price booms it helps create and the debt overhang it leaves behind. As Chapter 10 discusses, even loans that are paid off in full can—through their contribution to debt overhang effects—have harmful macroeconomic consequences. Even "good lending" can produce adverse externality effects.

Central banks/regulators therefore need to ensure that capital requirements for different types of credit reflect systemic and macroeconomic risks that it will never be rational for individual banks left to themselves to take into account. That can be achieved either through maximum gross leverage ratios (that is, capital requirements against the gross unweighted value of assets) or by setting risk weights for real estate lending significantly higher than individual bank assessments suggest are appropriate.

Regulating Shadow Banking: Less Liquid Markets for Credit Securities

The policy levers considered above would constrain (or in periods of downturn deliberately underpin) the ability of banks to provide credit to the real economy, either in total or by specific category. But the constraints could be undermined if credit creation shifted to the shadow bank sector.

As Chapter 6 argues, increased nonbank credit intermediation could in theory make the financial system more stable. But the pre-crisis developments that we label "shadow banking" replicated the distinctive features of banks—credit and money creation through maturity transformation—outside the constraints of bank regulation. Meanwhile, market reference pricing—for instance, using CDS spreads to infer the appropriate price of credit—increased the exposure of the credit intermediation system to the potential irrationality of liquid traded markets. And the very risk management devices supposed to contain the resulting risks—secured financing, mark-to-market accounting, and Value at Risk models—exacerbated the dangers. Shadow banking thus took the inherent instability of the credit and asset price cycle and hardwired it into contractual relationships, accounting rules, and pricing and risk-management models.

To manage the credit cycle, we must therefore constrain banklike activities outside the formal banking sector. The international Financial Stability Board has proposed principles and specific measures to achieve that end.[16] Crucial among them is the imposition of minimum "haircuts" in secured funding markets, such as repo markets, effectively imposing capital requirements at the level of the contract and not the institution. In the upswing of the cycle these would constrain the system's ability both to fund new credit to the real economy and to increase the scale and complexity of intrafinancial system links, since more collateral would be required to support any given level of activity.

But gaining agreement to an adequately robust approach has proved difficult. Too tight controls, the banking industry have warned, will reduce "liquidity" in crucial markets and impair the financial system's ability to provide new credit to the economy or to deliver the benefits of efficient price discovery. Similar arguments have been made against increases in the capital that banks have to hold against assets held for trading.

But if more liquidity and more credit are not limitlessly beneficial, these objections are invalid. If markets in subprime mortgage credit had been less liquid in the pre-crisis years, less subprime credit would have been extended, fewer lower income Americans would have been tempted into unaffordable debt, and the world financial system would have been more stable. Tight regulation of all nonbank activities that involve bank type risks should not be diluted out of fear that market liquidity or credit supply will be reduced.

Constraints on Borrowers and High Interest Lending

Bank capital and reserve requirements and shadow bank regulations seek to limit the quantity and volatility of credit supply. But constraints on shadow banking will inevitably be imperfect, and lending across international boundaries can undermine the impact of domestic rules. Moreover, to a degree supply-side quantity constraints work by means of price mechanisms, with higher capital or reserve requirements producing a higher price of credit. Their effectiveness can therefore be undermined if expectations of rising asset prices make borrowers inelastic in their response to increased interest rates. They need to be supplemented by quantitative constraints that limit borrower access to credit.

Maximum allowable LTV or LTI limits can be applied in the residential mortgage market and, somewhat less effectively, in commercial real estate. And they could be applied either as standards held constant throughout the economic cycle or varied across the cycle, tightened during real estate booms and relaxed in downswings.[17] Several emerging economies, and some advanced economies which managed to avoid the latest financial crisis, already apply such limits.[18] They should be part of the armory of macroprudential regulation.

Required minimum standards in mortgage credit underwriting also have a role to play. UK regulations now stipulate that mortgage lenders must not assume property price rises when assessing borrowers' ability to repay.[19] That principle should be applied in all countries.

Constraints on people's freedom to borrow are inevitably controversial. It is feared they will curtail home ownership and disadvantage people with limited initial wealth, who need to borrow aggressively to afford a home. And the immediate impact of tighter LTI or LTV limits, for any given level of house prices, will clearly disadvantage some specific individuals. But over the medium term, house prices are not a given, and easier credit access can drive price increases that squeeze buyers with limited initial wealth out of the market. Home ownership in the United Kingdom was on a downward trend in the pre-crisis decade not only in spite of, but in part because of, rapid growth of mortgage credit and the easy supply of high LTV and high LTI loans. The subprime mortgage boom in the United States ended in large losses of wealth for poorer Americans, which Mian and Sufi have described. More restricted mortgage credit supply can help make homes *more* affordable and limit the highly unequal impact of credit and asset price cycles on the distribution of wealth.

Restrictions on high interest unsecured consumer lending should also be introduced. Loans at the interest rates seen in the UK payday lending market—as much as 1,000% on an annual basis—can trap borrowers in debt dependency and exacerbate increasing inequality. Outright bans create the danger that lending moves into the informal economy. But there is a a strong case for tight regulation of pricing and credit risk assessment procedures and for limits on advertising.

Structural Reform: Ring-Fencing in and between Countries

A final set of policy levers could be important: changes to bank legal structures or mandates to constrain unnecessary capital flow and to encourage valuable forms of credit creation.

Several structural policies have already been implemented. In the United States the Volcker rule prevents commercial banks from engaging in proprietary trading. In Europe the Liikanen Group proposals require market-making and trading activities to be separated from traditional banking. The United Kingdom, following the Vickers commission, is committed to a ring-fence between "retail banking" and "wholesale banking." In addition several countries require international banks active in their markets to operate as subsidiaries rather than as branches, with capital and liquidity held at the national level and subject to national regulations and supervision.

The stated objective of these reforms is to improve the resilience of the financial system itself. Ring-fencing reduces the risk that problems in one part of the financial system produce knock-on consequences in others. It makes it easier to resolve major banks, giving resolution authorities the option of closing down some activities while ensuring the continuity of important economic functions. It reduces the likelihood that taxpayer support will be required to avoid chaotic bank failure.

All complex systems are potentially unstable. Physical engineers designing systems such as nuclear power plants deliberately create firewalls between subelements, even if doing so requires the sacrifice of maximum potential efficiency. The pre-crisis financial system was built on the hubristic belief that sophisticated risk management techniques could make a massively complicated and interrelated system stable. There would be a strong case for ring-fencing to increase resilience even if it involved sacrificing some theoretically attainable efficiency benefits.

But international capital flows often have nothing to do with the efficient allocation of capital, and a large proportion of credit creation plays no role in mobilizing investment. Ring- fencing might therefore be valuable precisely because it does curtail some forms of financial activity.

The Merits of Fragmentation

International banks with major operations in a country should operate as standalone subsidiaries, with sufficient capital and liquidity to survive parent bank failure. Many bankers strongly oppose that proposal, arguing that it leads to harmful "fragmentation" or "balkanization" of global financial markets, interrupting the free flow of capital and increasing the costs of operation, since capital and liquidity are "trapped" in national subsidiaries.

But the evidence does not suggest that all forms of capital flow are valuable. It suggests instead a hierarchy of value: foreign direct investment is beneficial due to the related transfer of technology and know-how; but short-term bank intermediated flows often exacerbate domestic credit and asset price cycles, and they sometimes drive foreign-exchange rates away from rational equilibrium levels.

Requiring banks to subsidiarize does not restrict valuable foreign direct investment or other long-term capital flows. It still leaves international banks able to compete in emerging markets, bringing the potential benefits of skill and technology transfer. It still leaves them able to finance expansion with parent company funding, provided it is long-term. But it puts some sand in the wheels of potentially harmful flows of short-term debt. It will sometimes, as opponents argue, increase funding costs and thus credit pricing, particularly during upswings of market exuberance. But if excessive credit supply can sometimes cause harm, that could be a positive result. Some fragmentation of global capital markets would be a good thing.

ENOUGH OF THE RIGHT SORT OF DEBT

Structural measures could also help ensure that the financial system provides enough of the right sort of debt. In autumn 2008 we suffered a crisis that originated in excessive lending to residential and commercial real estate in the United States and other countries; but in its immediate wake, the global supply of trade finance was severely squeezed, and credit supply to many small and medium enterprises not involved in real estate was restricted.[20] We have a financial system with a strong tendency to create excessive debt in residential and commercial real estate markets, but we still need to mobilize capital to support huge investments—for instance, in the area of clean energy—and debt finance will be essential to achieve that mobilization.

Faced with a free market bias toward real estate lending, interventions favoring other types of lending are justified. One option is to create institutions that are only allowed to lend money for specific purposes and whose capacity to do so is not vulnerable to losses arising from real estate loans. The German publicly owned banking group KfW has a mandate that requires particular focus on sustainable development and the supply of finance to small and medium enterprises. The United Kingdom's Green Investment Bank has been established to lend to clean energy projects. Such institutions are not dangerous diversions from efficient free market capital allocation, but are essential to offset the misallocation that entirely free markets can produce. Chapter 8 describes how the most successful developing economies deliberately directed credit flows toward productive investment: their example remains relevant today.

Economic textbooks typically assume that banks lend money to entrepreneurs and businesses to fund capital investment. Interventions to bring reality in line with theory can play a useful role.

Anti-Markets and Anti-Growth?

The reform agenda set out above represents a dramatic rejection of the pre-crisis orthodoxy. Some elements of it—such as the importance of countercyclical capital requirements—are already accepted by most central banks and financial regulators. But others go far beyond the post-crisis consensus in two ways: first in focusing on the *level* of leverage as well as the pace of credit growth, and second in arguing that we must influence the allocation of credit among alternative uses.

These elements will be criticized as dangerously interventionist, replacing the allocative wisdom of the market with imperfect public policy judgements. But free markets in credit creation can be chronically unwise and unstable. That was why such economists as Henry Simons, in every other respect an extreme free marketeer, believed that banks should be abolished. I do not go that far. But we need to recognize that free markets do not ensure a socially optimal quantity of private credit creation or its efficient allocation. We should not intervene in the allocation of credit to specific individuals or businesses; but we must constrain the overall quantity of credit and lean against the free market's potentially harmful bias toward the "speculative" finance of existing assets.

The program will also be criticized because it means "less credit to fuel economic growth." And there will indeed be less credit. But as Chapter 7 discusses, that does not mean less growth, since a large proportion of credit is not essential to economic growth; does not produce a proportionate increase in nominal demand; and leads to crisis, post-crisis debt overhang, and recession. Our explicit objective should be a less credit-intensive economy.

Too Much Discretion and Too Much Responsibility?

The reform agenda outlined above would equip central banks, as macroprudential authorities, with multiple tools and wide-ranging responsibilities. Some of the tools could take the form of constant rules, for instance, much higher capital requirements. But some require decisions made over time in response to the evolving economic cycle. Those decisions cannot be based on a precise science: they need to reflect judgments amid uncertainty.

Decisions on countercyclical capital buffers, for instance, need to reflect both the rate of credit growth and the level of leverage already achieved. But we do not know for certain how much private leverage is "too much." A paper by Stephen Cecchetti, former chief economist at the Bank for International Settlements reached the tentative conclusion that effects become negative if either corporate debt goes above 90% or household debt above 85% of GDP.[21] But it rightly stresses the uncertainty of any such estimates. Similarly in relation to asset prices, we know that credit-fueled bubbles cause harm, but deciding when the bubble has started and the size of the divergence from rational equilibrium values is an art, not a science.

Many central bankers and economists are therefore wary of the need for discretionary decisions. Many hanker for the clarity and simplicity of the pre-crisis orthodoxy. The combination of one objective (price stability) and one instrument (the interest rate) allowed clear accountability. It buttressed central bank independence, because central banks could pose as neutral technicians, devoted simply to attaining a defined objective that everyone agreed was desirable. It was a clear, precise, and intellectually elegant policy framework; and it ended in economic disaster.

Unavoidable uncertainty about precise optimal results cannot be an excuse for reverting to the comfort zone of the pre-crisis orthodoxy. We should address as best we can the fundamental drivers of credit-intensive growth discussed in Chapter 11. We should seek as best possible to reform tax regimes and to encourage the new forms of equity contract discussed in Chapter 12. We should rely as much as possible on constant rules, such as higher capital requirements, and on structural changes, such as ring-fencing, to build a system that is inherently more stable.

But we cannot escape the need for discretionary decisions in managing the instability and inefficiency of private credit creation. As Hayek, Minsky, and Simons rightly argued, private credit creation is inherently unstable, and there is no set of rules that can be defined once and forever to fix that problem.

Escaping the Debt Overhang

||||||||||||||||||||||||||||||||||||||||||||||||||||||||||||||||||||||||||||||||||||||

PART IV DESCRIBES THE POLICIES required to build less credit-intensive and more stable economies in the future. Part V answers a different question: how to escape from the debt overhang left behind by past policy mistakes.

Faced with deleveraging and too low inflation, all traditional policy levers appear to be blocked. But inadequate nominal demand is one problem to which there is always an answer, provided we are willing to consider all policy options, including overt money finance, creating additional fiat money to finance increased fiscal deficits.

Chapter 14 describes how that option works, why it may well be essential, and why there is no technical reason it must result in excessive inflation. Chapter 15 addresses the more difficult issue: whether we can design political constraints to guard against excessive use of this potentially valuable tool.

In some countries that should be feasible: in the eurozone it may prove impossible. But if fiat money creation is dismissed as too dangerous, we will suffer for longer from debt overhang and low growth, and increase the risk that excessive private credit creation leads again in the future to instability and crisis.

||||||||||||||||||||||||||||||||||||||||||||||||||||||||||||||||||||||||||||||||||||||||||||||||||||||||||||||||||||||||||||||||||||||||||||||||||||||||||||||||

FOURTEEN

MONETARY FINANCE—BREAKING THE TABOO

The current phase of the official policy approach is predicated on
the assumption that debt sustainability can be achieved through a
mix of austerity, forbearance and growth.... This claim is at odds
with the historical track record of most advanced economies.
—*Carmen Reinhart and Kenneth Rogoff, "Financial and Sovereign
Debt Crises, Some Lessons Learned and Those Forgotten"*[1]

Consider for example a tax cut for households and businesses that
it is explicitly coupled with incremental Bank of Japan purchases
of government debt -so that the tax cut is in effect financed by
money creation.
—*Ben Bernanke, "Some Thoughts on Monetary Policy in Japan"*[2]

SEVEN YEARS AFTER THE 2007–2008 financial crisis the world's major
economies are still suffering its consequences. Eurozone GDP has
not yet returned to pre-crisis levels: unemployment is still 12%, and
inflation is far below the ECB's close to 2% target. Japan continues to
struggle with low growth and relentlessly rising public debt. The United
Kingdom has begun to grow and create jobs, but GDP per capita is still
below the 2007 level, and average real earnings are still some 6–8%
below the pre-crisis peak. The U.S. recovery has been more robust, but
the employment rate remains far below 2007 levels. Inequality has continued to increase. Across the advanced economies many people are no
longer confident that capitalist economies will deliver rising prosperity
generation after generation.

There could be some supply-side explanations for this growth slow-down. Working age population growth has slowed and in Japan has turned negative. Some economists argue that the attainable rate of pro-ductivity growth has also declined.[3] But long-term developments in supply-side factors cannot possibly explain the sudden switch from ro-bust growth in many countries before 2008 to slow or nil growth for 7 years thereafter. Low rates of inflation and nominal GDP growth mean-while make it clear that inadequate demand has played a major role. For advanced economies to grow in line with potential and with about 2% inflation, we need nominal demand to grow at something like 4–5% per year. Since 2008, actual nominal domestic demand growth has been less than 3% per year in the United Kingdom and the United States, around zero in Japan, and less than 0.5% per year in the eurozone.[4] We will never get out of the current malaise, return inflation to target, or reduce debt levels unless we increase demand in our economies.

Faced with this malaise, it can seem that all policy levers are ineffec-tive: many central bankers indeed are keen to stress the limits to what they can achieve. But inadequate nominal demand is one of very few problems to which there is always an answer. Central banks and govern-ments together can create nominal demand in whatever quantity they choose by creating and spending fiat money. Doing so is considered taboo—a dangerous path toward inflationary perdition. But there is no technical reason money finance should produce excessive inflation, and by excluding this option, we have caused unnecessary economic harm. This chapter describes why money finance of fiscal deficits is technically feasible and desirable, why it may be the only way out of our current problems, and some specific ways in which we should now use this po-tentially powerful tool.

We Never Run Out of Ammunition

The fundamental reason recovery from the Great Recession has been slow and weak is the debt overhang described in Chapter 5. Collapsing credit supply played a crucial role in driving economies into recession in 2009, but thereafter debt overhang was the dominant factor, driving reduced private credit demand. Excessive private debt creation before the crisis left many households and consumers overleveraged and determined to pay down debt. Reduced private consumption and investment then depressed economic growth, producing large fiscal deficits and rising public debt to GDP. Leverage has not gone away, but simply shifted around the economy, from private to public sectors, or among countries: German deleveraging, for instance, has only been possible because Chinese leverage has soared. Overall, developed economy leverage, public and private combined, has continued to increase slowly, and total global leverage has increased significantly as emerging economy private credit grows at a fast pace.

Attempted deleveraging has thus depressed economic growth, but no overall deleveraging has actually been achieved. And none of our traditional policy levers seem able to overcome this dilemma.

TRADITIONAL FISCAL POLICY BLOCKED, AUSTERITY INEVITABLE?

After the crisis, fiscal deficits increased substantially as tax revenues fell and social expenditures rose. In the United States the fiscal deficit rose from 3.2% of GDP in 2007 to 13.5% in 2009, in the United Kingdom from 2.9% to 11.3%, and the eurozone aggregate deficit grew from 0.7% to 6.3%.[5] Those increased deficits helped prevent still deeper recession, providing a powerful stimulus to nominal demand in the face of private deleveraging.

There is indeed no doubt that if governments run fiscal deficits—spending more than they tax and borrowing the money to cover the difference—the immediate direct effect is increased nominal demand. But in some circumstances that direct effect can be stymied by the off-setting factors discussed in Chapter 7. If short-term interest rates have already been set by the central bank at an optimal level, increased fiscal deficits will provoke rate increases that slow the economy down. If the increased issue of government bonds produces a rise in long-term interest rates, a similar "crowding out effect" may result. And if individual or corporate taxpayers rationally anticipate that fiscal deficits today mean higher taxes in the future, they may save more today, refusing to spend tax cuts or cutting their private expenditure by as much as public spending rises (the so-called Ricardian equivalence effect.)

Pre-crisis macroeconomic theory therefore tended to the belief that fiscal policy had little potential to stimulate even nominal demand, let alone to produce an increase in real output. The counterargument, powerfully put by Brad DeLong and Lawrence Summers,[6] is that in the special circumstances of post-crisis recession, the offsetting factors do not apply. With central banks determined to keep interest rates close to zero, increased fiscal deficits will not provoke rate increases. There is underemployment and spare capacity, so the direct stimulus effect will produce additional real growth as well as price inflation; fiscal deficits might therefore pay for themselves, generating faster growth in GDP than in the stock of debt and thus actually reducing the future debt to GDP ratio. As a result, rational individuals and companies will not worry about how increased public debt can be repaid.

A strong case can therefore be made that fiscal policy stimulus should have been deployed even more aggressively in the aftermath of 2008. Some estimates suggest that UK GDP was depressed by 3% as result of unnecessarily aggressive fiscal consolidation after 2010.[7] And there is no doubt that in the eurozone, where the aggregate fiscal deficit has averaged 1.6% between 2008 and 2013 versus 7.2% in the United States and 6% in the United Kingdom, fiscal austerity has significantly depressed growth.

But the constraints on our ability to use fiscal stimulus must still be recognized. Even if in some circumstances incremental fiscal stimulus might reduce future public leverage relative to a no-action alternative, the large deficits actually run up have been accompanied by big increases in public debt to GDP—up from 72% to 105% in the United States, from 51% to 91% in the United Kingdom, and from 40% to 90% in Spain, for instance.[8] And while huge Japanese public deficits after 1990 may, as Richard Koo has argued, have helped offset the deflationary impact of private deleveraging, Japan is still left with the question of how its relentlessly rising public debt can be repaid. In the eurozone, fears that rising public debt burdens in peripheral countries might provoke default or eurozone exit did result in rising interest rates, exacerbating the danger that debts would become unsustainable and increasing the cost of credit to the private sector.

Thus there are limits to our ability to use traditional fiscal stimulus to escape the debt trap. Carmen Reinhart and Kenneth Rogoff's analysis suggests that if public debt levels rise above about 90% of GDP, adverse consequences for growth are likely to follow.[9] Controversy over their calculations shows that we must not overstate the importance of any one specific threshold. But their overall conclusion that high debt to GDP ratios will inevitably constrain the scope for fiscal policy stimulus is valid.

It is important not to misinterpret this finding. It most certainly does not mean that fiscal austerity is costless because of some so-called confidence-inducing effect. Indeed, the best interpretation of Reinhart and Rogoff's empirical results is that the adverse effect on growth that they observe derives primarily and directly from the fiscal tightening that high levels of accumulated debt appear to make necessary.

That makes it crucial to constrain public debt levels in the good years—and also crucial to restrict excessive private credit creation in the fashion described in Part IV, reducing the danger that excessive debt will shift to the public sector in the aftermath of crisis. But it also means that we need to find ways to stimulate nominal demand that do not result in rising public debt.

Ultra-loose Monetary Policy and Adverse Side Effects

For seven years, central banks have tried to use ultra-loose monetary policy to stimulate the economy. Short-term interest rates have been close to zero in the United States and the United Kingdom since 2009, in Japan for much longer, and in the eurozone since 2013. Quantitative easing—central bank purchases of government or other bonds—has been used in Japan, the United States, and the United Kingdom to drive down long-term interest rates; in March 2015 it was also finally deployed in the eurozone. And central bank liquidity and funding schemes—such as the Bank of England's Funding for Lending Scheme and the ECB's Targeted Long-term Repo Operation—have sought to ensure that real economy households or businesses, as well as financial market traders and investors, can borrow at low interest rates.

Those policies have almost certainly generated faster nominal demand growth than would otherwise have occurred and helped prevent either still lower inflation or still lower real growth. But they have suffered from two deficiencies. First, they have proved insufficient to deliver robust growth, with recovery still anemic and inflation falling below target in all major economies. Still lower (that is, negative) rates would have delivered more stimulus, but if central banks set rates at a more than marginally negative level, individuals and companies would convert bank deposits into currency notes and the stimulus effect would be undone.[10]

Kenneth Rogoff has argued that we should overcome this problem by abolishing paper currency, with all money held in deposit form:[11] central banks could then set interest rates at significantly negative levels. But that option is not available today: and if it were available and used, it would exacerbate the second deficiency of ultra-loose monetary policy—its adverse side effects. Quantitative easing works because low long-term yields drive up asset prices and wealth, and thus stimulate asset holders to consume or invest more; it is therefore bound to increase inequality. Sustained ultralow interest rates, meanwhile, are likely to encourage risky and highly leveraged financial speculation long before they stimulate real economy demand. And they can only stimulate real economy demand by encouraging a return to the private credit growth that first created the debt overhang problem. As Chapter 5 describes, the United Kingdom's Office of Budget Responsibility forecasts that UK private leverage, having declined slightly over the past 5 years, will by 2020 have risen to its highest ever level.

The IMF was therefore right to warn in its October 2014 Global Financial Stability Report that "the extended period of monetary accommodation and the accompanying search for yield is leading to credit mispricing and asset price pressures and increasing the danger that financial stability risks could derail the recovery."[12] But in its simultaneously published World Economic Outlook, the IMF also warned that increased nominal demand is needed and that "in advanced economies, this will require continued support from monetary policy."[13] With fiscal policy blocked, ultra-loose monetary policy thus seems simultaneously both dangerous and essential. Fortunately, however, there is an alternative.

Helicopter Money with Fractional Reserve Banks

It was Milton Friedman who explained most clearly why inadequate nominal demand is one problem to which there is always a possible solution. If an economy was suffering from deficient demand, he suggested, the government should print dollar bills and scatter them from a helicopter. People would pick them up and spend them: nominal GDP would increase: and some mix of higher inflation and higher real output would result.[14]

The precise impact of any given size of helicopter money drop would depend on how much people spent rather than saved their new-found financial wealth. But it would clearly be somewhat proportional to the value of bills printed and dropped. If they were only worth a few percentage points of current nominal GDP, the stimulus to either real growth or inflation would quite small. If they were worth many times nominal GDP, the effect would be large and primarily take the form of increased inflation, since the potential for real output growth is constrained by supply factors.

Thus while Friedman's example is very simple, it illustrates three crucial truths. We can always stimulate nominal demand by printing fiat money: if we print too much, we will generate harmful inflation; but if we print only a small amount, we will produce only small and potentially desirable effects.

The money drop from Friedman's helicopter is fiat money in currency note form—actual dollar bills. And as Chapter 7 describes, there are historical examples of governments that used printed currency to stimulate nominal demand but without generating dangerously high inflation. The Pennsylvania colony did so in the 1720s, and the Union government paid its soldiers with printed greenbacks in the American Civil War. However most money today is held in bank deposit, not paper currency, form.

But the essential principle of the helicopter money drop can be applied in the modern environment. A government could, for instance, pay $1,000 to all citizens by electronic transfer to their commercial bank deposit accounts. (Alternatively, it could cut tax rates or increase public expenditure.) The commercial banks in turn would be credited with additional reserves at the central bank, and the central bank would be credited with a money asset—a perpetual non-interest-bearing bond due from the government.[15] The "drop" is of electronic accounting entries rather than actual dollar bills, but the operation is in essence the same and so too would be the first round impact on nominal demand. Nominal demand would be stimulated, and the extent of that stimulus would be broadly proportional to the value of new money created.

Printing money in its modern electronic form is thus without doubt a technically possible alternative to either pure fiscal or pure monetary policy. It is indeed essentially a fusion of the two. It entails monetary finance of an increased fiscal deficit, and it would stimulate demand more certainly and with less adverse side effects than either pure fiscal or pure monetary policy. Compared with funded fiscal stimulus, it is bound to be more stimulative, since there is no danger of either crowding out or Ricardian equivalence effects: as Ben Bernanke put it in 2003, if consumers and businesses received a money-financed tax cut, they would certainly spend some of their windfall gain, since "no current or future debt servicing burden has been created to imply future taxes."[16] And compared with a pure monetary stimulus, it works through putting new spending power directly into the hands of a broad swath of households and businesses, rather than working through the indirect transmission mechanism of higher asset prices and induced private credit expansion. It does not rely on regenerating potentially harmful private credit growth, nor does it commit us to maintaining ultralow interest rates for a sustained period of time.

Our technical ability to stimulate nominal growth with money-financed deficits is not therefore in any doubt. A formal mathematical paper by Willem Buiter confirms the commonsense arguments of Friedman and Bernanke. His paper is titled "The Simple Analytics of Helicopter Money: Why It Works—Always."[17]

The crucial issue indeed is not whether money-financed fiscal deficits are feasible and potentially beneficial in the short term, but whether we can contain their long-term impact in a modern economy with fractional reserve banks. For though the first round impact of an electronic deposit drop is determined simply by its size, the exercise creates additional commercial bank reserves at the central bank and thus makes it easier for banks subsequently to create additional private credit, money, and spending power. While Chapter 7 describes private credit creation and fiat money creation as alternatives, in a fractional reserve banking system the latter can facilitate the former.

Thus the danger exists that the initial stimulative effect of money finance will be harmfully multiplied by subsequent private credit creation, producing more demand stimulus than desired. That danger would not arise in a system of 100% reserve banks of the sort that Irving Fisher and

Henry Simons supported in the 1930s, and that Milton Friedman recommended in 1948. In such a system the monetary base is the money supply, private credit and money creation play no role, and the final long-term stimulative effect of money finance is bound to be broadly proportionate to its initial size. For Fisher, Simons, and Friedman in 1948, 100% reserve banks and overt money finance of small fiscal deficits were thus a logically linked package. The latter made it unnecessary to rely on unstable private credit creation to grow nominal demand; the former both made private credit creation impossible and ensured that the long-term stimulative effect of money finance could be precisely controlled.

Fractional reserve banks thus complicate the implementation of money finance, but the model of 100% reserve banks also suggests the obvious solution: any dangers of excessive long-term demand stimulus can be offset if central banks impose reserve asset requirements. These requirements would force banks to hold a stipulated percentage of their total liabilities at the central bank and thus would constrain the banks' ability to create additional private credit and money.[18] Those ratios could be imposed on a discretionary basis over time, with the central bank increasing them if inflation threatened to move above target. But they could also in theory be deployed in an immediate and rule-driven fashion, increasing the required reserves of commercial banks at the same time as the electronic money drop and by precisely the same amount.

This would essentially impose a 100% reserve requirement on the new fiat money creation. We can in effect treat the banking system as if it were in part a 100% reserve system and in part a fractional reserve: we do not have to make an absolute either / or choice.

The precise future consequences of reserve requirements would also depend on whether the central bank paid interest on them and at what interest rate. Central banks can choose to pay whatever rate they want on required reserves, but the rate would have to be zero on at least some reserves to ensure that money finance today does not result in an interest expense for the central bank in the future or in central bank losses that would need to be paid for by government subsidy and ultimately by taxpayers.[19] Setting a zero interest rate for reserve remuneration might in turn seem to impair the central bank's ability to use reserve remuneration as a tool to bring market interest rates in line with its policy objective.

But central banks can overcome this problem, for instance, by paying zero interest rates on some reserves, while still paying the policy rate at the margin.[20]

Reserve requirements remunerated at a zero interest rate in turn effectively impose a tax on future credit creation. But as Chapters 12 and 13 argue, taxing credit creation might be a positively good thing. Our challenge is to find a policy mix that gets us out of the debt overhang created by past excessive credit creation without relying on new credit growth. Money-financed deficits today plus implicit taxes on credit intermediation tomorrow might well be the optimal combination.

Friedman was right: governments and central banks together can always overcome deficient nominal demand by printing and spending money. That is just as well, since without the option of money finance there may be no good way out of our debt overhang predicament.

Deleveraging—No Other Good Way Out?

Total economywide leverage in advanced economies, public and private combined, is now at levels only previously seen in the aftermath of major wars. Analysis of how deleveraging from previous peaks was achieved illustrates just how difficult it will be from today's levels.

The United Kingdom came out of the Second World War with public debts of 250% of GDP but was able to reduce these to 50% by 1970. That reduction was not achieved by paying down absolute debt levels; instead it resulted from 25 years in which nominal GDP grew at about 7% per year, while interest rates averaged much less. That nominal GDP growth rate in turn reflected both average inflation of more than 4% (well above current central bank targets), and a real growth rate of almost 3%, made possible both by significant demographic expansion and by technological catch up toward U.S. levels of productivity.[21] Moreover, a falling public debt ratio was accompanied by private debts rising slowly from low levels and constrained by quantitative credit controls. Residential mortgages were only provided by building societies (mutual savings and loans institutions), not by banks, and consumer credit availability was limited by rules on minimum down payments and payback periods. In 1964 total private sector bank debts, household and company combined, were still just 27% of GDP rather than the 120% reached by 2007.[22] The same pattern of rapid nominal GDP growth, low interest rates, and low but rising private leverage also lay behind the United States' success in cutting public debt from 120% of GDP in 1945 to 35% in 1970.[23] Across continental Europe, meanwhile, wartime debts were in many countries eroded by high inflation or debt writeoff in the immediate aftermath of the war.

The historical experience thus illustrates that public deleveraging is possible, but it also indicates how difficult simultaneous public and private deleveraging will be in today's changed circumstances. Demographic and technological factors will not allow the real growth rates observed in many advanced economies in the 1950s and 1960s; and if 2% inflation targets are considered sacrosanct, nominal GDP growth in many advanced economies is unlikely to exceed 4%. In some it will be lower still: the Bank of Japan estimates that Japan's potential growth rate is no more than 1%.[24] Even if it achieves its 2% inflation target, nominal GDP will grow at only 3%. Growing out of debt burdens will be far more difficult than in the post-war period.

Indeed, in some countries the mathematics make it impossible. The IMF Fiscal Monitor illustrates that Japan would need to turn today's primary deficit of 6.0% (that is, its fiscal deficit before interest expense) into a surplus of 5.6% by 2020 and to maintain that surplus for an entire decade to reduce net public debt to 80% of GDP by 2030.[25] This will simply not occur, and if attempted would push Japan into a deep deflationary depression in which public debt leverage, far from falling, would almost certainly rise. Japanese government debt will simply not be repaid in the normal sense of the word. Italy's public debt burden, at 132% of GDP and rising, is also now so high and the country's potential long-term growth so low that there is no clear "austerity plus growth" path to fiscal sustainability.[26]

Across the eurozone indeed, the "Fiscal Compact" requirement that all countries should reduce their debt stocks to a maximum of 60% of GDP through running primary budget surpluses is not credible. To achieve this objective, Greece would have to run a primary budget surplus of 7% of GDP for more than a decade; Ireland, Italy, and Portugal 5%; and Spain 4%. As Barry Eichengreen has pointed out, there are close to no historical examples of such large continued primary surpluses.[27]

They could only be compatible with robust growth if offset by rapid and potentially dangerous private credit growth either within the countries involved or in their export markets. And if, as is more likely, they produced low growth and sustained high unemployment, debt burdens would not in fact be reduced. In the face of such austerity, moreover, talented young people would be likely simply to leave their countries, reducing the tax base and walking away from their share of the inherited debts. Sometimes debts simply cannot be and will not be fully repaid.

Other ways out of the debt overhang will have to be found.

INFLATION AND FINANCIAL REPRESSION

As the UK post-war experience suggests, one option might be to accept many years or even decades in which interest rates are held below nominal GDP growth rates and probably indeed below inflation. One variant of this policy approach—floated by both Kenneth Rogoff and Olivier Blanchard—would entail accepting a higher inflation target than today's 2%.[28] Another would be to sustain interest rates close to zero for many more years.

But in essence this policy would be simply a continuation of today's ultra-loose monetary approach, reflecting a realistic assessment that it can only erode debt burdens significantly if maintained for far longer than currently hoped. It would therefore suffer from the disadvantages already discussed: it would help erode the value of existing debts but could only do so by stimulating new credit growth, and it would create incentives for risky financial speculation.

DEFAULT AND DEBT WRITE-OFF

If debts cannot be eroded away by either real growth or inflation, they could be reduced by default and debt restructuring. Rather than creditors receiving an undiminished nominal value degraded in real terms through inflation, the nominal value of debts could be reduced. Such debt write-offs could certainly play a useful role, but they cannot be a sufficient solution.

The extreme version of this option suggests that all we need is fiscal, monetary, and free market discipline. Governments should make their own debts sustainable by cutting expenditures or raising taxes; interest rates should return to normal levels; and in the face of subsequent recession, individuals, companies, and governments who are unable to pay their debts should default, providing a useful signal to creditors to be more careful about lending money in the future.

This policy is essentially the one proposed by U.S. Treasury Secretary Andrew Mellon in 1931—"liquidate labor, liquidate stocks, liquidate farms, liquidate real estate…. It will purge the rottenness out of the system."[29] And its consequences would be similar to those which followed in the early 1930s. For as Irving Fisher described in his theory of the "debt deflation" cycle, default and bankruptcy on a large scale drive a self-reinforcing cycle of collapsing nominal demand, as bankruptcy provokes fire sale reductions in asset prices, and as creditors facing unexpected losses themselves cut consumption and investment. The policy of applying pure free market discipline amounts indeed to a rejection of the consensus discussed in Chapter 7—that it is desirable by one means or another to achieve a slowly growing level of nominal demand.

The more realistic alternative involves negotiated debt write-downs and restructurings to reduce debts to sustainable levels, while avoiding the disruptive effect of bankruptcy and default. It can be applied to either private or public debts. But in neither sector can debt restructuring be sufficient alone to cope with the scale of today's debt overhang.

Atif Mian and Amir Sufi argue that the United States should have implemented a large-scale program of coordinated mortgage debt restructuring after 2008. By cutting mortgage debts to affordable levels, this would have reduced the severity of the household consumption cuts that drove the country into recession. Even without such a coordinated program, household debt write-offs have been greater in the United States than elsewhere, helping achieve a more rapid pace of household sector deleveraging. But Mian and Sufi are surely right to argue that a more extensive and officially mandated program of debt forgiveness would have spurred economic recovery.

But achieving sufficient private debt write-down to fix the debt overhang problem is made difficult by the dilemma discussed in Chapter 10—that even lending that is "good" from a private perspective can have an adverse macro effect. Overleveraged households and companies can act in ways that depress nominal demand even if they can and do repay their debts in full: indeed, it is the consumption and investment cuts they make to repay their debts that depress the economy. For private debt restructuring to be a complete solution it would therefore have to involve the write-down of debts that from a private perspective look sustainable. Orchestrating such a resolution in a fair, politically agreed-on, and nondisruptive fashion would be extremely difficult.

Public debt write-offs might potentially play a larger role. Greek public debt was reduced by a write-down of private sector in claims 2011 without significant market disruption, and public sector claims on Greece could be and almost certainly will be written down as well.[30] Public debt write-downs indeed can be used as an indirect way to deal with excessive private leverage. Excessive private credit creation produces crisis, debt overhang, and post-crisis deflation, and as a result, rising public debt burdens: leverage doesn't go away, it simply shifts from the private to the public sector. But once it has shifted to public debt, it may be easier to negotiate restructuring and write-down without harmful shocks to confidence. The absolute size of the write-downs is crucial, however. The restructuring and write-down of Greek government debt was easily absorbed by financial markets, because the total value written off was trivial in global terms. Write-downs of Japanese or Italian government debt sufficiently large to make the remaining debt clearly sustainable would be far more disruptive.

A COMBINATION OF LEVERS

Given the scale of the debt overhang created by past credit growth, there are no certain and costless routes to deleveraging and no one policy that will ensure an optimal result. A combination of policy levers is needed in response, varying by country. In Japan it is not possible that public debt will be reduced substantially as a percentage of GDP through the normal processes of growth plus fiscal consolidation. In the United States, starting with smaller debt to GDP than Japan's and with faster potential growth rate because of a still-growing population, a combination of continued loose monetary policy, growth, and market-driven debt write-down may prove sufficient without more radical policy action.

But whatever the mix of policies deployed, the money finance option should not be excluded as taboo. Indeed, in some countries it will be essential if we are to achieve adequate debt reduction and reasonable growth.

Overt Money Finance — Three Specific Options

Three specific uses of overt money finance should be considered: Bernanke's helicopter, one-off debt write-off, and radical bank recapitalization.

BERNANKE'S HELICOPTER

Ben Bernanke proposed in 2003 that Japan should execute a modern version of a helicopter money drop, paying for either tax cuts or increased public expenditure with central bank–created fiat money and making it clear that no new fiscal debt had been incurred and thus that no additional debt-servicing burden had been created. If Japan had followed that advice, it would now have higher nominal GDP, some mix of higher real output and a higher price level, and a lower level of debt to GDP.

Ideally the major advanced economies should have implemented Bernanke-style helicopter money drops in the immediate aftermath of the 2007–2008 crisis. If we had done so, the recession would not have been so deep, and we would now be further advanced in escaping the debt overhang. We would also almost certainly be further advanced in returning to normal interest rate levels. In the United Kingdom, for instance, the Bank of England has conducted quantitative easing asset purchases to the tune of £375 billion: these have stimulated the economy by pushing down long-term interest rates and increasing bond, equity, and property prices. If instead the UK government had devoted a fraction of that money (say, £35 billion) to tax cuts or expenditure increases funded with permanent fiat money, the likely effect would have been a stronger, more equitable, and less risky recovery.

In the United Kingdom, and the United States, the time for such policies may now have passed. For good or ill, we have used ultra-loose monetary policy to achieve at least some economic recovery. But in Japan and in the eurozone the case for money finance of increased fiscal deficits has become stronger over the past few years, given accumulating

evidence of chronically deficient demand. At the Jackson Hole conference in August 2014 ECB President Mario Draghi noted that without
some fiscal as well as monetary stimulus, recovery in the eurozone could
not be assured. But any fiscal stimulus funded with new public debt issues will raise questions about how the debt can be repaid. Ideally the
eurozone should now consider policies of the sort put forward by the
Italian economists Francesco Giavazzi and Guido Tabellini, who argue
for a simultaneous 3-year tax cut in all eurozone economies, funded by
long-term bonds, which the ECB buys and holds in perpetuity.[31] Chapter 15 discusses the political difficulties that may well make this ideal
policy unattainable in practice.

PUBLIC DEBT WRITE-OFFS

The Japanese did not follow Bernanke's advice in 2003. Instead they offset private deleveraging with large funded fiscal deficits, making a relentless rise in public debt to GDP the inevitable consequence. But they
could now write off some of that accumulated debt, putting themselves
in the position they would have been if they had accepted Bernanke's
advice.

In an attempt to counter deflation, the Bank of Japan has conducted
very large quantitative easing operations, buying government bonds
which by the end of 2014 amounted to 44% of GDP. It is now buying
government bonds at the rate of ¥80 trillion per year, a figure substantially larger than the fiscal deficit and net new debt issue, which is running at about ¥50 trillion per year. As a result, the amount of government debt not owned by the Bank of Japan is falling, and by 2017 net
government debt owned neither by the Bank nor by other government-
related entities (such as the social security fund) could be down to just
65% of GDP.

This seems indeed like some form of money finance. But the stated
objective of these quantitative easing operations is not to fund the government deficit but to stimulate the economy through the classic transmission mechanisms of ultra-loose monetary policy—very low long-
term interest rates, rising asset prices, and currency depreciation. And
the stated intent is that at some time the Bank of Japan will sell its government bond holdings back into the market, and that the government

will repay these bonds out of future fiscal surpluses. Official figures for Japanese public debt therefore include the debt that the Japanese government owes to the Bank of Japan, an institution that the government owns.

That debt could be written off and replaced on the asset side of the Bank of Japan's balance sheet with an accounting entry—a perpetual non-interest-bearing debt owed from the government to the bank. The immediate impact of this on both the bank's and the government's income would be nil, since the interest which the bank currently receives from the government is subsequently returned as dividend to the government as the bank's owner. So in one sense a write-off would simply bring public communication in line with the underlying economic reality. But clear communication of that reality would make it evident to the Japanese people, companies, and financial markets that the real public debt burden is significantly less than currently published figures suggest and could therefore have a positive effect on confidence and nominal demand.

The equivalent operation could also be used to cut stated debt levels and to reduce the apparent need for fiscal consolidation in other countries too. The Bank of England owns government bonds worth 23% of GDP. Writing some of them off would not remove entirely the need for further improvement in public finances, but it would reduce the required pace and severity of fiscal consolidation.

Bank Recapitalization

The third possible use of fiat money creation would not deal with the inherited debt overhang but would facilitate rapid progress to a sounder financial system without exacerbating the deleveraging problem.

Chapter 13 argues that bank capital requirements should be set far higher than those established by Basel III. But rapid progress to higher capital ratios could increase the pace of private-sector deleveraging: banks can meet the higher ratios by cutting loans rather than increasing capital. A possible answer is to require banks to increase ratios by raising new capital and to give banks a short period of time to raise it from the private sector, but with the backstop of government equity injection if private capital is not forthcoming. Government stakes could then be sold off over time.

But the problem is that if the government equity injection is actually required, government debt to GDP increases. So if public debt is already at troubling levels, we solve one problem but exacerbate another. Concerns about the impact that public recapitalization would have on already high fiscal deficit and debt levels undermined the effectiveness of the European bank stress tests in 2011. With such countries as Spain, Ireland, and Italy already struggling with high public debts and increasing government bond yields, they could not promise to put new capital into the banking system for fear of exacerbating market concerns about sovereign debt sustainability. It was impossible to promise a credible public backstop to private equity raising.

If, however, public recapitalization is financed by the central bank through a permanent increase in central bank money, the problem of future debt sustainability does not arise. Even for those who worry a lot about debt monetization, this option might be acceptable. Bernanke's helicopter money drop may be unacceptable if it takes the form of tax cuts or public expenditure increases: the medicine may taste so sweet that the temptation to use it to excess is overwhelming. But a helicopter money drop used solely for bank recapitalization would be more likely to be treated as undoubtedly one-off.

The Taboo

As Friedman illustrated, deficient nominal demand is one economic problem to which there is an obvious and always possible solution—money creation by government fiat. We have tools, moreover, that can ensure that the demand stimulus is appropriately modest rather than dangerously inflationary. And if money finance is excluded, escaping the debt overhang will be far more difficult and economic growth unnecessarily depressed.

But using central bank money to finance fiscal deficits or to write off past public debts remains a taboo policy, and for some good reasons. For if we first admit that money finance is possible, how will we ensure we do not use it to excess? The risks of money finance are thus not technical but political. Chapter 15 considers whether those political dangers can be overcome.

||||||||||||||||||||||||||||||||||||||||||||||||||||||||||||||||||||||||||||||||||||||||||||||||||||||||||||||||||||||||||||||||||||||||||||||||||||||||||||

FIFTEEN

BETWEEN DEBT AND THE DEVIL—
A CHOICE OF DANGERS

> Under the proposal, government expenditures would be financed
> entirely by tax revenues or the creation of money ... the chief
> function of the monetary authorities [would be] the creation of
> money to meet government deficits or the retirement of money
> when the government has a surplus.
> —*Milton Friedman, "A Monetary and Fiscal Framework for
> Economic Stability," June 1948*[1]

> There is no subtler, no surer means of overturning the existing
> basis of society than to debauch the currency.
> —*J. M. Keynes, "Inflation," 1919*[2]

I N A SPEECH IN SEPTEMBER 2012, Jens Weidman, president of the
Bundesbank, cited the story of Part Two of Goethe's *Faust* in which
Mephistopheles, agent of the devil, tempts the emperor to distribute
paper money, increasing spending power and writing off state debts. It
all starts well with an enjoyable boom, but it inevitably "degenerates into
inflation, destroying the monetary system."[3]

The printing of fiat money to finance public deficits is viewed by
many central bankers not as a technical policy error but as a sort of sin,
forbidden by a powerful taboo. Many central bank mandates, including
the ECB's, make monetary finance illegal. Most mainstream economists
and policymakers are very wary of expressing support for monetary finance, lest they be thought unsound. Ben Bernanke recommended it in
2003 but never repeated that advice after he became chair of the Federal

Reserve. Michael Woodford, one of the world's leading New Keynesian monetary theorists, effectively proposed it in his paper presented at the Jackson Hole conference in August 2012, but without explicitly saying the words.[4] So deep and effective is the taboo, indeed, that many people outside central banks believe that monetary finance of the sort described in Chapter 14 is not only undesirable but also in some sense impossible.

It is not impossible, but it may be undesirable, and the taboo may serve a good purpose. For once we admit that money finance is possible, there is no technical limit to how much fiat money can be created and how much nominal demand produced, and there are great temptations to create ever larger amounts. If governments are allowed to print money to finance deficits, they will be tempted to do so before elections, to spend it on favored political constituencies, and to run large fiscal deficits on a permanent basis rather than make tough choices about tax and public expenditure. Money finance can be used responsibly without producing harmful inflation—Japan in the early 1930s, under finance minister Takahashi, is a case in point. But it can also be used excessively, producing the hyperinflations of Weimar Germany or modern-day Zimbabwe.

Monetary finance is like a dangerous medicine, which when taken in small amounts can help cure severe illness but when taken in excess can be fatal. And so there is a good argument—the argument that Weidman makes—for locking up the medicine and throwing the key away. Doing so will have adverse consequences: it will make it harder to escape from the debt overhang and will depress growth for many years. But printing money might in the long term prove more harmful still, since it breaks the taboo and opens the way to excessive use in the future.

So should we lock up the medicine and throw away the key? I don't believe so for two reasons. First, because it is in principle possible to design institutional mechanisms to place appropriate constraints on excessive use. Second, because the alternative route to nominal demand growth—private credit creation—is just as dangerous. We face a choice of dangers, not inevitable perdition on the one side and perfection on the other. Moreover, once we recognize that reality, we may need to consider the possibility that money finance might be a desirable policy tool, not just in today's extreme circumstances but on a continuous basis.

Central Bank Independence and Fiscal Discipline

Low and stable inflation is not sufficient for financial and macroeconomic stability, but it is highly desirable, and central banks successfully delivered it in the pre-crisis years. Their ability to do so was underpinned by an increasing trend toward central bank independence. In emerging markets that had previously suffered high or hyperinflation, independent central banks were increasingly able to say no to government demands for monetary finance. And around the world central banks were increasingly free to set interest rates to meet inflation targets, whatever the government's short-term preferences. Using monetary finance to escape the debt overhang seems to remove the discipline.[5]

But in fact there is no reason the use of monetary finance cannot be appropriately constrained within precisely the same discipline of central bank independence. Central bank committees that today vote to approve interest rate movements or quantitative easing operations could also be given the power to approve or disapprove either a Bernanke-style helicopter money drop or a one-off government debt write-off. And they could determine the appropriate size of such operations in the light of their independent judgements on the prospects for inflation relative to target. In the United Kingdom, for instance, there is no reason why the Bank of England Monetary Policy Committee, if equipped with the legal power, could not have approved in 2009 and 2010 a £35 billion helicopter money operation to finance increased fiscal expenditure, instead of £375 billion of quantitative easing. And no reason it could not have refused to approve a larger helicopter money operation if it believed that would endanger inflation above the 2% target.

The problem of independent discipline is therefore soluble in principle. Significant coordination between fiscal and monetary authorities would nevertheless still be required. For while the central bank could be given the power to approve or disapprove a specific quantity of money finance, decisions on how to spend the money—whether by tax cuts or public expenditure increases and in what specific form—would inevitably be political. And since the precise use of the money would in itself have implications for the stimulative impact, fiscal and monetary authorities would need to discuss optimal policy design.

Such discussions are, however, nothing new, but inevitable and appropriate when economies face debt overhang and deflationary pressures. In the United Kingdom after 2008 the potential roles for exceptional liquidity measures, quantitative easing, and the Funding for Lending Scheme were extensively discussed between the governor of the Bank of England and the chancellor of the Exchequer. In Japan, the Bank of Japan's current program of quantitative and quantitative easing has been designed as part of a "three-arrow package" also involving fiscal and structural measures. Coordination of policy design does not diminish the central bank's ability to say no if it thinks the total size of the stimulus package will be excessive and will cause harmful inflation. As Ben Bernanke argued in 2003 "under [some circumstances] greater cooperation for a time between the central bank and the fiscal authorities is in no way inconsistent with the independence of the central bank."[6]

The potential to use monetary finance to escape from debt overhang and deflation should not therefore be excluded on the grounds that it will lead inevitably to excessive inflation and fiscal indiscipline. In countries with one central bank and one fiscal authority, the challenge of combining appropriate discipline with coordination should be soluble. Where it may not be, however, is in the eurozone.

The Eurozone Exception—An Unfixable Problem?

From 2011 to 2014 the eurozone was stuck in the doldrums, with zero growth and with inflation far below the ECB's "close to 2%" target. In spring 2015, as I finish this book, the ECB's massive quantitative easing program—and the resulting depreciation of the euro—seem at last to have stimulated some recovery. But the overall performance of the eurozone economy remains dire: GDP in 2014 was still 1% below the 2007 level, and GDP per capita was still further behind.[7] The eurozone faces an entire decade of no growth in living standards.

In many eurozone countries the private sector is attempting to deleverage after excessive pre-crisis borrowing; in most, the state is also attempting to pay down high public debts. From 2011 to 2014 the predominant policy assumption was that loose monetary policy alone could stimulate the economy, provided the "monetary policy transmission mechanism" was repaired. ECB promises to "do whatever it takes" to prevent exit from the eurozone led to declining government bond yields in peripheral countries: cheap ECB liquidity lines plus regulatory actions to force bank balance-sheet repair (stress tests and asset quality reviews) led to declining bank funding costs, and interest rates charged to households and companies fell to historically low levels. But robust economic growth has not returned, because demand is depressed by simultaneous public and private deleveraging.

The eurozone thus faces the same predicament as Japan did in the 1990s and with the same likely consequence—many years or even decades of slow growth and excessively low inflation. But the social and political consequences of a Japanese-style lost decade would be far more severe in the eurozone of separate nation-states, with significant ethnic and religious minorities, facing large and uncontrollable migration flows from unsettled countries to the south, than in culturally and ethnically homogeneous Japan. Rebooting the eurozone economy is vital, and without fiscal as well as monetary stimulus ideally combined in the form of monetary finance, that reboot will not be achieved.

While radical policy measures are most needed in the eurozone, however, it is also in the eurozone that they are least likely to be agreed on. Achieving the appropriate balance of discipline plus policy coordination is difficult but should be possible in economies with one central bank and one government. But in a eurozone with one central bank and multiple nations, the challenge is magnified by distributional issues and a lack of trust. For if national government debts can be written off and increased fiscal deficits financed by central bank money, which specific eurozone countries should benefit from this largesse? And once countries that borrowed excessively in the past realize that money finance is possible, what incentive do they have to avoid excessive public or private debts in the future? Such problems of moral hazard are difficult to address within one nation with one central bank, but they are far more so in the eurozone.

In principle there are technical solutions to these issues of distribution and discipline. As Francesco Giavazzi and Guido Tabellini have argued, the eurozone could agree to use central bank money to finance simultaneous tax cuts of exactly the same percentage of GDP in each eurozone country, so that there would be no transfer of spending power among nations.[8] And such a tax cut could be clearly time limited, with existing eurozone rules on deficit and debt reduction continuing to apply to the rest of public budgets.

But technical possibility is not enough, as there are widely divergent views in Europe about whether nominal demand is actually deficient, and low-debt countries such as Germany do not trust high-debt countries to stick to their commitments. Until the end of 2014, the ECB found it difficult to gain agreement even to large-scale but reversible quantitative easing operations, let alone to permanent money finance.

Today's eurozone structure may therefore make a Japanese-style "lost decade" inevitable. The required long-term solution, if the eurozone is to stay together and succeed, must entail significant federalization. Some public debts should be issued at the eurozone level, while others remain at national level as well as a national state level: national level debts should be subject to the market discipline of potential default, but federal level debt should become an undoubtedly safe asset underpinned by the potential backstop of central bank monetization. Private credit creation should be constrained by strong macroprudential tools coordinated at eurozone level but differentiated on a country-by-country basis to constrain national credit and asset price cycles.

The best pragmatic short-term strategy, meanwhile, may well involve operations that post facto turn out to be money finance, but whose essential nature can be denied for fear of legal and political challenges. If the European Investment Bank funds infrastructure investment, raising money with long-term bonds that the ECB buys, we edge closer to money finance without quite crossing the line.[9]

But if neither the long-term solution nor adequate short-term action is possible, it would be better for the eurozone to break up, ideally through the exit of potential hard-currency countries, such as Germany.[10] If it continues with structures and rules that make any form of monetary finance impossible, Europe will be condemned to an unnecessarily long period of slow growth and dangerously low inflation.

One-off Money Finance Only?

Faced with a debt overhang and deficient nominal demand, we must be willing to use the money finance option. There is, however, a strong argument for making that use "one-off" only, a response to exceptional circumstances, returning to the orthodox prohibition on monetary finance once robust growth has returned and inflation is back on target. If the policy is clearly one-off and is justified by extreme circumstances, it will be easier to contain the moral hazard risk: but if we accept money finance as a normal operation, deployed continuously year after year, the danger that future governments will abuse it is greatly increased.

But that was not what Milton Friedman proposed in 1948. Instead he argued that if a slow increase in nominal demand was desirable, it should be provided by the government running each year small fiscal deficits entirely financed with fiat money creation. If, say, the money stock stood at 50% of GDP and needed to grow at 4% per year (that is, by 2% of GDP) to support 4% nominal GDP growth, the government would each year run money-financed deficits of 2% of GDP.

So should we consider this more radical proposal? Friedman himself stressed that "The proposal has of course its dangers. Explicit control of the quantity of money by government and the explicit creation of money to meet actual government deficits may establish a climate favourable to irresponsible government action and to inflation."[11] Once governments know that they can fund 2% of GDP deficits with money rather than taxes, what is to stop them wanting to make that 3% or 4% or 5%?

For that reason my own strong preference is that any use of the money finance option should be one-off. But the logic of this book's analysis is that there could be circumstances in which a continuous role for money finance would be less risky than alternative policies.

Secular Stagnation — The Case for Continuous Money Finance?

Chapter 7 argues that much of the rapid credit growth before the 2007–2008 crisis was not essential to deliver economic growth. Credit to finance the purchase of existing real estate drove up leverage and asset prices but produced no necessary and fully proportionate increase in nominal demand. Rising consumer credit helped maintain adequate demand in the face of rising inequality, but it would not have been needed if inequality had not increased. If we make the reforms described in Part IV, we might therefore be able to achieve economic growth without still faster growth in private credit.

But it is also possible that if we constrain private credit growth to limit the risks of future crisis and debt overhang, we will then face a problem of deficient nominal demand. Credit extended against real estate does not necessarily produce a fully proportionate increase in nominal demand, but it may, by making people feel richer, stimulate expenditure to a significant extent. It is therefore possible, as Larry Summers has argued, that without rapid and potentially unstable credit growth, we might face a problem of secular stagnation.[12]

Structurally deficient nominal demand could arise if desired (ex ante) savings exceed desired (ex ante) investment, and forces at work in modern economies may make that imbalance inevitable. Investment needs, as Chapter 7 describes, may be reduced by the falling relative price of capital goods that incorporate ICT. And slower population growth reduces the need for each generation to accumulate additional capital stock. But demographic change in the form of increased longevity can simultaneously encourage people to accumulate large savings during working life to fund longer retirements, and the desire to bequeath wealth can, as Thomas Piketty argues, produce increased desired savings irrespective of whether additional investment in capital stock is required.

Through a variety of mechanisms, economies could therefore face a disconnect between savings aspirations and investment needs, with savings and investments only brought into balance by very low real interest rates. In 1990 the real rate of return available on 20-year index-linked government bonds in the United Kingdom and the United States was over 3%. By the 2007–2008 crisis that rate had already fallen to less than 1.5% and is now close to zero. Extremely low interest rates in turn helped induce the rapid credit growth that led to crisis.

It is therefore possible, though by no means certain, that we face not merely a severe debt overhang problem produced by excessive credit growth but also an underlying structural deficiency of nominal demand. If so, it seems we must accept either the instability of credit booms and busts, or sustained low growth, too low inflation, and debt levels that are never reduced.

But deficient nominal demand is one problem that can always be solved through fiat money creation. And if the secular stagnation threat is truly as severe as some economists argue, we could counter it by using money finance not as a one-off device but continuously over time. We would need as best possible to guard against excessive use, for instance, through legal limits on the maximum quantity of fiat money created each year or by locating decisions on allowable quantity in independent and inflation-targeting central banks. And there is a risk that such constraints would prove imperfect. But if the alternative is sustained slow growth and deflation, that might be a risk we have to accept.

Between Debt and the Devil

Allowing monetary finance is dangerous, since governments may create fiat money in excessive quantities and misallocate the resulting spending power to inefficient ends. But the alternative route to adequate nominal demand—by means of private credit creation—is also dangerous, since free financial markets left to themselves are bound to create credit in excessive quantities and allocate it inefficiently, generating unstable booms and busts, debt overhangs, and post-crisis recessions.

The United States was not printing fiat money in the decade before 2008, but a huge private credit boom produced a huge financial crisis. Far from printing fiat money to fund fiscal deficits, Ireland before 2008 was using fiscal surpluses to repay public debt: but it still suffered from a massive misallocation of capital investment into unprofitable real estate projects. China could have chosen in 2009 to offset the impact of the global recession with money-financed fiscal stimulus: it chose instead to use bank credit creation. But it is still left with excessive real estate and infrastructure investment in many cities and a severe debt overhang problem.

Pre-crisis macroeconomic orthodoxy combined total anathema against fiat money finance with an almost totally relaxed attitude to private credit creation. Optimal future policy must reflect the reality that we face a choice of dangers and must combine far tighter controls on private credit creation with the disciplined use of fiat money finance when needed. Our refusal to use that option until now has depressed economic growth; led to unnecessarily severe fiscal austerity; and, by committing us to sustained very low interest rates, increased the risks of future financial instability.

THE QUEEN'S QUESTION AND THE FATAL CONCEIT

[The] central problem of depression prevention has been solved, for all practical purposes, and has in fact been solved for many decades.

> —*Robert Lucas, president of the American Economic Association, 2003*[1]

Standard macroeconomic theory did not help foresee the crisis, nor has it helped understand it or craft solutions ... complete markets macroeconomic theories not only did not allow the key questions about insolvency and illiquidity to be answered. They did not allow such questions to be asked.

> —*Professor Willem Buiter, "The Unfortunate Uselessness of Most 'State-of-the-Art' Academic Monetary Economics," 2009*[2]

There are probably few genuinely "deep" (and therefore stable) parameters or relationships in economics, as distinct from in the physical sciences, where the laws of gravity are as good an approximation to reality one day as the next.

> —*Mervyn King, "Uncertainty in Macroeconomic Policy-Making," 2010*[3]

IN SPRING 2009, Queen Elizabeth visited the Economics Department of the London School of Economics to discuss the financial crisis. She asked a simple question: "Why did no one see it coming?" The response, delivered by letter some months later, was that there had been "a failure of the collective imagination of many bright people, both in this country and internationally, to understand the risks to the system as a whole."[4] But the truth is worse than that. The dominant strain of academic economics, and of policymaking orthodoxy, not only failed to see the crisis coming but asserted that better policy and increased financial sophistication had made financial crises far less likely than in the past. The president of the American Economic Association, Robert Lucas, was confident in 2003 that "the central problem of depression prevention has been solved." The IMF was sure in 2006 that financial innovation had "increased the resilience of the financial system" and made commercial bank failures less likely.

Ideas matter. They strongly influence the assumptions with which policymakers approach practical policy choices. They define other ideas as unsound, not worth considering, taboo. So it is vital not only to pursue different policies but also to challenge the assumptions, theories, and methodologies that underpin them.

In two key ways the dominant strain of modern economics ill served our understanding of financial and macroeconomic instability. Finance theory assumed that human beings are rational and financial markets efficient, and macroeconomics largely ignored the details of the financial system. A more complex financial system was therefore bound to make the economy more efficient, and the macroeconomy was bound to be stable as long as low inflation was achieved.

But underlying these specific failings was also a methodological and philosophical bias—a preference for mathematical precision and elegance at the expense of realism and a desire to arrive at certain answers that made possible unchanging public policy rules.

We need a new approach to economics and to public policy. The precrisis policy orthodoxy reflected overconfidence in the power of free financial markets to deliver optimal results. Ironically, indeed, its self-assurance replaced but mirrored the earlier mid-twentieth century confidence that government economic planning and direction could achieve superior performance. Our future approach must recognize that both markets and governments can fail, and that optimal policy inevitably involves a choice between alternative imperfections and alternative dangers.

Market Efficiency and Rationality—Mathematical Elegance over Reality

Part I describes the pre-crisis assumption that financial market completion was certain to produce positive results. Securitization, derivatives, and increased trading of credit securities made it possible to "slice and dice" risk and distribute it into the hands of those best placed to bear it. Visible and market-driven prices for credit derivatives and securities brought the wisdom of the market to bear on the pricing of credit to the real economy. More financial activity thus ensured both better allocative efficiency and greater stability.

That did not of course mean that there should be no regulation, nor that economists believed that the perfect equilibrium described by Kenneth Arrow and Gerald Debreu is attainable in the real world. Conduct regulation was needed to protect customers from exploitation, and microprudential regulation was required to offset the risks created by misaligned incentives. But there was a strong bias to believe that more financial activity was in general good and that rational profit-maximizing private firms would manage risks well enough to make the whole system stable. Regulators should therefore, it was believed, concentrate on identifying and correcting the specific imperfections standing in the way of still more efficient markets. We were getting closer to the "the utopia of finance for all."

That confidence was underpinned by the assumptions of the Efficient Market Hypothesis and the Rational Expectations Hypothesis. But the EMH suffers from the deficiencies described in Chapter 2, and the REH is equally unrealistic. It asserts that economic agents base their decisions on rational assessments of the probability distribution of future possible results, bringing to bear in that assessment all available information.[5] Indeed, agents (that is, ultimately people) have mental models of how the economy works (for instance, how different economic factors interact), which they use to transform available information into rational expectations, and these mental models are the same as those which economists who believe in the REH deploy to understand the world.

As economists Roman Frydman and Edmund Phelps have commented, this proposition is not only debatable, it is distinctly odd. "Why," they ask, "would the predictions of a particular economist's overarching account have any connection with how profit-seeking participants forecast outcomes in real world markets?"[6] The assumption is also at odds with what we know about actual human decisionmaking and about how human brains work. And it fails to face the reality that the future is not governed by mathematically defined probability distributions of results but by inherent uncertainty.

Indeed, for many people outside the citadel of academic economics, the triumph of such an unrealistic theory as the REH is deeply strange. But its origins lay in a well-intentioned desire to address what were rightly seen as deficiencies in the post-war Keynesian consensus. That consensus was based on a formalization of Keynes's theory into a set of mathematical relationships summed up in what is known as the ISLM model.[7] It sought to describe macroeconomic dynamics by focusing on aggregate flows of investment, consumption, and government spending, and on high-level relationships between, for instance, interest rates and investment levels. But it failed to specify why those aggregates should interact in the fashion proposed, given individual agents' behaviors, preferences, and expectations. The theory, critics argued, did not have "microfoundations." In particular, it failed to specify how people's behavior was determined by expectations about the future, why they held particular expectations, and how those expectations would evolve in the light of changing circumstances and public policies.

Seeking to define the microfoundations of macrobehavior was a valid and indeed vital intellectual objective. But the actual microfoundations developed, based on the assumption that expectations were wholly rational, were dangerously unrealistic. But they had one useful feature: they made economic theory and models mathematically tractable and thus capable of producing definitive and elegant mathematical results, which would not have been achievable with more realistic assumptions.

Sound policy for the future needs to reflect the reality that individuals are not wholly rational and financial markets far from perfectly efficient.

An Economy without Banks: The Strange Amnesia of Modern Macroeconomics

The second crucial failure was that modern macroeconomics largely ignored the operations of the financial system and in particular the role of banks. If the assumptions of the REH are rather odd, the fact that modern macroeconomics wrote the financial and banking system out of the script is even odder. After all, monetary policy works through credit markets and the banking system; changes in central bank interest rates affect the real economy because interest rates charged to bank borrowers or paid to bank depositors are changed. But modern macroeconomics had increasingly assumed that the financial system could be treated as a veil through which the impetus of monetary policy passes but without being affected by it. Any focus on the banking system as an autonomous creator of credit and purchasing power, which had been central to the thinking of earlier economists—such as Wicksell, Hayek, Fisher, and Simons—largely disappeared. Andrew Haldane, chief economist of the Bank of England, has estimated that in the decade preceding the 2007–2008 crisis, the Monetary Policy Committee of the Bank of England spent just 2% of its time discussing developments in the banking system.[8]

The roots of this strange amnesia are complex. As a fine historical account by the economist Mark Gertler sets out, the tendency to ignore the details of the financial system was found not just in the New Classical and New Keynesian schools that have dominated over the past three or four decades, but in earlier post-war Keynesianism and Monetarism.[9] Thus while Keynes himself wrote insightfully about financial system instability in both *The General Theory* and *Treatise on Money*, post-war Keynesian frameworks and models tended to focus on overall aggregates and broad policy tools—investment, the interest rate, fiscal deficits—and paid little attention to financial sector balance sheets. Some economists of the 1950s and 1960s, such as John Gurley and Edward Shaw, tried to redress the balance.[10] But from the 1970s on interest declined. The few economists who continued to insist on the vital importance of financial system dynamics and balance sheets—in particular, Hyman Minsky—were marginalized.

Chapter 10 discusses one reason for this declining interest—economists and policymakers drew the wrong conclusion from increasing evidence that money growth had no necessary and proportionate implications for current price inflation. Another factor at work was that taking the financial system out of theory and models made it possible to arrive at mathematically precise results.

For if one assumes that the financial system is of no macroeconomic importance, it becomes possible to analyze the dynamics of the macroeconomy with the use of models in which a single "representative household" contracts with a single "representative firm." This, in essence, is what goes on in standard Dynamic Stochastic General Equilibrium models, which have become important central bank tools, informing real-world policy choices. In these models, economies can be disturbed from smooth equilibrium paths by externally arising real shocks, such as political events, new raw material discoveries, or unexpected technological breakthroughs. And their path back to equilibrium can be complicated by the fact that prices and wages are "sticky," rather than adjusting in a perfectly smooth fashion. But they will never illustrate that the financial system can be itself a cause of instability, because that possibility is excluded by the initial assumptions.

You cannot see a crisis coming if you have theories and models that assume that the crisis is impossible.

The Underrated Value of Empirical Facts

Modern macroeconomics focused little attention on the role of banks. But when economists and financial theorists did describe banks, they usually made a dangerously simplistic assumption—that banks take deposits from households to lend money to businesses and entrepreneurs, allocating capital resources between alternative investment projects. In fact, as Chapter 4 describes, most bank lending in modern economies (or in the United States, most capital markets lending) is unrelated to new business investment but instead funds a competition among households for the ownership of already existing real estate.

That reality has been clearly shown by the historical analysis of Òscar Jordà, Moritz Schularick, and Alan Taylor. Their work shows the vital contribution to good economics of empirical analysis of real-world trends. Thomas Piketty's analysis of the changing historical relationship between wealth and income has similarly raised important issues that most modern macroeconomics has largely ignored. And detailed analysis of the importance of urban land in the growing wealth / income ratios that Piketty has documented in turn suggests crucial policy and theoretical issues on which Piketty himself has not focused.[11]

At the core of macroeconomic instability in modern economies lies the interaction between the limitless capacity of unconstrained private banking and shadow banking systems to create credit, money, and purchasing power, and the inelastic supply and rising demand for locationally specific urban land. Most modern macroeconomics has failed to focus on this interaction. That is in large part because it was uninterested in the empirical reality of what banks actually do.

In Academia's Defense

Inadequate economics thus played a major role in blinding policymakers to growing dangers in the financial system. It provided support for central bank policies focused too exclusively on low inflation and for regulatory policies that placed too much faith in efficient financial markets.

But as a criticism of economics overall, this might seem unfair. For many economists over the past 30 years have explained why financial markets do not always produce beneficial results and why they might be unstable. All of the arguments presented against the EMH in Chapter 2 draw on the work of leading economists, several of whom have been honored as Nobel laureates. Daniel Kahneman's work on behavioral economics has provided a compelling critique of simplistic assumptions of rationality. Robert Shiller and Andrei Shleifer's work provides a rich understanding of the dynamics of real world financial markets. James Mirrlees, Joseph Stiglitz, and George Akerlof have illustrated that inherent imperfections make it inevitable that markets can settle far from efficient equilibrium and that equilibria can be multiple and fragile. Joseph Stiglitz and Bruce Greenwald argued for many years before the crisis that "the focus of monetary policy should shift from the role of money in transactions to the role of monetary policy in affecting the supply of credit."[12] And recent excellent work on financial instability dynamics, such as that by Marcus Brunnermeier and Hyun Shin cited in Chapter 6, builds on ideas which were at least to some extent present in the academic literature over the past several decades.[13]

But the fact remains that while academic economics has not been monolithic, in the translation of ideas into public policy one oversimplistic strand dominated. The belief that market completion was bringing us closer to an efficient equilibrium did predispose regulators to believe that financial innovation and financial deepening must be good for the economy. And modern macroeconomic theory left us ill-equipped to understand how financial developments generate macroeconomic instability.

As Willem Buiter has put it,

> standard macroeconomic theory did not help foresee the crisis, nor has it helped understand it or craft solutions.... Complete markets macroeconomics theories not only did not allow the key questions about insolvency and illiquidity to be answered. They did not allow such questions to be asked.[14]

The Fatal Conceit and a Choice of Imperfections

Underlying the key failures of pre-crisis economics were thus common methodological roots: an attraction to argument by axiom and to apparently complete and certain models, and a willingness to ignore real world complexities. Theory in turn appeared to support universally applicable policy rules: financial liberalization was beneficial whether applied to equity or debt markets, to developed or emerging economies, and to domestic markets or international capital flows. And central banks could ensure macrostability provided they used interest rate policy rules to pursue clear inflation targets. In that search for certainty and rules, paradoxically, neoclassical orthodoxy mimicked the very faults that had previously affected its intellectual polar opposite—the ideology of socialist planning.

Friedrich Hayek argued that there was a "fatal conceit" in socialist planning that made it not only undesirable but also quite impossible.[15]

It assumed that it was possible for planning authorities to gain such comprehensive knowledge of both present conditions and future developments as to allow mathematically precise optimization. But for Hayek, effective economic organization and progress depended on the use of knowledge "which is not given to anyone in its totality"[16] and is inherently imperfect. No precisely rational, mathematical plan for the whole economy is therefore possible. And in its absence, economic and social progress is best achieved through processes of market-based exploration that are inherently imperfect and changing over time.

The pre-crisis orthodoxy suffered from not just a similar but in some senses the very same conceit. For the idea that free markets will always deliver optimal results and that financial stability will be achieved provided central banks pursue clear targets with predictable rules rests on the assumption that the future can be described by precise mathematical models and that rational human beings maximize their utility on the basis of rational expectations. As Roman Frydman and Michael Goldberg argue, a hubristic overconfidence follows, in which

> like a socialist planner, the economist thus believes that he can accomplish great feats, because he supposes that he has finally uncovered the fully determined mechanism which drives market outcomes and that his model adequately captures how market participants think about the future.[17]

Indeed, as Frydman and Goldberg point out, true believers in rational expectations share exactly the same belief in the possibility of rational optimization that motivated proponents of economic planning. Oscar Lange, who left the University of Chicago in the late 1940s to become a senior official in Poland's communist government, believed that planning was superior to the market because it would enable rational mathematical programming that the market itself could not perform. Robert Lucas, a leading proponent of rational expectations–based economics, conversely believes that "the mathematics of planning problems turned out to be just the right equipment needed to understand the decentralised interactions of a large number of producers."[18] The shared belief is that either rational agents or rational planners can produce socially optimal results in a mathematically predetermined world.

In the real world, however, we must deal with only partially rational human beings and inherently imperfect markets. And our understanding of future economic developments cannot be reduced to precise mathematical models, since the future is governed, as Frank Knight argued in a famous article in 1921, not by probability distributions of possible results, but by inherent irreducible uncertainty.[19] As a result, as John Maynard Keynes put it, "human decisions affecting the future, whether personal or political or economic, cannot depend on strict mathematical expectations, since the basis for making such calculations does not exist."[20] The social science of economics can never therefore reach the standards of mathematical precision established by Newtonian physics, and the economics profession's tendency to "physics envy" leads to a dangerous and unjustified confidence in the certainty of its conclusions.[21]

That unjustified confidence underpinned both the belief that ever more financial activity must be socially valuable and the idea that macroeconomic stability would be ensured provided central banks followed clear rules. Instead we need to accept that both governments and markets can play positive roles but that both are inherently imperfect instruments that, unless effectively constrained, can also create severe economic and social harm.

History tells us that discretionary government control over fiat money can lead to instability and hyperinflation. Societies have therefore attempted to place constraints or absolute limitations on this dangerous potential. The gold standard represented one such attempt, but its rigidities were unsustainable. The orthodoxy that developed before the 2007–2008 crisis was another: it assumed that as long as central banks were independent enough to refuse monetary finance of fiscal deficits, financial and macroeconomic stability would result.

But the crisis showed that simple rule also to be insufficient. That was because while excessive fiat money creation can be dangerous, so too can private credit and money creation. Free markets in private credit creation left to themselves can create too much of the wrong sort of debt, crisis, debt overhang, and post-crisis recession, and they can do so even if inflation is permanently low and stable.

Pre-crisis orthodoxy treated free market private credit creation as by definition optimal and fiat money creation as in all circumstances dangerous—the work indeed of the devil. But in fact we face a balance of risks and benefits. A totally relaxed attitude to private credit creation produced the crisis; and a total prohibition on fiat money creation has made recovery weaker than it could have been. Absolute beliefs and simple rules are dangerous.

There is no utopia of finance for all, which will result from the operation of free markets subject only to a simple set of macroeconomic rules. We cannot therefore avoid the need to intervene to offset the inefficiency and instability that free financial markets will inevitably generate.

But we should also be wary of any belief that policy interventions can produce an alternative utopia of perfect results. There are no perfect markets, and there can be no perfect planner. Markets are imperfect, because the future is uncertain and human beings are not fully rational; discretionary public policy produces imperfect results for exactly the same reasons.

We face a choice of imperfections, and some of the imperfections are unfixable. Equity markets will always display significant random noise and occasional large divergences from equilibrium values. But irrational equity markets can still produce socially useful by-products: the NASDAQ boom and bust left us with the companies of the Internet.[22] Rather than pursuing an unattainable utopia, we should identify where free markets have the greatest potential to diverge from social optimality and design public policies in response.[23]

That is above all in the market for credit creation and the resulting debt contracts. Those markets should be constrained by far stronger constant rules—such as much higher capital requirements. But public authorities cannot avoid the need also to make discretionary decisions, responding to continually evolving market conditions.

This proposition will be resisted. The idea that free financial markets plus simple macroeconomic rules will ensure social optimality is very elegant and appealing. But it was a fatal conceit that produced the disaster of 2007–2008, from whose consequences many ordinary citizens around the world are still suffering.

NOTES

Introduction

1. Reinhart and Rogoff (2013).
2. Lucas (2003).
3. U.S. Bureau of Labor Statistics, employment to population ratio (www.bls.gov). The ratio was 63% in 2007 and was about 58.5% during 2013, rising slightly to 59.3% in April 2015.
4. IMF World Economic Outlook Database, April 2015.
5. The London Interbank Offered Rate (LIBOR) provides a measure of the market price of interbank loans (in various currencies and for various maturities) and is used as a reference price for contracts in the lending and derivatives markets. It is set each day on the basis of inputs from major banks active in the interbank market. During 2008–2009 it became apparent that personnel responsible for input from some of the banks had manipulated their inputs to improve the value of their banks' trading positions. In response fines amounting to several billion U.S. dollars were imposed on several major international banks by various regulatory authorities, including the UK Financial Services Authority, the U.S. Commodity Futures Trading Commission, and the European Commission. Similar market rate manipulation has subsequently been discovered in the foreign exchange market, with very large fines again being imposed.
6. IMF Fiscal Monitor, April 2014, Table 1.6. The average 3.0% estimate reflects gross costs minus recoveries so far, but in some countries (e.g., the United Kingdom) there will be significant further recoveries as, for instance, equity stakes in Lloyds Bank and the Royal Bank of Scotland are sold.
7. IMF Fiscal Monitor, October 2014, Table 7, which shows increase on a gross debt basis from 72.5% to 106.5%. On a net debt basis (Table 8) the increase was from 44.7% to 73.6%.
8. Note that while throughout this book I use the phrase "banks create credit, money, and purchasing power" to capture the essence of how banks stimulate nominal demand, no particular importance should be attached to the quantity of the specific subsets of bank liabilities that are (somewhat arbitrarily) labeled as "money" in official statistics. By extending loans, banks create purchasing power, and at the moment when the loan is extended, the credit asset on the bank's balance sheet is matched by a money liability. However, holders of the money may subsequently switch their "money" into another category of claim against the bank or may transfer the money to another person or company, which then holds another category of claim. But once credit has been created by the extension of a loan, there is bound to be a matching bank liability of some sort, which can only be extinguished if the credit (i.e., loan) is repaid. More formally therefore we should say "banks create credit, purchasing power, and matching bank liabilities, some of which are rather arbitrarily labeled as 'money' in financial statistics." The division of bank liabilities between those labeled "money" and other liabilities is, however,

of secondary importance. Indeed, as Benjamin Friedman (2012, p. 302) has put it, "in retrospect the economics professions focus on money—meaning various subsets of instruments on the liability side of bank balance sheets in contrast to bank assets—turns out to have been a half-century long diversion which did not serve our profession well."

9. The counterargument could be made that the banking system before the crisis was subject to very significant regulation, and thus was not "left almost entirely to free market forces." But the crucial point is that while regulators did attempt (in retrospect, ineffectively) to ensure the stability of the *financial system itself* (i.e., to mitigate the risks of chaotic bank failure), there was almost no focus on the total amount of credit created nor on its allocation. The clear philosophy was that as long as the banking system itself is stable, whatever amount of credit is created and whatever the level of leverage resulting are bound to be optimal.

10. Weidman (2012), p. 3.

11. Friedman (1948).

12. See Richard Smethurst's (2009) biography of Takehashi Korekiyo and Barry Eichengreen's (2015) *Hall of Mirrors*.

Chapter 1

1. Rajan and Zingales (2004, p. 66).

2. The figures in the following paragraphs are taken from Haldane, Brennan, and Madouros (2010).

3. On some measures, indeed, finance had become even more dominant. Haldane shows that the UK financial industry's gross operating surplus—its profits before taxes—grew from just a few percent of all company profits in the 1960s and 1970s to 18%, almost a fifth, by 2007. And he illustrates a dramatic outperformance in terms of equity return. If an investor in 1900 had bought a typical portfolio of nonfinancial companies on the London stock exchange and also a portfolio of financial firms, his return from 1900 to 1970 would have been very similar. From 1970 to 2007, however, the total return on the financial portfolio would have been three times greater than on the nonfinancial stocks.

4. Greenwood and Scharfstein (2013).

5. Bank for International Settlements, Online statistics, long series on credit to the private nonfinancial sector (www.bis.org/statistics/).

Note that different official figures for private debt levels by country (e.g., from the Bank for International Settlements, the OECD, or from national databases) vary significantly, and as a result so do some figures quoted in major reports—for example, the Geneva report "Deleveraging, What Deleveraging?" (Buttiglione et al. 2014) or the McKinsey Global Institute (2015) report "Debt and (Not Much) Deleveraging." The figures for household debt are usually fairly consistent across different data sources. But figures for nonfinancial corporate debt or for financial institution debt often vary significantly because, for instance, of variable coverage of nonbank lending, and different treatments of lending by foreign banks into a country or by domestic banks out of the country. The direction of trends is however highly consistent across all the different data sources and reports. Figures for public debt tend to be more consistent, and the IMF Fiscal Monitor can be treated as a definitive source, applying standard definitions as best possible. Varying figures are, however, sometimes found for *net* public debt (after holdings by government-related entities), and estimates of public debt in recent years sometimes vary by several percentage points between different editions of the biannual Fiscal Monitor, in part because of changing estimates of recent-year GDP levels. As for private debt, the picture for trends over time is highly consistent, even if measures of absolute level vary.

6. Bank of England in Layard (2010, Chapter 1, Figure 1.23).

7. Investment Company Institute, 2014 Investment Company Factbook, Table 37, Total Net Assets of Money Market Funds by Type (www.icifactbook.org).

8. U.S. Federal Reserve, Data Download Program, nonfinancial sectors credit market instruments; liability (www.federalreserve.gov/datadownload/). In line with common market usage, the term "fixed income" financial assets is used here and elsewhere in the book to refer to all financial assets that are not equity in form and whose return to the investor is fixed by prior contract rather than being dependent on the economic performance of the business or project. But it can refer to assets—such as variable rate bonds or deposits—where the return varies with market interest rates

9. World Bank Global Financial Development Database.

10. Layard (2010, Figure 1.5). See Layard (2010, pp. 17–21) for detailed discussion of the evolution of bank balance sheets from the 1960s to 2007. See Sheppard (1971) for the evolution of the system from 1880 to 1962.

11. Historical data series provided by Argus Media for the four main futures contacts now being traded—the CME (NYMEX) WTI Light Sweet Crude, CME Brent, ICE WTI, and ICE Brent. In 2013 total annual volume for the four contacts was 352 million, representing 352 billion barrels of oil (contracts are for 1000 barrels), compared with around 33 billion barrels of oil produced and consumed.

12. Bank for International Settlements, May 2008, Semiannual Survey. Hong Kong.

13. Bank for International Settlements, May 2013, Statistical Release: OTC Derivatives at end December 2012, Graph 2.

14. BIS Quarterly Review, March 2008, p. 88.

15. BIS Quarterly Review, December 2008.

16. European Banking Authority, High Earners, 2012 Data.

17. Philippon and Reshef (2012).

18. Dudley and Hubbard (2004, p. 3).

19. IMF Global Financial Stability Report: Market Developments and Issues, April 2006, p. 51.

20. See A. Palmer, "Playing with Fire," *The Economist*, print edition, February 25, 2012.

21. Dudley and Hubbard (2004, p. 17).

22. King (2012, p. 5).

23. For example, see Rousseau and Sylla (2003).

24. Levine (2005).

25. Rajan and Zingales (2004, p. 66). It is important to note, however, that one of the authors of that book, Raghuram Rajan, was also one of the few economists who subsequently understood and warned about the growing risks in shadow banking activities before the crisis. See Chapter 6.

Chapter 2

1. Shiller (2000, p. 203).
2. "Maturity transformation" is achieved when a bank (or other financial intermediary) has longer term assets than liabilities, thus enabling end investors / savers to hold claims of shorter maturity than the assets that they indirectly finance. "Liquidity transformation" is achieved when medium- or long-term financial instruments, such as equities or bonds, are traded in liquid markets, thus enabling investors to sell them quickly when they wish; this also makes it possible for investors who wish to hold immediately redeemable claims to finance long-term financial commitments to companies.
3. Levine (2005).
4. Smith (1977 [1776]).
5. Arrow and Debreu (1954).
6. Named after the Italian economist Vilfredo Pareto (1848–1923).
7. Fama (1970). For an excellent summary of the EMH propositions and their deficiencies, see Shleifer (2000).
8. Jensen (1978, p. 1).
9. Kindleberger (1978).
10. Dash (1999).
11. MacKay (1841).
12. Shiller (1992, 2000).
13. Haldane (2010, p. 3).
14. Kahneman and Tversky (1973, 1979).
15. Shleifer (2000, p. 13).
16. Keynes (1973 [1936], p. 156).
17. Soros (2013).
18. Knight (1921).
19. Frydman and Goldberg (2011).
20. Tobin (1984, p. 5).
21. Wolfe (1987).
22. Stiglitz (2001). See also Stiglitz (1989).
23. Lewis (2014).
24. Summers and Summers (1989, 1990).
25. The literature includes French and Roll (1986), Edwards (1993), Umlauf (1993), and Hu (1998).
26. Stiglitz (2001). See also Lipsey and Lancaster (1956).
27. Janeway (2012).

Chapter 3

1. Kindleberger and Aliber (2005, pp. 9–10). The first edition (by Kindleberger) was published in 1978. Reproduced with permission of Palgrave Macmillan.
2. BIS Statistics, long series on credit to the private nonfinancial sector (www.bis .org/statistics/).

3. The figures for Chinese leverage are drawn from People's Bank of China, Statistics and Analysis Department, online database. They reflect the Bank's "total social finance" definition. Other estimates of Chinese leverage, using different definitions, show higher levels: for example, the McKinsey Global Institute (2015) report shows an increase from 158% in 2007 to 282% in 2014, or from 134% to 217% if intrafinancial system debt is excluded. All the different figures, however, illustrate a dramatic increase of about 80–100% in real economy leverage above pre-crisis levels and still higher increases when intrafinancial system debt is included.

4. Graeber (2012).

5. Aristotle (2000).

6. For formal analysis of the concept of "costly state verification" (i.e., the fact that finding the truth about project returns can be a costly and difficult process), see Townsend (1979).

7. Bagehot (1878, p. 5).

8. Gerschenkron (1962).

9. Gennaioli, Shleifer, and Vishny (2012, p. 466).

10. BIS Statistics, Long series on credit to the private nonfinancial sector (www.bis.org/statistics/).

11. Bernanke (2000, p. 53).

12. Fisher (1933).

13. Thus for instance, in Gertler and Kiyotaki (2009, p. 11) the bank intermediation channel is described as follows: "At the beginning of the period each bank raises deposits dt from households in the retail financial market at the deposit rate R_{t+1}. After the retail market closes, investment opportunities for nonfinancial firms arrive randomly."

14. Bank of England components of M4. This percentage is calculated as (notes + coins)/(notes + coins + retail and wholesale deposits). If one simply focused on retail deposits instead of both retail and wholesale deposits, the balance would be 96% and 4%.

15. Wicksell (1936).

16. Wicksell also noted that the degree of constraint might vary between a closed economy and one linked with others through international trade and payments systems. In particular he noted that if countries running deficits had to make international payments in metallic commodities (e.g., gold) or in foreign currencies linked to gold, this might constrain their ability to expand domestic credit. This constraint effectively disappeared with the collapse of the Bretton Woods system in 1971, and the development of global interbank markets, as Chapter 6 describes.

17. Woodford (2003).

Chapter 4

1. Jordà, Schularick, and Taylor (2014a, pp. 2, 10).

2. For instance, see descriptions in Townsend (1979), Rajan and Zingales (2004), and Levine (2005).

3. Bank of England Interactive Database, Sectoral analysis of M4 and M4 lending; also see Bank of England Interactive Database, Industrial analysis of monetary financial institutions lending to UK residents.

4. Bank of England Interactive Database, Unsecured net lending (www.bankofengland .co.uk/boeapps/iadb/).

5. U.S. Federal Reserve estimate covering revolving consumer debt and excluding debt secured by real estate, as well as automobile loans, loans for mobile homes, trailers, or vacations. This measure, at $860 billion in 2013, is a subset of total unsecured consumer. See www.federalreserve.gov/releases/g19/current/.

6. Thus if people value consumption in excess of their income today more than they will value the same amount of consumption in the future, the ability to borrow money today (consuming more than their income) and to repay it later (consuming less than their income) can, economic theory argues, produce a higher level of "utility" or "wealth" than if their consumption had to be equal to their income in all periods. This may often be the case, and it means that credit to finance consumption can be a socially useful activity. But the social value has nothing to do with the mobilization and allocation of capital on which most favorable assessments of financial deepening rest.

7. Hayek (2008 [1931]) and Minsky (2008 [1986]).

8. Central Statistics Office Ireland (www.cso.ie/en/media/csoie/releasespublications/ documents/construction/current/constructhousing.pdf).

9. Minsky also used the word "Ponzi" to describe the stage of the cycle in which new debt is required not only to finance capital repayments on existing debt, but even to repay the interest on the debt.

10. Y. Sun, P. Mitra, and A. Simone (2013) "The Driving Force behind the Boom and Bust in Construction in Europe." Working Paper 13/181. Washington, DC: International Monetary Fund (www.imf.org/).

11. In Minsky's description of the self-reinforcing cycle of increasing unsustainable investment, increases in the price of the existing stock of assets play a crucial role; as existing asset prices increase, it seems to make sense to invest in new similar assets. But what Minsky does not consider is a pure play case, where the existing asset is in absolutely finite supply, and where there is no actual new investment, and indeed no need for new investment.

12. Jordà, Schularick, and Taylor (2014a, pp. 2, 10).

13. Piketty (2014).

14. Knoll, Schularick, and Steger (2014).

15. Brynjolfsson and McAfee (2014).

16. IMF World Economic Outlook, April 2015, chapter 4, figure 4.5. The figure also demonstrates that the price of capital investment "structures" has *risen* by about 20% relative to current goods and services. Machines are getting cheaper and physical buildings more expensive.

17. Federal Deposit and Insurance Corporation, and Bank of England.

18. Calomiris and Haber (2014).

19. Case-Shiller Index and U.S. Federal Reserve; European Central Bank (2009) "Structural Issues Report: Housing Finance in the Euro Area," March.

20. See Mian and Sufi (2014) and Chapter 6 for discussions of credit and house price growth in "elastic" and "inelastic" cities.

21. For example, see Borio and Drehman (2009), Borio (2012), and Muellbauer et al. (2012).

Chapter 5

1. Mian and Sufi (2014, p. 9). The University of Chicago Press, Chicago 60637. The University of Chicago Press Ltd., London. © 2014 by Atif Mian and Amir Sufi. All rights reserved. Published in 2014. Printed in the United States of America.

2. Buttiglione et al. (2014, p. 11).

3. Koo (2008).

4. Werner (2003).

5. Piketty and Zucman (2013).

6. Werner (2003).

7. Werner (2003, chapter 9). As Richard Werner points out, reported value may sometimes have been excessive even relative to best estimates of then-current prices. In some cases he describes, banks that had decided to only lend up to 70% LTV colluded with borrowers to increase the estimated value of specific land plots, so that larger loans could be justified. But since the very process of extending larger loans would in itself tend to increase the market price, the question of what the "true" market price really was, is itself somewhat debatable. The crucial point is that the market price was not an exogenous given but the endogenous result of the quantity of credit extended.

8. Jordà, Schularick, and Taylor (2014a, p. 37).

9. Mian and Sufi (2014).

10. See Eggertsson and Krugman (2012) for formal analysis of the negative impact on demand arising from the asymmetry of response between net debtors and net creditors.

11. Bank for International Settlements, Online statistics, Long series on credit to the private nonfinancial sector (www.bis.org/statistics/).

12. Bank for International Settlements, Online statistics, Long series on credit to the private nonfinancial sector (www.bis.org/statistics/).

13. Government debt figures can be expressed either on a gross basis or net after deducting holdings of government debt by institutions that are themselves quasi-government (e.g., Social Security funds). The IMF Fiscal Monitor provides the figures on both bases. In Japan's case the difference is large; for example, in 2013 gross debt was 243% of GDP and net was 134%. But even on a net basis, Japan's debt has relentlessly increased and is now at levels that make repayment through normal processes impossible. Net figures in the IMF definition do not, however, deduct holdings by central banks. The implications of Bank of Japan holdings of government debt for debt sustainability and appropriate policy are discussed in Chapter 14.

14. Figures for public debt are on a gross basis from IMF Fiscal Monitor, April 2015, Table A7. On a net basis (Table A8) the increase is from 50% to 79% in the United States and from 30% to 59% in Spain.

15. Buttiglione et al. (2014).

16. See UK Office of Budget Responsibility: *The Economic and Fiscal Outlook*, March 2014. This estimate makes allowance for likely future proceeds from, for instance, the sale of government equity stakes and is therefore considerably lower than the IMF estimates of gross costs before recoveries referred to in the Introduction, note 4. Latest OBR estimates, published as this book goes to print, are lower still.

17. Buttiglione et al. (2014).
18. See Chapter 3, note 3, for a discussion of alternative figures for Chinese leverage.
19. Buttiglione et al. (2014).
20. The argument that increased fiscal deficits could sometimes be so stimulative that they will "pay for themselves" and thus not produce an increase in public debt levels is considered in Chapter 14.
21. Kapetanios et al. (2012).
22. See Bank of England (2012).
23. UK Office of National Statistics,Wealth and Asset Survey, Gross Household Financial Wealth by Decile, released on April 2, 2015 (www.ons.gov.uk). In 2006–2008 the top 10% owned 65.5%; by 2010–2012 this had increased to 70.8%. This increase in percentage share reflects the fact that wealthier people hold a larger proportion of their financial assets in marketable securities (e.g., equities and bonds), which increase in value when rates fall, while less wealthy people hold a larger share in bank deposits, which face a fall in interest income when rates fall but no increase in capital value.
24. UK Office of Budget Responsibility, November 2014. The latest OBR Report of July 2015 suggests slightly slower pace of increase but with combined public and private leverage in 2020 still higher than ever before.

Chapter 6

1. IMF Global Financial Stability Report: Market Developments and Issues, April 2006, p. 51.
2. A. Palmer, "Playing with Fire," *The Economist,* print edition, February 25, 2012.
3. Reinhart and Rogoff (2009).
4. Schularick and Taylor (2012, p. 9). Four per cent refers to the annual probability in any one country: thus across say 100 countries, it would imply four crises per annum.
5. Kindleberger and Aliber (2005, p. 6).
6. Dudley and Hubbard (2004, p. 3).
7. See Coggan (2011) for an excellent discussion of the links between global capital flows and domestic liberalization.
8. Eichengreen (2008).
9. U.S. Flow of Funds, cited in Layard (2010, Figurte 1.20). See pages 23–27 for detailed discussion of the growth of securitization.
10. Rajan and Zingales (2004, p. 47).
11. Dudley and Hubbard (2004, p. 17).
12. Greenspan (2005, p. 2).
13. See Lewis (2011, p. 93), where the phrase is attributed to Greg Lipmann of Deutsche Bank.
14. Greenspan (2005, p. 2).
15. IMF Global Financial Stability Report: Market Developments and Issues, April 2006, p. 51.
16. Hudson and Mandelbrot (2004).
17. Taleb (2007).
18. Brunnermeier and Pedersen (2009); Shin (2010).

19. Gorton and Metrick (2012).

20. Securities Industry and Financial Markets Association, Repo Fact Sheet 2014 (www.sifma.org/research/).

21. Financial Services Authority (2011).

22. Dudley and Hubbard (2004, pp. 17, 21).

23. One other category of credit which has grown rapidly in the United States and is now growing rapidly in the United Kingdom is student debt, incurred to finance university tuition fees and living expenses. This debt could be seen as financing "investment" in human capital. But there are growing signs that much of it will prove unrepayable, with the returns from this investment not always sufficient to ensure debt sustainability. The issues relating to student debt—and how it fits in the framework of credit categories presented in this book—deserve further attention.

24. The asset management drivers of shadow banking activity have been explored in various articles by Zoltan Pozsar, Manmohan Singh, and James Aitkin. For example, see Pozsar (2011, 2015), and Singh and Aitkin (2010).

25. Financial Stability Board (2012b).

26. For instance, it is often possible to boost return for a number of years in an apparently low-risk fashion by taking positions (effectively out of the money options) that carry a small risk of significant loss but may not crystallize for many years. And the apparent benefits of highly active investment strategies (e.g., by hedge funds) are often illusory once account is taken of "survivor bias"—the tendency for published returns to reflect only those funds that were successful and remained open to new investment. See Lack (2012).

Chapter 7

1. Minsky (2008 [1986], p. 117–18). *Stabilizing an Unstable Economy*, H. Minsky, McGraw Hill-Education, © McGraw Hill-Education.

2. Eccles (1951, p. 76). It is not known who owns the copyright. Publisher Random House had no information and we are awaiting confirmation from The University of Utah Marriott Library, which holds some of Eccles papers, that the University does not have the rights of Eccles's estate.

3. In theory the problem of the zero lower bound could be removed by abolishing paper money, so that all money took deposit form, as proposed by Kenneth Rogoff (2014). How this option (if feasible) would change the pros and cons of stimulating nominal demand by means of ultralow interest rates and quantitative easing is discussed in Chapter 14.

4. Even in a pure metallic money system, however, the meaning of the "pace of circulation" is less precise than often assumed. As Richard Werner (2005) has pointed out, the original specification of the quantity theory of money suggested that the money stock might bear a somewhat stable relationship to the value of *transactions* in the economy ($MV = PT$, with V relatively stable), rather than to the value of nominal GDP ($MV = PY$). And since the relationship between transactions (T) and real income (Y) can vary (e.g., due to changes in the extent to which economic relationships are within rather than between firms), V defined as PT/M can move differently from V defined as PY/M. So

even in a pure metallic economy, while spending power must be to a degree constrained by the amount of chosen metal available, the relationship between money stock and nominal demand would not be precise.

5. See the description of the Lyon fairs in Martin (2013, chapter 6).

6. It is easiest to think of the deficit as taking the form of an explicit payment to each citizen of money that is transferred to their accounts at the savings bank (with the rest of the government budget being in balance). But it could also arise simply because the government had total expenditures higher than tax revenues, with a resulting *net* payment of money from the government to citizens. The central bank balance sheet could then be made to "balance" by recording on the asset side of its balance sheet a perpetual non-interest-bearing claim against the government. But this is not strictly necessary, since there is no absolute need for a central bank balance sheet to balance.

7. As cited in Werner (2005, pp. 166–67).

8. Friedman (1948).

9. For discussion of the Pennsylvania case, see Jackson and Dyson (2013).

10. See Smethurst (2009) and Eichengreen (2015).

11. Friedman and Schwartz (1963).

12. Smith (1999 [1776], Book V, Chapter 2, p. 410).

13. It is worth noting that while the initial origins of the Weimar hyperinflation lay in money-financed fiscal deficits, its subsequent acceleration was also strongly driven by the Reichsbank's willingness to refinance the credit extended to the private sector by commercial banks. This illustrates that the dynamics of fiat money and private money creation can in practice sometimes be interlinked. See Bresciani-Turroni (1937 [1931]).

14. Friedman and Schwartz (1963).

15. Simons (1936, pp. 9–10).

16. One consequence of central bank liquidity provision is, however, that the dividing line between private credit creation and fiat money creation is not as absolute as it first seems. While central bank operations to provide market liquidity are always designed to be reversed in a micro sense, they often tend over time to produce an increase in the monetary base; and if, as in some regimes, this monetary base is non-interest bearing, the result is as if governments had financed a small part of the budget deficit with central bank money.

17. In fact in Keynes's own writings, it is sometimes unclear whether he assumed that stimulative fiscal deficits should normally or always be debt financed. In one passage in *The General Theory*, he observes that "if the Treasury were to fill old bottles with banknotes, bury them at suitable depths in disused coalmines" and then let people dig them up and spend the banknotes, "there need be no more unemployment, and the real income of the community … would probably become a good deal greater" (Keynes 1973 [1936], p. 129). What is described here is effectively a money-financed fiscal deficit not a debt-financed one.

18. See Barro (1974, 1989), and Sargent and Wallace (1981).

19. In these circumstances central banks may be unable (because of the zero lower bound) to set interest rates low enough to achieve their desired inflation targets and will not therefore respond to fiscal stimulus by raising interest rates. See Chapter 14 and DeLong and Summers (2012).

20. Another possibility is that the public debt is never formally monetized but that (1) maturing public debt is continually replaced by new public debt issues, with the public

debt to GDP ratio continually rising; and (2) the interest rate on public debt continually falls, steadily approaching zero, so that the interest expense on public debt always appears affordable. In these circumstances it would appear that there is no limit to how high public debt to GDP could rise. In essence indeed, debt that is perpetual and non-interest-bearing is money: so the greater the likelihood that debt will be perpetually rolled over, and the lower the interest rate paid on it, the less important is distinction between debt and money finance. Japan's current experience is testing the limits of the distinction.

21. Keynes (1930, pp. 41–43).

22. What is not important, however, is whether the assets deriving from credit creation are defined as "money" according to the arbitrary definitions used in financial statistics. Credit creation by banks must result in the emergence of some category of bank liability, and thus of some category of financial asset held by the nonbank sector. But this claim may take multiple forms (e.g., a deposit at bank, or ownership of a debt security issued by a bank). And the claims linking the real economy and the banks can be either direct (e.g., a company or household bank deposit) or indirect (with, e.g., a company or household holding an account at a money market mutual fund, which in turn holds a debt security issued by a bank). Thus while Keynes's categorization of the different uses of money is insightful, it is best understood as an explanation of the consequences of different categories of credit extension, rather than implying that the balance between those bank liabilities that we count has "money" and those counted as "non-money" is of any particular importance. See also the Chapter 10, note 14 discussion of the meaningless of the concept of a "demand for money," which, as the economist Benjamin Friedman has commented, has proved to be a "half-century long diversion which did not serve our profession well" (Friedman 2012, p. 302).

23. Bank of England and UK Blue Book, National Income and Accounts. Note that the increase in mortgage debt is understated, because it does not count securitized mortgage lending, which increased significantly during that time period.

24. Werner (2003).

25. See figures 9.1 and 9.2 in Werner (2003).

26. Brynjolfsson and McAfee (2014).

27. Keynes (1973 [1936], p. 96).

28. The motivations that lead "poorer" or at least "less rich" people (i.e., people with median or even above average incomes but who are still not participating in rapid income growth) to seek to maintain consumption in excess of income through borrowing have been explored by Robert Frank in a series of papers (Frank 2001, 2007; Frank, Levine, and Dijk 2010).

29. Eccles (1951, p. 76).

30. Rajan (2011, Chapter 1)

31. Rancière and Kumhof (2010). In Kumhof and Rancière's model the inequality is between the top 5% and the other 95%. This may well reflect a reality that the quantitatively important element of the stimulus to credit intensity arising from inequality derives not from the behavior of the truly poor (e.g., the bottom quartile) but from the efforts of the middle / less rich to keep up with the expenditure patterns of, say, the top decile or top few percent of the income distribution. Bordo and Meissner (2012) find no *general* link between inequality, credit booms, and financial crises, but they argue that rising inequality did play a role within the origins of the 2007–2008 crisis. Van Treeck and Sturn (2012) point out that before the crisis both the actual extent of permanent (rather

than transitory) inequality and its potential importance were downplayed in a political climate in which concerns about inequality were unwelcome, and in which the easy availability of credit was seen as an integral part of the American dream.

32. Mian and Sufi (2014, p. 23).

33. Report by Savills, quoted in "Private Landlords Gain the Most from Rising Property Market," *Financial Times,* January 18, 2014.

34. Graeber (2012).

35. For detailed exposition of this argument, see Pettis (2013).

36. The concept of "secular stagnation" (implying a chronic deficiency of private nominal demand, which can only be overcome by appropriate government policy intervention) was originally associated with the work of the mid-twentieth-century economist Alvin Hansen. It was revived by Larry Summers in his remarks to the fourteenth Jacques Polak Annual Research Conference, Washington, DC, November 8, 2013.

37. Bank of England, Interactive Database.

38. The longer-term picture is inherently difficult to discern. Index-linked bonds were not issued before the 1980s. Estimates of ex ante required / expected real returns before then therefore rely on comparing ex post nominal realized returns with inflation rates; but this is not a robust methodology in periods that saw large and unanticipated variations in inflation rates. But David Miles (2005) has presented a plausible argument that today's real interest rates are well below those typical throughout the nineteenth century, when less volatile inflation rates make inference from ex post realized returns a more valid technique.

39. Bernanke (2005).

40. McKinsey Global Institute (2010).

41. Turner (2010).

42. IMF World Economic Outlook, April 2015, chapter 4, figure 4.5.

43. See Wolf (2014) and other articles by Martin Wolf.

44. See Turner (2014, appendix 3).

45. See, for example, Lawrence Summers, "Why Public Investment Really Is a Free Lunch," *Financial Times,* October 6, 2014.

Chapter 8

1. Hayek (1984 [1925], p. 21).

2. Studwell (2013, p. 139). Excerpt from *HOW ASIA WORKS,* copyright © 2013 by Joe Studwell. Used by permission of Grove/Atlantic, Inc. Any third party use of this material, outside this publication, is prohibited.

3. Maddison (2001).

4. IMF World Economic Outlook database; Maddison (2001).

5. Indeed even earlier catch-up countries, such as Germany and the United States, were blessed by the nonexistence of the Washington consensus in the mid-nineteenth century. For as the development economist Ho-Joon Chang (2007) argues persuasively, their catch-up development models also involved either high tariffs (as in the case of the United States) or state encouragement of initial industrial development (in the case of Prussia / Germany).

The very early stages of Japanese industrial catch up in the late nineteenth century, after the Meiji restoration, were also based on state-led economic development and on admiration for the development theories of the German economist Friedrich List, who quite explicitly rejected the idea that free trade and free markets would drive economic catch up. See List and Colwell (1856).

6. Studwell (2013).

7. The word "machine" is used here to mean a software system as much as a piece of physical equipment. It covers anything that automates a function that previously required human activity, whether physical or mental. The importance of investment in "machines" in this sense is therefore in no way diminished by the shift from manufacturing to services, or from hardware to software in the modern economy.

8. Capital investment in itself, unaccompanied by technological progress, will of course be subject to diminishing marginal returns. And, as Chapter 4 discusses, one of the features of the modern economy is that many "machines," particularly in the form of software, are falling in relative price: some capital investment goods are getting much cheaper. But even for advanced economies technological progress is still embedded in new generations of machines (whether hardware or software), and without the devotion of some resources to investment rather than to the production of current goods and services, no economic growth could occur.

9. This does not imply that the increased rate of growth achieved by higher investment continues forever. Indeed, in the long term a higher rate of investment cannot permanently increase the growth rate above the pace determined by technological progress and increasing total factor productivity, since once a higher capital/output ratio has first been achieved, high investment is needed simply to keep that ratio stable. But that still leaves the attainable pace of growth during the *transition* to a higher capital stock per capita, and thus to a higher attainable standard of living, highly dependent on the investment rate.

10. Young (1995). Young's insight is sometimes misinterpreted as implying that there is thus something inferior about the Asian growth path, and that a less capital-intensive path would have been better. In fact it simply illustrates that the only available path to rapid catch up is one that entails high investment.

11. Fiat money creation might, for instance, reduce real consumption by generating inflation, which reduces real incomes. In a sense therefore, fiat money creation can impose an "inflation tax." But other transmission mechanisms are also possible.

12. Hayek (1933, pp. 118–19). In this passage Hayek also attacks the idea that this transfer of resources must work by means of inflation. It therefore seems at times as if he is attacking the very idea that "forced savings" are achieved by credit creation. In fact he is clear that his objection to the phrase "forced savings" was just that he felt it an unfortunate expression, which, in the form described by others, could be misunderstood. He was absolutely clear that "every grant of additional credit involves 'forced savings.'"

13. This pattern of response—savings rates increasing as the interest rate paid declines—of course contradicts the simple textbook assumption that the quantity of savings is a positive function of the interest rate. But a wealth of empirical data shows that such backward-sloping supply curves for savings can and do exist, given individuals' need to accumulate a given level of resources for retirement.

14. For example, see Joe Studwell's (2013) description of the role of the "Berkeley Mafia" in Indonesia.

15. See Werner (2003, chapter 9).

16. IMF World Economic Outlook database.

17. Lardy (2006).

18. Wen Jiabao comments at press conference following conclusion of National People's Congress, March 15, 2007.

19. See Chapter 3, note 3, for discussion of the various different estimates of Chinese leverage, all of which however, illustrate the same dramatic increase. The "total social finance" measure includes significant lending to state-owned firms, and to local government as well as private firms. And in an economy where the dividing lines between state and private enterprise continue to be fuzzy, it is not precisely comparable with measures of private-sector credit in other economies. But it does primarily reflect credit that is supposed to be repaid either out of household income or out of profits generated by investments, rather than out of taxation revenues.

20. IMF Fiscal Monitor, October 2014.

21. Fueki et al. (2010).

Chapter 9

1. Rey (2013, p. 312).

2. Committee on the Global Financial System (2009, p. 2). www.bis.org

3. IMF Balance of Payments Statistics, October 2013.

4. For example, see Mathias (1969).

5. Broner et al. (2013).

6. The danger of asymmetric responses to current-account imbalances between net debtor and net creditor nations—the former compelled to restrict demand, the latter under no equivalent pressure to stimulate it—was central to Keynes's concerns about the operation of the international monetary system and to his arguments at the Bretton Woods conference in favor of some form of global central bank (see Skidelsky 2004). Indeed, potentially asymmetric responses between nations represent simply a particularly risky subset of the more general asymmetry between net debtors and net creditors (whether between nations, companies, or households), which Eggertsson and Krugman (2012) have explored.

7. Broner et al. (2013).

8. Committee on the Global Financial System (2009, p. 2).

9. Rey (2013, p. 312).

10. European Commission (1990).

11. IMF World Economic Outlook database.

12. The overhang is now as much in the public sector, where debt levels soared after the crisis, as in the private sector. Eurozone developments thus illustrate the general principle described in Chapter 5, that once private debt has grown to unsustainable levels, it doesn't go away after a crisis but simply shifts to the public sector. After a financial crisis, excessive private credit creation is thus effectively socialized. In addition however, the specific character of the European System of Central Banks results in another form of debt socialization—the growth of "Target 2 balances." Before the crisis, banks

and other investors in current-account surplus countries were willing to provide funding to banks in deficit countries, which in turn financed credit extension to household and corporate sectors. After the crisis, new flows dried up, with surplus country investors seeking to deposit money in safe domestic assets (e.g., domestic bank deposits) and with domestic banks in turn placing increased reserves at their national central banks. But meanwhile, the national central banks of deficit countries had to extend central bank liquidity support to their domestic banks, and they funded that support by borrowing from the rest of the eurozone through the intercentral bank payment system, which is known as "Target 2": effectively, they borrowed from the central banks of the surplus countries. Private flows that had previously passed from surplus country private banks to deficit country private banks thus now flowed by means of the European System of Central Banks. From close to zero in 2007, Target 2 balances grew to reach a peak in 2012, at which time deficit country central banks owed the rest of the system more than €1 trillion. That figure fell to a still enormous €600 billion by the end 2014.

13. IMF Fiscal Monitor, October 2014.

14. Figures for the eurozone are from ECB Statistical Data Warehouse, National Accounts, Main Aggregates http://sdw.ecb.europa.eu). Figures for the United States, the United Kingdom, and Japan calculated from change in nominal GDP (from the IMF World Economic Outlook database) minus increase in net exports (from the World Bank World Development Indicators database).

Chapter 10

1. Minsky (1970, p. 2).

2. Hayek (1933, p. 102).

3. I am indebted to Avinash Persaud for the idea of the "bad apple" theory of financial crisis. As Persaud (2013) has commented, "politicians are drawn to the bad apple theory of financial crisis: crises are caused by bad people doing bad things.... It absolves them from responsibility for creating an unsustainable financial system," and it reflects a misunderstanding of the underlying causes of financial instability "that condemns us to repeat boom and bust."

4. Ahamed (2009).

5. See Financial Services Authority, Final Notice to Bank of Scotland, March 10, 2012, and Final Notice to Peter Cummings, September 12, 2012.

6. Koo (2008).

7. Financial Services Authority (2011).

8. Shin (2005).

9. In September 2009, the international Financial Stability Board agreed to and published *Principles for Sound Compensation Practices*. These were reflected in subsequent UK Financial Services Authority regulations and in European Union directives applicable with the force of law across the European Union. Elsewhere in the world, the Principles have been applied at best as guidelines.

10. Chuck Prince, interview in Japan, *Financial Times*, July 9, 2007.

11. Greenspan (2005, p. 1).

12. Rajan (2005). The criticisms were set out in a paper by Don Kohn (www.federal reserve.gov/boarddocs/speeches/2005) and by Larry Summers among others in the general discussion paper (www.kansascityfed.org/publicat/sympos/2005/pdf/GD5-2005.pdf).

13. Comments by Blanchard in an interview with Portfolio.hu on October 3, 2012 (www.portfolio.hu/en).

14. The implication of this is that the very concept of the "demand for money," which played a central role in monetarist theory, is not only of little value but is close to meaningless. In the standard theory, the demand for money is driven by (1) the level of nominal income Y, since the higher Y is, the greater the need to hold money for transactions purposes, and (2) the interest rate i, which determines the opportunity cost of holding non-interest-bearing money rather than bonds. But in a world where most money is not held for transactions purposes, where most is interest bearing, and where what is called "money" is a somewhat arbitrarily defined subset of bank liabilities, this function bears little relation to reality (see Turner 2013a). It is therefore more useful to think about banking system liabilities in general, and those specific subsets that we label "money," as arising as an automatic by-product of the credit creation process rather than being something for which there is a specific "demand." Indeed, as Professor Benjamin Friedman (2012, p. 302) has put it, "in retrospect the economic profession's focus on money—meaning various subsets of instruments on the liability side of bank balance sheets in contrast to bank assets—turns out to have been a half-century long diversion which did not serve our profession well."

15. McKinsey Global Institute debt database. The 54% figure is for household plus nonfinancial corporate debt but excludes the debt of financial institutions.

16. A new OECD report, published in June 2015, estimates that the impact of rising private credit growth turns negative when private credit exceeds about 90% of GDP. See OECD (2015).

17. Admati and Hellwig (2013).

Chapter 11

1. Lloyds Banking Group, Halifax House Price Index, Historical House Price Data (www.lloydsbankinggroup.com/media/economic-insight/halifax-house-price-index/).

2. Japan Real Estate Institute, Urban Land Price Index, Six Large City Areas (www .reinet.or.jp/).

3. For discussion of the specific market features and public policy choices that can have an influence on the severity of credit and real estate price cycles in different countries, see Muellbauer (2010, 2012, 2014), Muellbauer and Durca (2014), and Muellbauer et al. (2012).

4. McKinsey Global Institute (2015).

5. George (1884).

6. Piketty (2014).

7. Brynjolfsson and McAfee (2014). Thus at the top of the income distribution, powerful network externality and brand effects deliver huge returns to the best, fastest, and luckiest app or game developers, irrespective of whether the next best would have been almost as good. And throughout the income distribution, employers filling high-skilled

jobs that have been made more productive by complementary ICT capital may rationally choose to pay whatever is needed to get the most skilled job applicant, rather than being willing to employ adequately but slightly less skilled applicants at a lower rate. For fuller consideration of this argument, see Turner (2012, 2014).

8. Piketty (2014).

9. IMF World Economic Outlook database

10. IMF World Economic Outlook database. The latest estimate for the current account surplus in 2015 is 3.2% of Chinese GDP.

11. In 2008 China's GDP (at market exchange rates) was $4.54 trillion and 7.2% of global GDP; in 2015 it is forecast to be $11.21 trillion and 15.04% of global GDP (IMF World Economic Outlook database). China's forecast current account surplus of 3.2% of Chinese GDP will therefore equal 0.48% of global GDP.

12. IMF World Economic Outlook database. The forecast figure for 2015 is 3.3%.

13. IMF World Economic Outlook, April 2015, Table A2. In contrast, real domestic demand grew by 7.4% in the United States, 4.4% in the United Kingdom, and 3.8% in Japan.

14. IMF World Economic Outlook database.

15. Tilford (2015).

16. Comments by Tim Geithner (www.bloomberg.com/news/2010-10-22/geithner -push-for-g-20-trade-gap-targets-opposed-before-g-20-talks-start.html).

Chapter 12

1. Simons (1936, pp. 3, 9–10). Simons, JOURNAL OF POLITICAL ECONOMY, *"Rules versus Authorities in Monetary Policy,"* 44:1 (1936) Journal of Political Economy © 1936 The University of Chicago Press.

2. Mian and Sufi (2014, p. 168). The University of Chicago Press, Chicago 60637. The University of Chicago Press Ltd., London. © 2014 by Atif Mian and Amir Sufi. All rights reserved. Published in 2014. Printed in the United States of America.

3. Knight (1933). The proposal went through several iterations over the subsequent years, with different memoranda signed by different combinations of authors. Key supporters included Henry Simons, Irving Fisher, and Frank Knight.

4. Fisher (1936).

5. Friedman (1948).

6. Benes and Kumhof (2012).

7. Jackson and Dyson (2013).

8. Cochrane (2014).

9. "Imputed rent" is the economic benefit that owner occupiers derive from being able to live rent free in their property. In most countries if someone rents out a property, they pay income tax on the rent received, but when they "rent it to themselves," no income tax is payable. Property can thus become one form of wealth on which the return is not taxed, and is thus tax advantaged versus other forms. In the United Kingdom, imputed rent was taxed under Schedule A of the tax code until 1963. Such economists as Mervyn King, Tony Atkinson, and John Muellbauer have at various times proposed that tax should ideally be imposed on imputed rent. See T. Callan (1992) "Taxing

Imputed Rent from Owner Occupation," *Fiscal Studies* 13(1): 58–70 for a summary of the relevant literature.

10. Whether a reserve asset requirement (i.e., a requirement for banks to hold a given quantity of "reserves" on deposit at the central bank) imposes a tax on credit intermediation depends on whether the central bank pays interest on these reserves and at what rate. If the interest rate paid (on either some or all of the reserves) is below the market interest rate, a tax is effectively imposed. Chapter 14 discusses the potential role of reserve requirements, and their remuneration, in the context of money finance operations.

11. Shiller (2013).

12. Some modern Islamic finance scholars, however, increasingly stress both the macroeconomic stability and the ethical arguments, seeking to integrate them into a unified theory. See Askari et al. (2012).

13. Irfan (2014).

Chapter 13

1. Kindleberger and Aliber (2005, p. 75). Reproduced with permission of Palgrave Macmillan.

2. In particular, sustainable levels of both private and public debt are dependent on potential future rates of growth. High growth rates make it feasible to deleverage through rapid nominal GDP growth rather than through debt repayment. Low potential growth rates, such as Japan's or Italy's, make aggregate deleveraging close to impossible, facing economies with the choice between either perpetually rising public debt (as the private sector deleverages) or simultaneously attempted debt pay down in both public and private sectors, generating deflation. Chapter 14 discusses the policy implications.

3. White (2012).

4. Stein (2013, p. 9).

5. Borio and Drehmann (2009, p. 17).

6. See Hense (2015) for empirical analysis of variations in the interest elasticity of demand for credit across sectors and over time.

7. Internationally agreed-on bank capital requirements stipulate that banks hold a minimum percentage of "risk-weighted assets" in total capital (which includes both equity and long-term subordinated debt). In addition, the subset of that total that is equity has to exceed a smaller minimum percentage.

8. Before the 2007–2008 crisis, the Basel II rules required banks to hold total capital equal to at least 8% of weighted-risk assets, with at least half of that (i.e., 4%) in "Tier 1" capital (which excluded some but not all categories of debt) and at least half of Tier 1 capital (i.e., 2%) in equity. Since the crisis, under the Basel III regime, the equity requirement ("Core Tier 1") has been increased to 4.5%. In addition banks are normally required to hold a capital conservation buffer of 2.5%, and globally systemically important banks are required to hold surcharges ranging from 0.5% to 2.5%. Total requirements therefore now amount to about 7–9.5%, depending on how "systemically important" the bank is judged to be.

The total impact of the Basel III regime, however, has been still more significant than the increase in the required ratio suggests, because (1) the definition of what counts as equity in the numerator of the ratio has been tightened, and (2) various regulatory changes have increased the calculated value of risk-weighted assets with, for instance, large increases in the weights attached to trading assets.

9. Admati and Hellwig (2013).

10. See Modigliani and Miller (1958) for the classic theoretical statement of this proposition.

11. Bank for International Settlements (2010) *Guidance for National Authorities Operating the Counter Cyclical Capital Buffer*, December. Basel.

12. Reserve requirements define the amount of "reserves" (i.e., deposits) that commercial banks are required to hold at the central bank. They are therefore assets for the commercial bank and liabilities for the central bank. The required level of these reserves can be defined as a minimum percentage of either the commercial bank's total assets or its total liabilities. Since total bank assets will tend to be closely related to total bank liabilities, this choice is not crucial. Whether defined as a percentage of assets or liabilities, the minimum percentage requirement effectively constrains the quantity of loans (or total assets) that a bank can hold as a multiple of its central bank reserves.

13. Commercial bank reserves at the central bank (which are liabilities of the central bank and, along with notes and coins, form the monetary base) can only be created by central bank operations (e.g., by buying other assets from commercial banks and crediting them in return with additional reserves). Any individual bank can increase its own reserves at the central bank (e.g., by selling assets to and receiving reserves from other banks), but this does not increase the aggregate amount of central bank reserves in the system.

14. In theory, however, it would be possible to set reserve requirements at rates that varied by category of asset or loan.

15. Under Basel rules, major banks that are deemed sophisticated enough to perform the analysis are covered by the Internal Ratings Based approach, making their own assessments of credit risks and effectively setting their own risk weights (though subject to some regulatory challenge). Other banks are required to use standardized weights set down by regulatory rules. Even the standardized weights, however, do not attempt to allow for the systemic and macroeconomic risks that can result from the growth of large aggregate quantities of loans (e.g., residential mortgages) which at a micro level seem relatively low risk.

16. Financial Stability Board (2012a,b).

17. Both LTV and LTI constraints may have a role to role to play, but there are strong arguments in principle for preferring LTI rules. Maximum LTVs can still allow unsustainable growth of leverage relative to income and thus to debt servicing capacity, since the denominator (property value) can itself increase. Maximum LTI rules more directly address the issue of debt servicing capacity and more clearly constrain the danger of self-reinforcing credit and asset price cycles.

18. For instance, Canada imposes maximum LTV limits (varied over time) on mortgages that are insured through the Canada Mortgage and Housing Corporation. Germany's mortgage credit availability is constrained by the rules or conventions determining eligibility for inclusion as collateral held against "Pfandbriefe" covered bonds.

19. Financial Services Authority, Mortgage Market Review, Final Rules, October 25, 2012.

20. Lending to companies not involved in real estate might also be squeezed out by the growth of real estate lending in the upswing of the cycle (and not solely after a finan-

cial crisis has impaired bank lending capacity). Research by Chakraborty, Goldstein, and MacKinlay (2014, p. 1) covering the United States from 1988 to 2006 suggests that "banks which are active in strong housing markets increase mortgage lending and decrease commercial lending. Firms which borrow from these banks have significantly lower investment."

21. Cecchetti, Mohanty, and Zampolli (2011). See also Cecchetti and Kharroubi (2015). The latest OECD report on Finance and Inclusive Growth (OECD 2015) meanwhile suggests that the effects turn negative when total private credit (household and corporate combined) exceeds about 90%.

Chapter 14

1. Reinhart and Rogoff (2013, p. 1).
2. Bernanke (2003, p. 10).
3. Gordon (2012).
4. See Chapter 9, note 14 for sources.
5. IMF World Economic Outlook database.
6. DeLong and Summers (2012).
7. Jordà and Taylor (2013). Jordà and Taylor's findings differ from those of Alesina and Ardagna (2009), who in an influential study of data from 1970 to 2007, argued that austerity could be "expansionary." Crucially, Jordà and Taylor find that the adverse impact of austerity occurs mainly when economies are already weak—fiscal contraction seems to delay recovery from recession, but it has much smaller contractionary effects when the economy is strong. This may suggest that fiscal austerity—that is, attempted public-sector deleveraging—is harmful when the private sector is also deleveraging and that the adverse effect derives from the attempted simultaneous deleveraging of both sectors. An IMF study (Guajardo, Leigh, and Pescatori 2011) also cast doubt on Alesina and Ardagna's analysis.
8. IMF Fiscal Monitor, October 2014, Table 7, General Government Gross Debt. On a net debt basis, after accounting for public debt owned by government related entities, the figures are the United States, 50% to 81%; the United Kingdom, 47% to 85%; and Spain, 30% to 69% (Table 9).
9. Reinhart and Rogoff (2010).
10. The interest rate at which this conversion effect will become significant is unclear. Prior to 2015 many commentators assumed that it would be difficult for central banks to set interest rates below about −0.25% In January 2015, however, the Swiss central bank set an interest rate of −0.75% on deposits without inducing a major shift from deposits to notes. But it is clear that there must be some point at which a large shift would occur.
11. Ken Rogoff, "Time to Phase Out Paper Money," *Financial Times*, May 29, 2014.
12. IMF Global Financial Stability Report, October 2014, p. 1.
13. IMF World Economic Outlook, October 2014, Executive Summary, p. xv.
14. Friedman (2006 [1969], p. 4).
15. A bond that is perpetual and non-interest-bearing is effectively equivalent to money. After the operation described, the central bank's balance sheet would thus end

up with additional matching non-interest-bearing assets and liabilities. And its current and future profit and loss account would be unaffected, as long as the additional commercial bank reserves were remunerated at a zero interest rate—see note 19.

16. Bernanke (2003, p. 11).

17. Buiter (2014). See also Galí (2014). Galí provides a formal analysis of money-financed stimulus under both classical and new Keynesian frameworks and compares it with the effects of a more conventional debt-financed stimulus. He concludes that "under a realistic calibration of nominal rigidities, money financed fiscal stimulus is shown to have very strong effects on economic activity, with relatively mild inflationary consequences" (Galí 2014, p. 1).

The only possible reason money financed deficits might *not* stimulate nominal demand is if agents (i.e., companies and households) expected that the money finance would be reversed in the future, with a government running budget surpluses and withdrawing from circulation the money it had initially created. If anticipated in advance, this could negate the stimulative impact of money finance in the same way that Ricardian equivalent-type anticipation can in theory negate the stimulative impact of bond-financed deficits. Indeed, in theory the impact of all monetary and fiscal policy stimuli depends on expectations as to future fiscal/monetary authority actions; see Turner (2013a) for discussion of the numerous possible variants of expectation effects. But even in a world where households and companies did attempt to generate rational expectations of future government/central bank action, there is almost certainly a crucial *signaling* difference between money finance and bond finance: the use of money finance signals that it is the authorities' intent that the stimulus will be permanent and the money never withdrawn; conversely, the use of bond finance signals that it is the authorities' current intent that the bonds will be repaid, potentially offsetting the stimulus effect.

18. Alternatively, a government could, if the long-term stimulus turned out to be more than desired, run primary budget surpluses and retire money, as discussed in note 17. This indeed was the offsetting contractionary policy that Milton Friedman (1948) envisaged. And as note 17 discusses, the anticipated possibility of such "future withdrawal" could in theory undermine the initial effectiveness of the money finance stimulus: but it would only do so if the anticipated "future withdrawal" was so great as to offset not only the excessive and unintended element of stimulus, but also all of the stimulus.

19. Since the central bank (as per note 15) holds a non-interest-bearing bond from the government, it would make a loss if its matching liability (additional commercial bank reserves at the central bank) were interest-bearing. While there is in fact no absolute necessity for central banks to be solvent in accounting terms (since they can ultimately always "print money"), ongoing losses would have one of two consequences: either (1) the government would have to offset the central bank losses by means of subsidy from the budget (but doing so would require it to raise taxes or cut expenditure), imposing a future contractionary effect on the economy, or (2) the central bank would use its capacity to print yet more money, producing a potentially excessive stimulus and harmfully high inflation. Remunerating the newly created commercial bank reserves at zero interest rates prevents a loss from occurring and thus averts either of these two future dangers.

20. Thus, for instance, a central bank, having first cooperated with the government in a money-financed "helicopter money" drop, can require commercial banks to hold

a given percentage of their total liabilities (or their total assets) in zero-remunerated reserves, while continuing to pay a positive interest rate on reserves held above this percentage (and continuing to make borrowing facilities available at that or a higher positive rate).

21. UK Debt Office; UK Office of National Statistics.

22. Layard (2010, Figure 1.9). The figures are for lending to the household and non-financial corporate sector by UK banks and building societies. In addition, companies in both years borrowed from corporate bond markets, and in 2007 (though far less so in 1964) there was also significant borrowing from foreign banks.

23. Historical Data on Federal Debt Held by the Public, July 2010, U.S. Congressional Budget Office, Washington, DC.

24. Fueki et al. (2010).

25. IMF Fiscal Monitor, October 2014.

26. Figure on a gross basis as per IMF Fiscal Monitor, April 2015, Table A7. On a net basis, the figure is 110%.

27. Eichengreen (2014).

28. Rogoff (2011) and Blanchard, Dell'Ariccia, and Mauro (2010). Note, indeed, that Blanchard, Dell'Ariccia, and Mauro argue not simply for a temporarily higher inflation rate to facilitate deleveraging but for a permanently higher inflation target.

29. Quoted in Herbert Hoover (1952) *The Memoirs of Herbert Hoover*, Volume 3, *The Great Depression*. New York, Macmillan, p. 30. Available as a pdf at www.ecomm code.com/hoover/ebooks/pdf.

30. Indeed, in essence public-sector debt claims against Greece have already (even at the time of this writing in March 2015) been written down, but through the indirect mechanism of interest rate reductions and maturity extensions, reducing the net present value of future debt repayments. If a debt liability from a government to an official lender (e.g., from Greece to the rest of the eurozone) were made perpetual and non-interest-bearing, in terms of economic substance it would have been entirely written off, but the nominal capital value could still be counted as outstanding. Debt maturity extension and interest rate reductions simply represent points along the spectrum toward full write-off, while preserving the fiction that no write-off has occurred.

31. Giavazzi and Tabellini (2014).

Chapter 15

1. Friedman (1948, pp. 247, 250).

2. Keynes (1991 [1919], p. 78). © The Royal Economic Society 1931, 1972, 2010, 2013 published by Cambridge University Press, used by permission.

3. Weidman (2012, p. 3).

4. Woodford argued that it was essential to deploy "policy actions that should stimulate spending immediately without relying too much on expectational channels." He argued that "the most obvious source of a boost to current aggregate demand that would not depend solely on expectational channels is fiscal stimulus." And he discussed the need to finance some of this fiscal stimulus with base money creation, and to be clear that some part "of the current increase in base money is intended to be permanent." But

he never quite says that he is essentially repeating Bernanke's call for an increased fiscal deficit financed with central bank money (Woodford 2012, pp. 86–87).

5. The desire to define pre-set rules that ensure discipline, rather than relying on responsible discretionary decisionmaking over time, lies in particular at the core of the German "ordo-liberal" tradition. The absolute prohibition of money finance has therefore been a central Bundesbank philosophy and is embedded in the legal framework that governs the European Central Bank. Turner (2015) argues, however, that the policy option of money finance can be made compatible with the ordo-liberal tradition and can be governed by appropriate rules rather than totally prohibited.

6. Bernanke (2003, p. 12).

7. IMF World Economic Outlook database.

8. Giavazzi and Tabellini (2014).

9. Indeed, several examples can be found in history of operations that post facto amounted to money finance, and were bound to do so, but where the reality of money finance was not overtly stated in advance. From the early 1940s to 1951, the U.S. Federal Reserve conducted open market operations designed to ensure that the long-term interest rate remained at 2.5% whatever the size of the fiscal deficit. As a result, the monetary base increased. Following the 1951 Federal Reserve–Treasury Accord, this policy ceased. But there was no "exit," no reversal; the monetary base ceased rising in nominal terms, but it did not reduce, and such stabilization rather than reduction proved compatible with a return to low inflation. Post facto a significant proportion of U.S. fiscal deficits from the early 1940s to 1951 was money financed: formally at the time, they were financed with interest-bearing debt that the Federal Reserve bought in what we would now call "quantitative easing operations."

10. There are good arguments for believing that if the eurozone does break up, it would be better for a small number of "hard-currency" countries to leave and face subsequent appreciation versus the euro, than for a small number of "soft-currency" countries to leave and devalue. In the latter case (1) any debts that do not redenominate in the new national currency (e.g., because extended from foreign counterparties or governed by foreign law) would rise in value, imposing a larger debt burden and (2) overshooting devaluation could create inflation and could be reinforced by capital flight. In the former case, in contrast, (1) some debtors whose debt remained in euros would enjoy a windfall gain, and conversely, some investors would suffer windfall loss, but the net effect would probably be less likely to provoke major disruptions, and (2) the depressive impact of overshooting appreciation could be offset by appropriate stimulus policy. Ironically, such policies would almost certainly involve foreign exchange intervention, with the central banks of the appreciating currencies buying the bonds of the remaining euro members.

11. Friedman (1948, p. 264).

12. See the Chapter 7 discussion of secular stagnation and Chapter 7, note 36.

Epilogue

1. Lucas (2003, p. 1).

2. Buiter (2009, p. 1).

3. King (2010, p. 4).

4. Letter to the Queen by the British Academy, signed by Tim Besley and Peter Hennessy, 2009.

5. Muth (1961).

6. Frydman and Phelps (2013, p. 6).

7. There is, however, a lively debate as to whether the ISLM framework, first developed by Sir John Hicks in 1937 in an attempt to reconcile Keynesian theory with pre-Keynesian classical economics, does indeed reflect the essence of Keynes's macroeconomic theory. For example, see Leijonhufvud (1968).

8. Haldane (2014, chart 13).

9. Gertler (1988).

10. Gurley and Shaw (1955).

11. The large and growing importance of urban land within total wealth suggests that theories of wealth and income distribution that build on traditional two-factor models of the economy (with the quantities and elasticities of substitution between labor L and capital K determining factor shares and returns) are inadequate. Instead we have to see irreproducible land as another key factor. Joseph Stiglitz (2015) explores this three-factor model, commenting that "it was the omission of land that represents the most important lacunae in my 1969 theory of the equilibrium distribution of wealth and income." See also Turner (2014) for discussion of the implications of modern economies that are increasingly both "hi-tech" (with high returns to network externalities and ideas) and "hi-touch" (with high returns to the most physical thing of all—land).

12. Greenwald and Stiglitz (2003, p. 104).

13. See Quadrini (2011) for analysis of the treatment of financial stability issues in mainstream pre-crisis economics.

14. Buiter (2009, p. 1).

15. Hayek (1988).

16. Hayek (1945, p. 519).

17. Frydman and Goldberg (2011, p. 67).

18. Lucas (2001, p. 14).

19. Knight (1921).

20. Keynes (1973 [1936], pp. 162–63).

21. Soros (2013).

22. Janeway (2012).

23. As Karl Popper (1957) puts it in *The Poverty of Historicism*, while utopian social engineering is dangerous, "piecemeal engineering" that focuses on specific defined problems and objectives is possible and essential.

Admati, A. R., and M. F. Hellwig (2013) *The Bankers' New Clothes: What's Wrong with Banking and What to Do about It*. Princeton, NJ: Princeton University Press.

Adrian, T., and H. S. Shin (2009) "Money, Liquidity and Monetary Policy." Staff Report 360. New York: Federal Reserve Bank of New York.

Ahamed, L. (2009) *Lords of Finance: The Bankers Who Broke the World*. New York: Random House.

Alesina, A., and S. Ardagna (2009) "Large Changes in Fiscal Policy: Taxes versus Spending." Working Paper 15438. Cambridge, MA: National Bureau of Economic Research.

Aristotle (2000) *Politics*. Translated by Benjamin Jowett. Mineola, NY: Dover Publications.

Arrow, K. J., and G. Debreu (1954) "Existence of an Equilibrium for a Competitive Economy." *Econometrica* 22: 265–90.

Askari, H., Iqbal, Z., A. Mirakhor, and N. Krichene (2012) *Risk Sharing in Finance: The Islamic Finance Alternative*. New York: Wiley.

Bagehot, W. (1878) *Lombard Street: A Description of the Money Market*. London: C. Kegan Paul.

Bank of England (2012) "The Distributional Effects of Asset Purchases." *Quarterly Bulletin* Q3. Available at: www.bankofengland.co.uk/publications/Documents/quarterly bulletin/qb120306.pdf.

Barro, R. (1974) "Are Government Bonds Net Wealth?" *Journal of Political Economy* 82(6): 1095–1117.

—— (1989) "The Ricardian Approach to Budget Deficits." *Journal of Economic Perspectives* 3(2): 37–54.

Benes, J., and M. Kumhof (2012) *The Chicago Plan Revisited*. Washington, DC: International Monetary Fund.

Bernanke, B. S. (1983) "Non-monetary Effects of the Financial Crisis in the Propagation of the Great Depression." *American Economic Review* 73(3): 257–76.

—— (2000) *Essays on the Great Depression*. Princeton, NJ: Princeton University Press.

—— (2003) "Some Thoughts on Monetary Policy in Japan." Tokyo, May.

—— (2005) "The Global Saving Glut and the U.S. Current Account Deficit." Remarks at the Sandridge Lecture, Virginia, Federal Research Board, March 10.

Bhagwati, J. (1998) "Capital Myth: The Difference between Trade in Widgets and Dollars," *Foreign Affairs* 77(3): 7–12. Available at: www.foreignaffairs.com/articles/asia.

Bhide, A. (2013) "The Hidden Costs of Debt Market Liquidity." Working Paper 79. New York: Centre on Capitalism and Society, Columbia University.

Blanchard, O., G. Dell'Ariccia, and P. Mauro (2010) "Rethinking Macroeconomic Policy." *Journal of Money, Credit and Banking* 42(s1): 199–215.

Bootle, R., and V. Redwood (2011) "Does Inflation Offer a Way out of the Debt Crisis?" *Global Economics Focus*, June 13. London: Capital Economics (www.capitaleconomics.com).

Bordo, M. D., and C. M. Meissner (2012) "Does Inequality Lead to a Financial Crisis?" *Journal of International Money and Finance* 31(8): 2147–61.

Borio, C. (2012) "The Financial Cycle and Macroeconomics: What Have We Learnt?" No. 395. Basel: Bank for International Settlements.

Borio, C., and M. Drehmann (2009) "Financial Instability and Macroeconomics: Bridging the Gulf." Paper prepared for the Twelfth Annual International Banking Conference, The International Financial Crisis: Have the Rules of Finance Changed? Chicago, September 24–25.

Bresciani-Turroni, C. (1937) [1931] *The Economics of Inflation—A Study of Currency Depreciation in Post War Germany.* London: George Allen & Unwin.

Broner, F., T. Didier, A. Erce, and S. Schmukler (2013) "Gross Capital Flows: Dynamics and Crises." *Journal of Monetary Economics* 60: 113–33.

Brunnermeier, M., and L. Pedersen (2009) "Market Liquidity and Funding Liquidity." *Review of Financial Studies* 22(6): 2201–38.

Brynjolfsson, E., and A. McAfee (2014) *The Second Machine Age: Work, Progress, and Prosperity in a Time of Brilliant Technologies.* New York: W. W. Norton and Company.

Buiter, W. (2009) "The Unfortunate Uselessness of Most 'State of the Art' Academic Monetary Economics." VOXeu.org, March 6.

———. (2014) "The Simple Analytics of Helicopter Money: Why It Works—Always." *Economics: The Open-Access, Open-Assessment E-Journal* 8: 1–51. (http://dx.doi.org/10.5018/economics-ejournal.ja.2014–28).

Buttiglione, L., P. R. Lane, L. Reichlin, and V. Reinhart (2014) "Deleveraging, What Deleveraging?" Geneva Report on the World Economy 16. Geneva: International Center for Monetary and Banking Studies, and Centre for Economic Policy Research.

Calomiris, C., and S. Haber (2014) *Fragile by Design: The Political Origins of Banking Crises and Scarce Credit.* Princeton, NJ: Princeton University Press.

Cassidy, J. (2009) *How Markets Fail: The Logic of Economic Calamities.* London: Macmillan.

Cecchetti, S. G., and E. Kharroubi (2015) "Why Does Financial Sector Growth Crowd Out Real Economic Growth?" Working Paper 490. Basel: Bank for International Settlements.

Cecchetti, S. G., M. S. Mohanty, and F. Zampolli (2011) "The Real Effects of Debt." Basel: Bank for International Settlements, Monetary and Economic Department.

Chakraborty, I., I. Goldstein, and A. MacKinlay (2013) "Dark Side of Housing Price Appreciation." VOXeu.org, November 25.

——— (2014) "Do Asset Price Booms Have Negative Real Effects?" Social Science Research Network, September 22.

Chang, H. J. (2002) *Kicking away the Ladder.* London: Anthem Press.

———. (2007) *Bad Samaritans: The Myth of Free Trade and the Secret History of Capitalism.* New York: Bloomsbury.

Cochrane, J. (2013) "Financial Reform in 12 Minutes." Remarks presented at the conference The US Financial System—Five Years after the Crisis, Brookings Institution and Hoover Institution, Washington, DC, October 1.

———. (2014) "Toward a Run-Free Financial System." April 16. Available at: http://faculty.chicagobooth.edu/john.cochrane/research/papers/run_free.pdf.

Coggan, P. (2011) *Paper Promises: Money, Debt and the New World Order.* London: Penguin UK.

Committee on the Global Financial System (2009) "Capital Flows and Emerging Market Economies." CGFS Paper 33. Basel.

Daniel, R., and H. Scheule (2013) *Credit Securitisations and Derivatives: Challenges for the Global Markets.* New York: John Wiley & Sons.

Dash, M. (1999) *Tulipomania: The Story of the World's Most Coveted Flower and the Extraordinary Passions It Aroused.* New York: Crown.

DeLong, J. B., and L. H. Summers (2012) "Fiscal Policy in a Depressed Economy." *Brookings Papers on Economic Activity* 233–97.

Dudley, W. C., and G. Hubbard (2004) *How Capital Markets Enhance Economic Performance and Facilitate Job Creation.* New York: Goldman Sachs Markets Institute.

Eccles, M. S. (1951) *Beckoning Frontiers: Public and Personal Recollections.* New York: Knopf.

Edwards, F. R. (1993) "Taxing Transactions in Futures Markets: Objectives and Effects." *Journal of Financial Services Research* 7(1): 75–91.

Eggertsson, G. B., and P. Krugman (2012) "Debt, Deleveraging, and the Liquidity Trap: A Fisher-Minsky-Koo Approach." *Quarterly Journal of Economics* 127(3): 1469–1513.

Eichengreen, B. (2008) *Globalizing Capital: A History of the International Monetary System,* second edition. Princeton, NJ: Princeton University Press.

—— (2014) "The Bond Markets Dance." *Financial Times,* November 17 (FT.com).

—— (2015) *Hall of Mirrors: The Great Depression, the Great Recession, and the Uses— and Misuses—of History.* New York: Oxford University Press.

European Commission (1990) "One Market, One Money: An Evaluation of the Potential Benefits and Costs of Forming an Economic and Monetary Union." European Economy, Commission of the European Communities, Directorate-General for Economic and Financial Affairs No. 44, October. Available at: http://ec.europa.eu/economy _finance/publications/publication7454_en.pdf.

Fama, E. F. (1965) "The Behavior of Stock-Market Prices." *Journal of Business* 38(1): 34–105.

—— (1970) "Efficient Capital Markets: A Review of Theory and Empirical Work." *Journal of Finance* 25(2): 383–417.

Fama, E. F., L. Fisher, M. Jensen, and R. Roll (1969) "The Adjustment of Stock Prices to New Information." *International Economic Review* 10(1): 1–21.

Ferguson, C. (2012) *Inside Job: The Financiers Who Pulled Off the Heist of the Century.* London: Oneworld Publications.

Financial Services Authority (2011) "Report on the Failure of the Royal Bank of Scotland." Board Report. London.

Financial Stability Board (2012a) "Global Shadow Banking Monitoring Report." Basel.

—— (2012b) "Securities Lending and Repos: Market Overview and Financial Stability Issues." Basel.

Fisher, I. (1933) "The Debt-Deflation Theory of Great Depressions." *Econometrica* 1(4): 337–57.

—— (1936) "100% Money and the Public Debt." *Economic Forum* Spring: 406–20.

Frank, R. (2001) *Luxury Fever: Why Money Fails to Satisfy in an Era of Excess.* New York: Simon and Schuster.

—— (2007) *Falling Behind: How Rising Inequality Harms the Middle Class.* Berkeley: University of California Press.

Frank, R. H., A. S. Levine, and O. Dijk (2010) "Expenditure Cascades." Social Science Research Network, SSRN 1690612.

French, K. R., and R. Roll (1986) "Stock Return Variances: The Arrival of Information and the Reaction of Traders." *Journal of Financial Economics* 17(1): 5–26.

Friedman, B. (2012) "Monetary Policy, Fiscal Policy and the Efficiency of Our Financial System: Lessons from the Financial Crisis." *International Journal of Central Banking* 8: 301–9. Available at: http://scholar.harvard.edu/files/bfriedman/files/lessons_financial _crisis_ijcb_jan_2012.pdf.

Friedman, M. (1948) "A Monetary and Fiscal Framework for Economic Stability." *American Economic Review* 38(3): 245–64.

—— (2006) [1969] *The Optimum Quantity of Money: And Other Essays.* Piscataway, NJ: Transaction Publishers.

Friedman, M., and A. Schwartz (1963) *A Monetary History of the United States 1867–1960.* Princeton, NJ: Princeton University Press.

Frydman, R., and M. D. Goldberg (2011) *Beyond Mechanical Markets: Asset Price Swings, Risk, and the Role of the State.* Princeton, NJ: Princeton University Press.

Frydman, R., and E. S. Phelps (eds.) (2013) *Rethinking Expectations: The Way Forward for Macroeconomics.* Princeton, NJ: Princeton University Press.

Fueki, T., I. Fukunaga, H. Ichiue, T. Sekine, and T. Shirota (2010) "Measuring Potential Growth in Japan: Some Practical Caveats." Bank of Japan Review Series 2010-E1. Tokyo: Bank of Japan.

Galí, J. (2014) "The Effects of a Money-Financed Fiscal Stimulus." Barcelona: Centre de Recerca en Economia Internacional, Universitat Pompeu Fabra and Barcelona. Available at: http://crei.cat/people/gali/gmoney.pdf.

Gennaioli, N., A. Shleifer, and R. Vishny. (2012) "Neglected Risks, Financial Innovation, and Financial Fragility." *Journal of Financial Economics* 104(3): 452–68.

George, H. (1884) *Progress and Poverty: An Inquiry into the Cause of Industrial Depressions, and of Increase of Want with Increase of Wealth. The Remedy.* London: W. Reeves.

Gerschenkron, A. (1962) *Economic Backwardness in Historical Perspective: A Book of Essays.* Cambridge, MA: Belknap Press of Harvard University Press.

Gertler, M. L. (1988) "Financial Structure and Aggregate Economic Activity: An Overview." *Journal of Money, Credit and Banking* 20(3): 559–88.

Gertler, M. L., and N. Kiyotaki (2009) *Financial Intermediation and Credit Policy in Business Cycle Analysis: Handbook of Monetary Economics.* New York and Princeton, NJ: New York University Press and Princeton University Press.

Giavazzi, F., and G. Tabellini (2014) "How to Jump Start the Eurozone Economy." VOXeu.org, August 21. Available at: www.voxeu.org/article/how-jumpstart-eurozone -economy.

Goethe, J.W. von (2007) *Faust—a tragedy in two parts.* London: Wordsworth Classics of World Literature.

Gordon, R. J. (2012) "Is US Economic Growth Over? Faltering Innovation Confronts the Six Headwinds." Policy Insight 63. New York: Center for Economic Policy Research.

Gorton, G., and A. Metrick (2012) "Securitized Banking and the Run on Repo." *Journal of Financial Economics* 104(3): 425–51.

Graeber, D. (2012) *Debt: The First 5000 Years.* London: Penguin UK.

Greenspan, A. (2005) "Risk Transfer and Financial Stability." Speech at the Federal Reserve Bank of Chicago, May 5.

Greenwald, B., and J. Stiglitz (2003) *Towards a New Paradigm in Monetary Economics.* Cambridge: Cambridge University Press.

Greenwood, R., and D. Scharfstein (2013) "The Growth of Finance." *Journal of Economic Perspectives* 27(2): 3–28.

Guajardo, J., D. Leigh, and A. Pescatori (2011) "Expansionary Austerity: New International Evidence." Working Paper 11/158. Washington, DC: International Monetary Fund.

Gurley, J. G., and E. S. Shaw (1955) "Financial Aspects of Economic Development." *American Economic Review* 45: 515–38.

Haldane, A. G. (2010) "Patience and Finance." Remarks at the Oxford China Business Forum, Beijing, September. Available at: www.bankofengland.co.uk/publications/speeches/2010/speech445.Pdf.

—— (2014) "Central Bank Psychology" (Chart 13). Speech at the conference of the Royal Society of Medicine, London, November.

Haldane, A. G., S. Brennan, and V. Madouros (2010) "What Is the Contribution of the Financial Sector: Miracle or Mirage?" in R. Layard (ed.), *The Future of Finance*. London: London School of Economics and Political Science.

Hayek, F. A. (1933) *Monetary Theory and the Trade Cycle*. New York: Harcourt, Brace & Company.

—— (1945) "The Use of Knowledge in Society." *American Economic Review* 35(4): 519–30.

—— (1984) [1925] *Money, Capital and Fluctuations: Early Essays*. London: Routledge and Kegan Paul.

—— (1988) *The Fatal Conceit: The Errors of Socialism*. London: Routledge.

—— (2008) [1931] *Prices and Production and Other Works: F.A. Hayek on Money, the Business Cycle and the Gold Standard*, edited by Joseph Salerno. Auburn, AL: Ludwig von Mises Institute.

Heaton, J., and Lo, A. W. (1994) "Securities Transaction Taxes: What Would Be Their Effects on Financial Markets and Institutions?" In S. Hammond (ed.), *Securities Transaction Taxes: False Hopes and Unintended Consequences*. Chicago: Irwin Professional Publishers.

Hense, F. (2015) "Interest Rate Elasticity of Bank Loans: The Case for Sector-Specific Capital Requirements." CFS Working Paper 504. Frankfurt: Center for Financial Studies. Available at: www.ifk-cfs.de/research/years/working-papers.html.

Hu, S. Y. (1998) "The Effects of the Stock Transaction Tax on the Stock Market—Experiences from Asian Markets." *Pacific-Basin Finance Journal* 6(3): 347–64.

Hudson, R. L., and B. B. Mandelbrot (2004) *The (Mis)Behavior of Markets: A Fractal View of Risk, Ruin, and Reward*. New York: Basic Books.

International Monetary Fund (2005) "Evaluation Report on the IMF's Approach to Capital Account Liberalization." August 9. Washington, DC: International Monetary Fund, Independent Evaluation Office.

Irfan, H. (2014) *Heaven's Bankers: Inside the Hidden World of Islamic Finance*. London: Constable.

Jackson, A., and B. Dyson (2013) *Modernising Money. Why Our Monetary System Is Broken and How It Can Be Fixed*. London: Positive Money.

Janeway, W. H. (2012) *Doing Capitalism in the Innovation Economy: Markets, Speculation and the State*. Cambridge: Cambridge University Press.

Jensen, M. C. (1978) "Some Anomalous Evidence Regarding Market Efficiency." *Journal of Financial Economics* 6(2): 95–101.

Johnson, S., and J. Kwak (2011) *13 Bankers: The Wall Street Takeover and the Next Financial Meltdown*. London: Random House.

Jordà, Ò., and A. M. Taylor (2013) "The Time for Austerity: Estimating the Average Treatment Effect of Fiscal Policy." Working Paper 19414. Cambridge, MA: National Bureau of Economic Research.

Jordà, Ò., M. Schularick, and A. Taylor (2013) "When Credit Bites Back: Leverage, Business Cycles and Crises." *Journal of Money, Credit and Banking* 45: 3–28.

—— (2014a) "The Great Mortgaging: Housing Finance, Crises and Business Cycles." Working Paper 20501. Cambridge, MA: National Bureau of Economic Research.

—— (2014b) "The Great Leveraging." In V. Acharya, T. Beck, D. Evanoff, G. Kaufman, and R. Portes (eds.), *The Social Value of the Financial Sector: Too Big to Fail or Just Too Big?* World Scientific Studies in International Economics 29. Hackensack, NJ: World Scientific.

—— (2015) "Betting the House." *Journal of International Economics*, Volume 96, Supplement 1, July 2015, Pages S2-S18. 37th Annual NBER International Seminar on Macroeconomics.

Kahneman, D., and A. Tversky (1973) "On the Psychology of Prediction." *Psychological Review* 80: 237–51.

—— A. (1979) "Prospect Theory: An Analysis of Decision under Risk." *Econometrica* 47(2): 263–91.

Kapetanios, G., H. Mumtaz, H. Stevens, and K. Theodoridis (2012) "Assessing the Economy-wide Effects of Quantitative Easing." Working Paper 443. London: Bank of England.

Kay, J. (2012) "The Kay Review of UK Equity Markets and Long-Term Decision Making." Final Report (July). Review commissioned by the UK Department for Business, Innovation and Skills, London.

Keynes, J. M. (1930) *A Treatise on Money*, 2 volumes. London: Macmillan & Company.

—— (1971) A Treatise on Money. *The Pure Theory of Money*, vol. 5, *The Collected Writings of J. M. Keynes*. London and Cambridge: Macmillan and Cambridge University Press (for the Royal Economic Society).

—— (1973) [1936] *The General Theory of Employment, Interest and Money*, vol. 7, *The Collected Writings of J. M. Keynes*. London: Macmillan (for the Royal Economic Society).

Keynes, J. M., "The Collected Writings of John Maynard Keynes, Vol. 9: Essays in Persuasion," edited by Elizabeth Johnson, Donald Moggridge, 1978. © The Royal Economic Society 1931, 1972, 2010, 2013, published by Cambridge University Press, translated with permission.

Kindleberger, C. P. (1978) *Manias, Panics and Crashes: A History of Financial Crises*. New York: Palgrave Macmillan.

Kindleberger, C. P., and R. Aliber (2005) *Manias, Panics and Crashes: A History of Financial Crises*, fifth edition. Hoboken, NJ: John Wiley & Sons.

King, M. (2010) "Uncertainty in Macroeconomic Policy-Making: Art or Science?" Presentation at the Royal Society conference on Handling Uncertainty in Science, London, March 22.

—— (2012) "Twenty Years of Inflation Targeting," The Stamp Memorial Lecture, London School of Economics and Political Science.

Kiyotaki, N., and J. Moore (1995) "Credit Cycles." Working Paper 5083. Cambridge, MA: National Bureau of Economic Research.

Knight, F. (1921) *Risk, Uncertainty and Profit*. New York: Hart, Schaffner and Marx.

—— (1933) "Memorandum on Banking Reform." Franklin D. Roosevelt Presidential Library, President's Personal File 431, March.

Knoll, K., M. Schularick, and T. Steger (2014) "No Price Like Home: Global House Prices, 1870–2012." Discussion Paper 10166. New York: Center for Economic Policy Research.

Koo, R. C. (2011) *The Holy Grail of Macroeconomics: Lessons from Japan's Great Recession*. New York: John Wiley & Sons.

Lack, S. (2012) *The Hedge Fund Mirage: The Illusion of Big Money and Why It's Too Good to Be True*. New York: John Wiley & Sons.

Lardy, N. (2006) "China: Toward a Consumption-Driven Growth Path." Working Paper PB06-6. Washington, DC: Peterson Institute for International Economics.

Layard, R., ed. (2010) *The Future of Finance: The LSE Report*. London: London School of Economics and Political Science.

Leijonhufvud, A. (1968) *On Keynesian Economics and the Economics of Keynes*. Oxford: Oxford University Press.

Levine, R. (2005) "Finance and Growth: Theory and Evidence." In P. Aghion and S. Durlauf (eds.), *Handbook of Economic Growth*, 1B. The Netherlands: Elsevier.

Lewis, M. (2011) *The Big Short: Inside the Doomsday Machine*. New York: W. W. Norton and Company.

——. (2014) *Flash Boys: A Wall Street Revolt*. New York: W. W. Norton and Company.

Lipsey, R. G., and K. Lancaster (1956) "The General Theory of Second Best." *Review of Economic Studies* 24(1): 11–32.

List, F., and S. Colwell. (1856) *National System of Political Economy*. New York: J. B. Lippincott & Company.

Lucas, Jr., R. E. (1972) "Expectations and the Neutrality of Money." *Journal of Economic Theory* 4(2): 103–24.

—— (2001) "Professional Memoir." Chicago: University of Chicago. (http://home.u chicago.edu).

—— (2003) "Macroeconomic Priorities." Presidential Address to the American Economic Association, Washington, DC, January 4.

MacKay, C. (1841) *Extraordinary Popular Delusions and the Madness of Crowds*. New York: Farrar, Straus and Giroux.

Maddison, A. (2001) *The World Economy. A Millennial Perspective*. Paris: OECD Development Centre.

Martin, F. (2013) *Money: The Unauthorised Biography*. London: Random House.

Mathias, P. (1969) *The First Industrial Nation: The Economic History of Britain 1700–1914*. London: Methuen & Co.

Mazzucato, M. (2013) *The Entrepreneurial State: Debunking Public vs. Private Sector Myths*. London: Anthem Press.

McKinsey Global Institute (2010) "Farewell to Cheap Capital? The Implications of Long-term Shifts in Global Investment and Saving." (www.mckinsey.com/insights/global _capital_markets/farewell_cheap_capital).

—— (2015) "Debt and (Not Much) Deleveraging." (www.mckinsey.com/insights/eco nomic_studies/debt_and_not_much_deleveraging).

Mian, A., and A. Sufi (2014) *House of Debt*. Chicago: University of Chicago Press.

Miles, D. (2005) "Where Should Long-Term Interest Rates Be Today? A 300 Year View." London: Morgan Stanley Equity Research.

Minsky, H. P. (1970) "Financial Instability Revisited: The Economics of Disaster." Hyman P. Minsky Archive, Paper no. 80.

——. (2008) [1986] *Stabilizing an Unstable Economy*. New York: McGraw-Hill.

Modigliani, F., and M. H. Miller (1958) "The Cost of Capital, Corporation Finance and the Theory of Investment." *American Economic Review* 48(3): 261–97.

Muellbauer, J. (2010) "Household Decisions, Credit Markets and the Macroeconomy: Implications for the Design of Central Bank Models." Discussion Paper 306. Basel: Bank for International Settlements. Available at: http://ideas.repec.org/p/bis/biswps/306.html.

—— (2012) "When Is a Housing Market Overheated Enough to Threaten Stability?" Discussion Paper 623, Department of Economics. Oxford: University of Oxford.

—— (2014) "Combatting Eurozone Deflation: QE for the People." VOXeu.org, December. Available at: www.voxeu.org/article/combatting-eurozone-deflation-qe-people.

Muellbauer, J., and J. Duca (2014) "Tobin LIVES: Integrating Evolving Credit Market Architecture into Flow-of-Funds Based Macro-Models." In B. Winkler, A. van Riet, and P. Bull (eds.), *A Flow-of-Funds Perspective on the Financial Crisis*, vol. 2. London: Palgrave Macmillan.

Muellbauer, J., J. Duca, and A. Murphy (2011) "House Prices and Credit Constraints: Making Sense of the U.S. Experience." *Economic Journal* 121(552): 533–51.

Muellbauer, J., J. Aron, J. Duca, K. Murata, and A. Murphy (2012) "Credit, Housing Collateral and Consumption in the UK, U.S., and Japan." *Review of Income and Wealth* 58 (3): 397–423.

Muth, J. F. (1961) "Rational Expectations and the Theory of Price Movements." *Econometrica* 29: 315–35.

OECD, *Finance and Inclusive Growth*, OECD Economic Policy Paper, Number 14, June 2015.

Persaud, A. (2013) "The Passing of a Reform Moment." LiveMint, July 21. Available at: www.livemint.com/Opinion/BscqIYIfGx0j5EXHMGVlmO/The-passing-of-a-reform -moment.html.

Pettis, M. (2013) *The Great Rebalancing: Trade, Conflict, and the Perilous Road Ahead for the World Economy*. Princeton, NJ: Princeton University Press.

Philippon, T. (2008) "The Evolution of the US Financial Industry from 1860 to 2007: Theory and Evidence." NBER/CEPR paper. Cambridge, MA: National Bureau of Economic Research. Available at: http://economics.stanford.edu/files/Philippon5_20.pdf.

Philippon, T., and A. Reshef (2012) "Wages and Human Capital in the US Finance Industry: 1909–2006." *Quarterly Journal of Economics* 127(4): 1551–1609.

Piketty, T. (2014) *Capital in the Twenty-First Century*. Cambridge, MA: Harvard University Press.

Piketty, T., and E. Saez. (2003) "Income Inequality in the United States, 1913–1998." *Quarterly Journal of Economics* 118(1): 1–41. Updated 2012 Excel tables available at: http://elsa.berkeley.edu/~saez/.

Piketty, T., and G. Zucman (2013) "Capital is Back: Wealth-Income Ratios in Rich Countries 1700–2010." *Quarterly Journal of Economics* 129(3): 1255–1310. Updated 2014 version available at http://qje.oxfordjournals.org/content/129/3/1255.

Popper, K. (1957) *The Poverty of Historicism*. London: Routledge Classics and Kegan Paul.

Pozsar, Z. (2011) "Institutional Cash Pools and the Triffin Dilemma of the US Banking System." Washington, DC: International Monetary Fund.

—— (2013) "Shadow Banking and the Global Financial Ecosystem." VOXeu.org. Available at: www.voxeu.org/article/global-financial-ecosystem-0.

—— (2015) "A Macro View of Shadow Banking: Levered Betas and Wholesale Funding in the Context of Secular Stagnation." Working Paper, Shadow Banking Colloquium, Institute for New Economic Thinking, New York, January. Available at: http://ineteconomics.org/sites/inet.civicactions.net/files/Macro_View_Final.XcxMB4.pdf.

Prasad, E. S., R. G. Rajan, and A. Subramanian (2007) "Foreign Capital and Economic Growth." Working Paper 13619. Cambridge, MA: National Bureau of Economic Research.

Quadrini, V. (2011) "Financial Frictions in Macroeconomic Fluctuations." *Economic Quarterly* 97(3): 209–54.

Rajan, R. G. (2005) "Has Financial Development Made the World Riskier?" Working Paper 11728. Cambridge, MA: National Bureau of Economic Research. Available at www.nber.org/papers/w11728.pdf.

—— (2011) *Fault Lines: How Hidden Fractures Still Threaten the World Economy.* Princeton, NJ: Princeton University Press.

Rajan, R. G., and L. Zingales (2004) *Saving Capitalism from the Capitalists: Unleashing the Power of Financial Markets to Create Wealth and Spread Opportunity.* Princeton, NJ: Princeton University Press.

Rancière, R., and M. Kumhof (2010) "Inequality, Leverage and Crises." Working Paper 10/268. Washington, DC: International Monetary Fund.

Reinhart, C. M., and K. Rogoff (2009) *This Time Is Different: Eight Centuries of Financial Folly.* Princeton, NJ: Princeton University Press.

—— (2010) "Growth in a Time of Debt." Working Paper 15639. Cambridge, MA: National Bureau of Economic Research.

—— (2013) "Financial and Sovereign Debt Crises: Some Lessons Learned and Those Forgotten." Working Paper 13/266. Washington, DC: International Monetary Fund.

Rey, H. (2013) "Dilemma Not Trilemma: The Global Financial Cycle and Monetary Policy Independence." In Global Dimensions of Unconventional Monetary Policy, Jackson Hole Economic Symposium, Federal Reserve Bank of Kansas City, August 24.

Rodrik, D., and A. Subramanian (2009) "Why Did Financial Globalization Disappoint?" *IMF Staff Papers* 56(1): 112–38.

Rogoff, K. (2011) "The Bullets Yet to Be Fired to Stop the Crisis," *Financial Times*, August 8.

—— (2014) "Time to Phase Out Paper Money," *Financial Times*, May 29.

Roll, R. (1989) "Price Volatility, International Market Links, and Their Implications for Regulatory Policies. *Journal of Financial Services Research* 3(2): 211–46.

Rousseau, P. L., and R. Sylla (2003) "Financial Systems, Economic Growth, and Globalization." In M. D. Bordo, A. M. Taylor, and J. G. Williamson (eds.), *Globalization in Historical Perspective.* Chicago: University of Chicago Press.

Sargent, T., and N. Wallace (1981) "Some Unpleasant Monetarist Arithmetic." Quarterly Review 531. Federal Reserve Bank of Minneapolis.

Schularick, M., and A. M. Taylor (2012) "Credit Booms Gone Bust: Monetary Policy, Leverage Cycles, and Financial Crises, 1870–2008." *American Economic Review* 102(4): 1029–61.

Schumpeter, J. A. (1912) *Theorie der Wirtschaftlichen Entwicklung.* Leipzig: Dunker & Humblot.

—— (1934) *The Theory of Economic Development.* Translated by R. Opie. Cambridge, MA: Harvard University Press.

Schwert, G. W., and P. J. Seguin (1993) "Securities Transaction Taxes: An Overview of Costs, Benefits and Unresolved Questions." *Financial Analysts Journal* 49(5): 27–35.

Sheppard, D. K. (1971) *The Growth and Role of UK Financial Institutions 1880–1962.* London: Methuen & Co.

Shiller, R. J. (1992) *Market Volatility.* Cambridge, MA: MIT Press.

—— (2000) *Irrational Exuberance.* Princeton, NJ: Princeton University Press.

—— (2013) *Finance and the Good Society.* Princeton, NJ: Princeton University Press.

Shiller, R. J., and G. A. Akerlof (2009) *Animal Spirits: How Human Psychology Drives the Economy, and Why It Matters for Global Capitalism.* Princeton, NJ: Princeton University Press.

Shin, H. S. (2005) "Commentary: Has Financial Development Made the World Riskier?" In The Greenspan Era: Lessons for the Future, Jackson Hole Economic Symposium, Federal Reserve Bank of Kansas City, August. Available at: www.kc.frb.org/publicat/sympos/2005/sym05prg.htm.

—— (2010) *Risk and Liquidity.* Clarendon Lectures in Finance. Oxford: Oxford University Press.

Shleifer, A. (2000) *Inefficient Markets: An Introduction to Behavioural Finance.* Oxford: Oxford University Press.

Simons, H. C. (1936) "Rules versus Authorities in Monetary Policy." *Journal of Political Economy* 44(1): 1–30.

Singh, M., and J. Aitkin (2010) "The (Sizeable) Role of Rehypothecation in the Shadow Banking System." Working Paper WP/10/172, Washington, DC: International Monetary Fund. Available at: www.imf.org/external/pubs/ft/wp/2010/wp10172.pdf.

Skidelsky, R. (2003) *John Maynard Keynes: 1883–1946: Economist, Philosopher, Statesman.* London: Pan Macmillan.

Smethurst, R. (2009) *From Foot Soldier to Finance Minister: Takahashi Korekiyo, Japan's Keynes.* Cambridge, MA: Harvard University Press.

Smith, A. (1999) [1776] *The Wealth of Nations,* Books I–III. London: Penguin Classics.

Soros, G. (2008) *The Crash of 2008 and What It Means: The New Paradigm for Financial Markets.* New York: PublicAffairs.

—— (2013) "Fallibility, Reflexivity, and the Human Uncertainty Principle." *Journal of Economic Methodology* 20(4): 309–29.

Stein, J. C. (2013) "Overheating in Credit Markets: Origins, Measurement, and Policy Responses." Speech delivered at the symposium Restoring Household Financial Stability after the Great Recession: Why Household Balance Sheets Matter, Federal Reserve Bank of St. Louis, St. Louis, MO, February.

Stiglitz, J. E. (1989) "Using Tax Policy to Curb Speculative Short-Term Trading." *Journal of Financial Services Research* 3(2): 101–15.

———— (2001) "Information and the Change in the Paradigm in Economics." Nobel Prize Lecture, December 8. Stockholm: Nobel Foundation. Available at: www.nobelprize .org/nobel_prizes/economic-sciences/laureates/2001/stiglitz-lecture.html.

———— (2015) "New Theoretical Perspectives on the Distribution of Income and Wealth among Individuals." Published in four parts, Working Papers 21189-92, NBER, May. New York: Columbia University. http://www.nber.org/authors/joseph_stiglitz.

Studwell, J. (2013) *How Asia Works: Success and Failure in the World's Most Dynamic Region*. New York: Grove Press

Summers, L. H. (2013) Speech at the IMF Economic Forum, panel on Policy Responses to Crises, Fourteenth Jacques Polak Annual Research Conference on Crises: Yesterday and Today, Washington, DC, Novermber 8. Panel participation available on video at: www.imf.org/external/mmedia/view.aspx?vid=2821294542001.

Summers, L. H., and V. P. Summers (1989) "When Financial Markets Work Too Well: A Cautious Case for a Securities Transactions Tax." *Journal of Financial Services* Research 3(2–3): 261–86.

———— (1990) "The Case for a Securities Transactions Excise Tax." *Tax Notes* 13: 879–84.

Taleb, N. N. (2007) *The Black Swan: The Impact of the Highly Improbable*. London: Random House.

Tilford, S. (2015) "German Rebalancing: Waiting for Godot?" Policy Brief, March. London: Centre for European Reform. Available at: www.cer.org.uk/publications/archive/ policy-brief/2015/germany-rebalancing-waiting-godot.

Tobin, J. (1984) *On the Efficiency of the Financial System*. London: Lloyds Bank Review.

Townsend, R. M. (1979) "Optimal Contracts and Competitive Markets with Costly State Verification." *Journal of Economic Theory* 21(2): 265–93.

Turner, A. (2001) *Just Capital: The Liberal Economy*. London: Macmillan.

———— (2010) "What Do Banks Do? Why Do Credit Booms and Busts Occur and What Can Public Policy Do about It?" In R. Layard (ed.), *The Future of Finance: The LSE Report*. London: London School of Economics and Political Science.

———— (2012) *Economics after the Crisis: Objectives and Means*. Cambridge, MA: MIT Press.

———— (2013a) "Credit, Money and Leverage: What Wicksell, Hayek and Fisher Knew and Modern Macro-economics Forgot." September 12. Stockholm: Stockholm School of Economics.

———— (2013b) "Debt, Money, and Mephistopheles: How Do We Get out of This Mess?" Lecture at Cass Business School, London, February 6.

———— (2014) "Wealth, Debt, Inequality and Low Interest Rates: Four Big Trends and Some Implications." Speech at Cass Business School, London, March 26.

———— (2015) "Credit, Money and Ordo-Liberalism." Lecture at the Center for Financial Studies, Goethe University Frankfurt, February.

Umlauf, S. R. (1993) "Transaction Taxes and the Behavior of the Swedish Stock Market." *Journal of Financial Economics* 33(2): 227–40.

Van Treeck, T., and S. Sturn (2012) *Income Inequality as a Cause of the Great Recession? A Survey of Current Debates*. Geneva: International Labour Organisation, Conditions of Work and Employment Branch.

Weidmann, J. (2012) "Money Creation and Responsibility." Speech at the 18th Colloquium of the Institute for Bank Historical Research (IBF), Frankfurt, September 18.

Werner, R. (2003) *Princes of the Yen: Japan's Central Bankers and the Transformation of the Economy.* Armonk, NY: M. E. Sharpe.

—— (2005) *New Paradigm in Macroeconomics: Solving the Riddle of Japanese Macroeconomic Performance.* New York: Palgrave Macmillan.

White, W. R. (2012) "Ultra-easy Monetary Policy and the Law of Unintended Consequences." Working Paper 126. Dallas: Federal Reserve Bank of Dallas, Globalization and Monetary Policy Institute.

Wicksell, K. (1936) *Interest and Prices.* London: Macmillan (for the Royal Economic Society).

Wilkinson, R. G., and K. Pickett (2011) *The Spirit Level.* Saybrook, CT: Tantor Media.

Wolf, M. (2014) *The Shifts and the Shocks: What We've Learned—and Have Still to Learn—from the Financial Crisis.* New York: Penguin Press.

Wolfe, T. (1987) *The Bonfire of the Vanities.* New York: Farrar, Straus and Giroux.

Woodford, M. (2003) *Interest and Prices: Foundations of a Theory of Monetary Policy.* Princeton, NJ: Princeton University Press.

—— (2012) "Methods of Policy Accommodation at the Interest-Rate Lower Bound." In The Changing Policy Landscape, Jackson Hole Symposium, Federal Reserve Bank of Kansas City. Available at: www.kansascityfed.org/publications/research/escp/symposiums/escp-2012.

Young, A. (1995) "The Tyranny of Numbers: Confronting the Statistical Realities of the East Asian Growth Experience." *Quarterly Journal of Economics* 110(3): 641–80.

INDEX